Migration and Diaspora in Modern Asia

Migration is at the heart of Asian history. For centuries, migrants have tracked the routes and seas of their ancestors – merchants, pilgrims, soldiers, sailors – along the Silk Road and across the Indian Ocean and the China Sea. Over the last 150 years, however, migration within Asia and beyond has been greater than at any other time in history.

Sunil S. Amrith's engaging and deeply informative book crosses a vast terrain, from the Middle East to India and China, tracing the history of modern migration against the background of empires, their dissolution, and the onset of modernity. Animated by the voices of Asian migrants, it tells the stories of those forced to flee from war and revolution, and those who left their homes and their families in search of a better life.

These stories of Asian diasporas can be joyful or poignant, but they all speak of an engagement with new landscapes and new peoples. Migration has been central to making Asian societies as complex and diverse as they are today.

SUNIL S. AMRITH is Senior Lecturer in History at Birkbeck College, University of London. He is the author of *Decolonizing International Health: India and Southeast Asia, 1930–65* (2006), and his articles have been published in numerous journals, such as the *American Historical Review* and *Past and Present*.

T0371053

New Approaches to Asian History

This dynamic new series will publish books on the milestones in Asian history, those that have come to define particular periods or mark turning-points in the political, cultural, and social evolution of the region. Books are intended as introductions for students to be used in the classroom. They are written by scholars whose credentials are well established in their particular fields and who have, in many cases, taught the subject across a number of years.

Books in the Series

Judith M. Brown, *Global South Asians: Introducing the Modern Diaspora*
Diana Lary, *China's Republic*
Peter A. Lorge, *The Asian Military Revolution: From Gunpowder to the Bomb*
Ian Talbot and Gurharpal Singh, *The Partition of India*
Stephen F. Dale, *The Muslim Empires of the Ottomans, Safavids, and Mughals*
Diana Lary, *The Chinese People at War*

For Ruth

Migration and Diaspora in Modern Asia

Sunil S. Amrith

University of London

CAMBRIDGE
UNIVERSITY PRESS

University Printing House, Cambridge CB2 8BS, United Kingdom

One Liberty Plaza, 20th Floor, New York, NY 10006, USA

477 Williamstown Road, Port Melbourne, VIC 3207, Australia

4843/24, 2nd Floor, Ansari Road, Daryaganj, Delhi - 110002, India

79 Anson Road, #06-04/06, Singapore 079906

Cambridge University Press is part of the University of Cambridge.

It furthers the University's mission by disseminating knowledge in the pursuit of education, learning and research at the highest international levels of excellence.

www.cambridge.org
Information on this title: www.cambridge.org/9780521727020

© Cambridge University Press 2011

First published 2011

A catalogue record for this publication is available from the British Library

Library of Congress Cataloging in Publication data
Amrith, Sunil S., 1979–
    Migration and diaspora in modern Asia / Sunil S. Amrith.
        p.   cm. – (New approaches to Asian history)
    Includes bibliographical references and index.
    ISBN 978-0-521-89835-5 (hardback) – ISBN 978-0-521-72702-0 (pbk.)
    1. Asia – Emigration and immigration – History.   2. Asian diaspora.   3. Asians –
    Migrations.   4. Immigrants – Asia – History.   5. Refugees – Asia – History.   I. Title.
    JV8490.A73   2011
    304.8095–dc22   2010031761

ISBN 978-0-521-89835-5 Hardback
ISBN 978-0-521-72702-0 Paperback

Contents

List of Plates, Tables, and Maps   *page* viii
Acknowledgements   xi
Select Timeline   xiii
Glossary   xvii

  Introduction   1

1 Asia's Great Migrations, 1850–1930   18

2 The Making of Asian Diasporas, 1850–1930   57

3 War, Revolution, and Refugees, 1930–1950   89

4 Migration, Development, and the Asian City,
  1950–1970   117

5 Asian Migrants in the Age of Globalization,
  1970–2010   151

  Conclusion   193

  Guide to Further Reading   201
  Index   207

List of Plates, Tables, and Maps

Plates

1.1	The SS 'Benalder' (1880)	*page* 26
1.2	Tamil Women on Maria Watta Estate (1895)	35
1.3	Boat Population of Canton, China (1900)	39
2.1	The Ginza, Tokyo (1904)	60
2.2	Malayan Pilgrims Return from Mecca (1949)	70
2.3	The Khoo Kongsi in Penang (2008)	78
2.4	The Ying Fo Hui Guan, Singapore (2010)	79
2.5	Chinese Girls' School, Singapore (undated, c. early 20th century)	80
2.6	Mariamman Temple, Penang (2009)	83
2.7	Image of Mazu, Temple of Heavenly Blessings, Singapore (2010)	85
3.1	Group Photograph of Singapore Overseas Chinese Association (1937)	102
5.1	Construction Site in Dubai (2008)	163
5.2	Vendor of Calling Cards in Singapore (2010)	180
5.3	Remittance Centre, Singapore (2010)	182
5.4	Migrant Family's House in Rural Kerala (2008)	183
C.1	Food Stall in Singapore (c. 2010)	199

Tables

1.1	Indian and Chinese Migration to Southeast Asia, 1891–1938	30
3.1	Wartime Refugees in China, 1937–1945	100
5.1	Population of Asia's 'Mega-Cities'	157
5.2	Estimated Stocks of Migrant Workers in Asia	168

Maps

1	Routes of Migration in Asia, c. 1870–1930	xix
2	Routes of Migration in Asia, c. 1980–2010	xix
3	India	xx
4	China	xx
5	Southeast Asia	xxi

Acknowledgements

This is a history of migration in modern Asia, written for anyone coming to the subject for the first time, and with students particularly in mind. It has its origins in a course I have taught at Birkbeck College since 2006. I have gained much from my diverse group of adult students at Birkbeck, and this book reflects what I have learned from many classroom discussions.

At Birkbeck, I would particularly like to thank Hilary Sapire, Chandak Sengoopta, and Naoko Shimazu for their solidarity: working with them is a pleasure and an education. I completed the book during a sabbatical year at Harvard University. I am grateful to Emma Rothschild for making this possible and for her unfailing support and intellectual example over many years. Tim Harper inspired many of the ideas in this book, and I owe a great deal to his friendship and kindness, as I do to the warm encouragement of Sugata Bose.

I am grateful to the staff of the following libraries and archives for their assistance and expertise: the British Library in London; Harvard University's Widener Memorial Library; the library of Singapore's Institute of Southeast Asian Studies (ISEAS); the National Archives of Singapore; the National Archives of India; and the Nehru Memorial Library. I acknowledge the generous financial support of the British Academy in the form of a Large Research Grant, and travel grants from Birkbeck College and the University of London's Central Research Fund.

I would like to express my appreciation and thanks to the following for kindly granting me permission to use photographic and archival material: National Archives of Singapore, for Plates 1.1, 2.2, and 3.1; Library of Congress, Washington, D.C., Prints & Photographs Division, for Plates 1.2, 1.3, 2.1, and 2.5; and Wellcome Library, London, for the cover illustration.

The four anonymous readers of the original proposal, and in particular the reader who commented on the finished manuscript, provided invaluable comments. For discussions that have helped to shape my ideas, I am grateful to Seema Alavi, Christopher Bayly, Chua Ai Lin, Mark Frost, Henrietta Harrison, Sumit Mandal, Ian Miller, Kavita Sivaramakrishnan, Michael Szonyi, A.R. Venkatachalapathy, and Kirsty Walker. It has been a great pleasure working with Cambridge University Press commissioning editor Marigold Acland, whose support and enthusiasm have made this book possible. I would like also to thank Joy Mizan for her work in bringing it to production, and Ronald Cohen for his stellar editorial work on the manuscript.

My greatest debts are to my family. My parents, Jairam and Shantha Amrith, have always taken a keen interest in my work; I am sure their lives' journeys sparked my interest in migration in the first place. I share an interest in migration with my sister, Megha Amrith, who is an anthropologist. I have learned much from her work, and I draw a great deal of inspiration from her example. My wife, Ruth Coffey, contributed many ideas to the design of this book; she accompanied me on photographic expeditions and brought to the project the sheer range of her enthusiasms. But the book is dedicated to her for other, more important, reasons.

Select Timeline

1405–33	Admiral Zheng He's naval expeditions to Southeast Asia and Indian Ocean
1498	Vasco da Gama reaches India
1511	Portuguese conquest of Melaka
1521	First Spanish expedition to the Philippines
1619	Dutch East India Company establishes a base at Batavia
1644	Manchu conquest of China, establishing the Qing dynasty (1644–1912)
1720	Establishment of small Chinese agricultural settlements on Sumatra
1740	Massacre of Chinese residents in Batavia
1757	Battle of Plassey. English East India Company takes control of Bengal
1786	British settlement in Penang
1819	British settlement in Singapore
1834	Beginning of Indian indentured migration overseas
1837	Abolition of slavery in the British Empire
1839–42	First Opium War
1845	Peninsular & Oriental Mail Service crosses Indian Ocean to Singapore
1851–64	Taiping Rebellion
1853	Inauguration of the Great Indian Peninsular Railway
1856–60	Second Opium War
1857	Indian Mutiny–Rebellion
1858	Establishment of Crown Rule in India
1867	Meiji Restoration in Japan
1869	Opening of the Suez Canal
1870s	British penetration into Malay Peninsula
1870s	Massive increase in Indian and Chinese emigration to Southeast Asia
1876–79	Famines in India and China
1878	First Chinese overseas consulate – in Singapore

1885	Completion of British conquest of Burma. Increase in Indian migration follows
1893	Official end of Chinese ban on overseas migration
1895	Formation of the Federated Malay States
1895	First Sino-Japanese war. Japanese colonization of Taiwan
1896	First Chinese students arrive in Japan
1896–1902	Famines in India and China
1898–1902	Construction and opening of Manchurian Railway
1905	Japanese military victory over Russia
1910	Japanese colonization of Korea
1910–17	Indentured labour abolished in the British Empire
1911	Chinese Revolution
1922	Indian Emigration Act seeks closer control over overseas migration from India
1926–27	Peak years of Indian and Chinese migration to Southeast Asia
1929	Wall Street crash precipitates global economic crisis
1930	British Malaya begins to enforce immigration restrictions
1930–31	Saya San Rebellion in Burma
1931	Japanese conquest of Manchuria
1932	Discovery of oil in Bahrain. Small-scale flows of migrant labour begin.
1934–45	Chinese Communist Party's 'Long March'
1937–45	Second Sino-Japanese War
1941–45	Japanese conquest of Southeast Asia. Second World War in the Pacific
1942	Indian refugee exodus from Burma
1943–44	Bengal famine
1945–49	Chinese Civil War
1945–49	Indonesian Revolution. Republic of Indonesia inaugurated in 1949
1945–54	Vietnamese declaration of independence and war of independence. French defeat at Dien Bien Phu in 1954
1946	Independence of the Philippines
1947	Partition of India. Independence of India and Pakistan
1948	Independence of Burma
1948	Independence of Sri Lanka
1948	Communist insurrection and declaration of Emergency in British Malaya
1949	Communist victory in Chinese Civil War. Inauguration of People's Republic of China and establishment of nationalist state on Taiwan

1955–59	Construction of Bhilai steel plant in India
1957–65	Independence of Malaya in 1957. Malaya becomes Malaysia with the addition of Singapore, Sabah, and Sarawak in 1963. Singapore becomes an independent city-state in 1965
1958–61	China's Great Leap Forward, resulting in mass famine
1962	Military coup in Burma
1964	India–Sri Lanka accord on 'repatriation' of Tamils
1965	Indonesian military coup installs General Suharto. Mass killings
1966–76	Chinese Cultural Revolution
1969	'Racial riots' in Malaysia
1971	Formation of Bangladesh. India-Pakistan war
1973	Oil crisis as OPEC increases price of oil
1973	Beginning of large-scale migration from South Asia to the Gulf states
1975	Fall of Saigon. American exit from Vietnam. Beginning of refugee crisis of Vietnamese 'boat people' (through 1990s)
1975–79	Pol Pot regime carries out Cambodian genocide, which ends with Vietnamese invasion
1978	Chinese economic reforms begin
1979	Islamic Revolution in Iran
1979	Russian invasion of Afghanistan. Beginning of Afghan refugee outflow
1983	Anti-Tamil pogroms in Sri Lanka
1991	Beginning of economic liberalization in India
1997–98	Asian financial crisis
2001–	US-led invasion of Afghanistan
2008	Collapse of Lehman Brothers bank sparks global financial crisis
2009	Sri Lankan military defeats the Liberation Tigers of Tamil Eelam

Glossary

Baba (m.)/*Nyonya* (f.)	Local-born Chinese in Singapore and Malaysia: the descendents of early Chinese settlers who married local women and adapted aspects of local cultural practice.
bumiputera	'Son of the soil': political term for indigenous inhabitants of the Malay Peninsula, primarily ethnic Malays.
dalit	Preferred modern term for low-caste or 'untouchable' groups in India, used as a term of self-description by many such communities.
hajj	Muslim pilgrimage to Mecca.
hawala	Informal, trust-based remittance networks that have existed for hundreds of years across the Indian Ocean.
hukou	Chinese system of residential permits introduced in the 1950s.
kangany	Tamil term for an existing plantation worker/ foreman who returned home to recruit workers on commission.
kongsi/gongsi	Overseas Chinese brotherhood of labourers and capitalists.
laoxiang	Chinese for homeland or 'home place'.
maistry	Term used in colonial Burma for '*kangany*'.
mestizo	In this book, refers to mixed Chinese/Filipino community, predominantly Catholic.
mui tsai	'Little sister' in Cantonese: a form of domestic service in China, and among overseas Chinese communities, not easily distinguished from adoption.
Nanyang	Chinese term for Southeast Asia ('Southern Ocean').

Peranakan	Indonesian term for descendents of early Chinese settlers who had married local women and adopted elements of indigenous culture.
sardar	Used widely in South Asian languages to denote a 'leader'; in this book, usually a labour boss/foreman.
totok	Used in colonial Indonesia to refer to recent immigrants ('pure Chinese') from China, distinguished from the Peranakan.
Transmigrasi	Indonesian programme of planned internal resettlement from Java to Sumatra and outer islands.
zifa	'Self-starters': voluntary Chinese migrants to Manchuria.

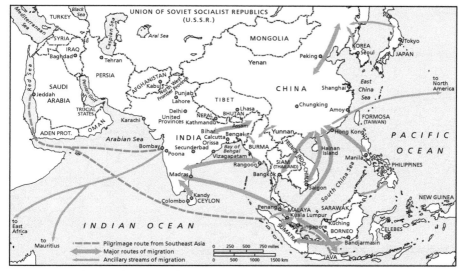

Map 1. **Routes of Migration in Asia, c. 1870–1930**

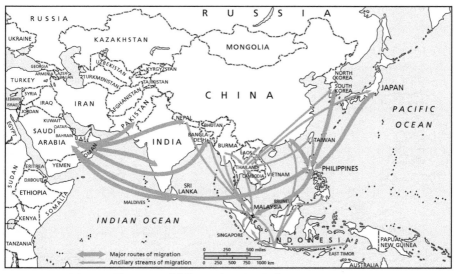

Map 2. **Routes of Migration in Asia, c. 1980–2010**

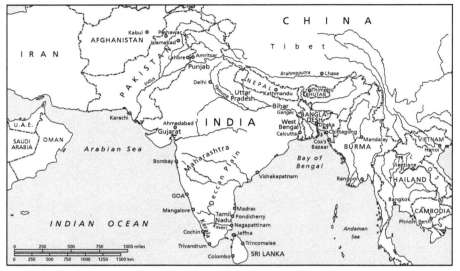

Map 3. **India**

Map 4. **China**

Map 5. **Southeast Asia**

Introduction

> Why should any man take upon himself all the risks of sailing abroad
> to seek a livelihood?
>
> *Farmer in Shantou, China, c. 1934*

Over the past 150 years, the scale of human migration within Asia has
been vast, greater than at any other time and place in human history. This
book argues that migrants have been central to enduring and significant
changes in modern Asian history: to economic and environmental transformations; to the spread of new political ideas and religious practices; to
social and demographic change. Until recently, most histories of Asia have
emphasized the perspectives of states, empires, and sedentary peoples.
This book seeks to place migrants at the heart of modern Asian history.

Migration has been a widespread experience in many regions of Asia,
but one that has, over time, come to be seen by states (and many historians)
as anomalous or exceptional. 'We imagine that mobility is border crossing, as though borders came first, and mobility, second', David Ludden
wrote in 2003. Historians have been too quick to project into the past the
modern world of nation-states with strict controls over movement into
and out of their territories. This book seeks to consider Asian history in
more mobile terms, by emphasizing the importance of movement and by
seeking to illustrate the connections that migrants made between distant
places. Borders did not pre-date mobility. Many of the routes that Asian
migrants followed in the age of mass migration built on much older traditions of circulation: along the Silk Road, across the Indian Ocean and
the China Sea. Over the twentieth century, however, borders constrained
and restricted mobility. They provoked many attempts at evasion.

This is a history of Asian migration since 1850; it is also a history
of states' continuing attempts to control migration, and of individuals'
and communities' efforts to resist, subvert, or adapt to such controls.[1]

---

[1] David Ludden, 'Presidential Address: Maps in the Mind and the Mobility of Asia',
Journal of Asian Studies, 62, 4 (2003), 1057–1078: 1062.

Who Is a Migrant?

Are any and all people who move, migrants? Does it help to treat as a singular phenomenon such different kinds of mobility as seasonal movement for agricultural work, forced displacement in times of conflict, the voluntary movement of individuals and families in search of opportunity, and even religious pilgrimage? In this book, 'migration' is used as shorthand for many kinds of mobility that are connected in many ways.

One thing these different kinds of mobility have in common is that they created connections beyond the local. Mobility in its many forms widened people's social networks and their imaginative worlds. Migration, whether short-term or long-term, over shorter or longer distances, changed hundreds of millions of people's sense of the world they lived in. Looking broadly at migration undermines the boundaries that have shaped historical research, and placed Indian, Chinese, and Indonesian history – or histories of South, Southeast, and East Asia – into separate boxes. The inter-regional connections that people forged through migration were both cause and consequence of the expansion of states and markets, the spread of the printing press, and the growth of modern militaries.

This book will show throughout that different forms of human mobility are connected. The migration of men for military service spurred the conflicts that displaced many others as refugees. Short-term seasonal migration could pave the way for family members to undertake longer journeys. An initial journey under conditions of indenture could establish social networks that later led to a further wave of free migration by relatives. The movement of students and pilgrims in search of enlightenment or blessings could turn, unplanned, into long-term settlement.

Finally, the book will show that the experience of migration could reach across generations. Many people descended from migrants continued to maintain cultural, familial, and political links with the lands of their ancestors; to the extent that they did, their lives continued to be shaped by histories of migration. The question of how long a migrant would remain a migrant was not always a matter of choice. Experiences varied. In some cases, migrant origins were erased or forgotten over time, as the descendents of migrants assimilated into local populations. But at other times and in other places, even those who chose to cut their links with the lands of their forebears were reminded constantly of their alien origins – origins that were marked on their identity cards, in the neighbourhoods they lived in, in persistent popular prejudices and stereotypes. In the twentieth-century world of nation-states, migrant origins in the distant past could remain a reason for exclusion or discrimination – even, in extreme cases, expulsion.

While developing these commonalities and connections between different kinds and experiences of migration, the book will distinguish between broad patterns of mobility in modern Asian history:

1. The migration of soldiers, sailors, and administrators in the service of states and empires. Through the twentieth century, this category would expand to include the movement of professionals and technicians.
2. The migration of large numbers of people as a result of war and political violence: captives, refugees, displaced people. Throughout the period covered by this book, millions of Asians were uprooted by violence: periods of particularly acute or widespread conflict saw major surges in this kind of forced mobility.
3. The movements over long distances, but sometimes for short periods, of students, pilgrims, and intellectuals: writers, journalists, publishers, teachers. Though their numbers were small, such people were at the forefront of cultural and social change.
4. Labour migration over long distances – this includes the vast migrations to tropical plantations in the nineteenth century, and the movement of unskilled and skilled labour in the construction and service industries in more recent times.
5. Long-distance, often overland, movement for settlement in sparsely populated lands, both state-sanctioned and spontaneous. This is a process that we might call 'colonization', and one that more or less came to an end in the mid-twentieth century, as new land was used up.
6. Seasonal migration for agricultural work, most often over short distances, and involving more women than men. This sort of migration was a constant over the entire period considered by the book, and involved the greatest number of people. It is the least likely to be counted in censuses and official statistics.
7. Urbanization: over the period covered by this book, migration from rural to urban areas grew in scale and significance, and now constitutes the most common form of migration in Asia – in China, above all.

Until the middle of the twentieth century, the common distinction between internal and international migration meant little in the Asian context. Most migration took place within and across the boundaries of empires. In the twentieth century, internal migration within empires turned abruptly into international migration, as new nations were formed and new borders drawn.

This book does not attempt to be comprehensive. Long-distance movement features more prominently than localized migration. The case studies often focus on overseas or cross-continental migration, though long-distance internal migration to urban areas plays a significant role in the second half of the book (Chapters 4 and 5). The justification for this focus, apart from constraints of space, is that focusing on long-distance migration presents us with a good way of studying more general social, cultural, and economic effects of migration – not least because long-distance migration was facilitated by and connected with local and regional movements.[2]

Underlying all of these movements was a fundamental feature of Asian migration until the mid-twentieth century: the tendency toward circular migration, or 'sojourning'. Agricultural colonists, scholars, and contract labourers alike maintained close ties with their home regions as they moved away. Wherever possible, they travelled back and forth between their home regions and the places to which they moved for work, alternating periods at home with periods away. Historians of Chinese migration have argued that sojourning represents a distinctively Chinese approach to migration: a practice of temporary residence away from home, with the intention of return – a kind of experimental migration. But this book suggests that this pattern of circulation was equally characteristic of other streams of Asian migration, including migration from the Indian subcontinent. Here, too, an important story of historical change unfolds: sojourning became easier as transportation became easier and cheaper, and then progressively more complicated, as modern states in the twentieth century made increasingly insistent demands of exclusive loyalty.

The pattern of sojourning is by no means exclusive to the Asian experience: both intra-European and trans-Atlantic migrations were often circular in nature; so, too, were many patterns of regional migration within Africa. Nevertheless, a far greater proportion of European migrants settled permanently at their destinations compared with Chinese or Indian migrants within Asia: the transience of migration was particularly, but not exclusively, characteristic of the Asian experience.

Explaining Asia's Mobility Revolution

The traditional picture of Asian societies as static and immobile before European colonization needs revision. The changes that historians have associated with 'early modernity', including increased human mobility, were as fully experienced in Asia as elsewhere. Mobile merchants, itinerant pilgrims, soldiers, and sailors all traversed long distances in Asia,

---

[2] Patrick Manning, *Migration in World History* (London: Routledge, 2005).

long before the nineteenth century (Chapter 1). There was a change in scale in mobility around the middle of the nineteenth century. That moment of acceleration and expansion provides the chronological starting point for this book. In terms of the numbers of people involved, the distances they travelled, and the environmental and economic transformations they brought about, the second half of the nineteenth century represented the start of Asia's mobility revolution.

What were the main drivers of Asia's mobility revolution? Four key factors will recur throughout the book, in different combinations over time. First, the nineteenth century witnessed a transformation in the scale and destructiveness of warfare and political violence, with lasting consequences. Military technology became more lethal. The protracted process of European conquest in Asia provoked regional conflicts and mobilized millions: soldiers, camp followers, refugees, political exiles, forced labourers. Periods of spectacular violence forced mass migrations: the catastrophic civil war of China's Taiping Rebellion; the wars of conquest and resistance in Indonesia; the Japanese conquest of Southeast Asia after 1941. More recently, civil strife or imperial wars in Vietnam, Cambodia, Burma (now Myanmar), Iraq, northeast India, and Afghanistan, have displaced hundreds of thousands.

The second causal factor is perhaps even more significant in the long term: the history of uneven economic development in Asia. The expansion of capitalism in colonial Asia was patchy, and it had variable effects. Pockets of modern industry and plantation-style agriculture coexisted with large, impoverished regions of increasingly precarious subsistence cultivation. New demands – for instance, the need to pay taxes – led millions of young men, and a growing number of women, to seek employment in the cash economy. These patterns of development and impoverishment have changed significantly over time, but unevenness persists as a spur to migration. To the present day, the high-growth economies of Southeast Asia continue to attract labour from poor regions of Bangladesh, India, Burma, and Nepal. The migration from poorer inland provinces to burgeoning industrial cities in contemporary China is the most rapid in human history. This book seeks to avoid the language, common to migration scholarship, of 'push' and 'pull' factors, which suggests that migrants merely respond to economic forces beyond their control. Nevertheless, it is a demonstrable and enduring feature of the history of Asian migration that economic inequality explains both the motivations for migration and the specific patterns of mobility.

The third driving force for migration is the expansion in the reach, the capacities, and the ambitions of colonial and post-colonial states.

It took the armed force of expanding European empires to make the global export of Indian indentured labour in the nineteenth century both viable and profitable. Conversely, in seeking to escape the attentions and exactions of expanding states and their militaries, millions more uprooted themselves. In the twentieth century, the creation of new nation-states across Asia proved a further impetus to migration. Finding themselves on the wrong side of the new borders that divided Asia after 1945, millions of people moved as refugees. As post-colonial states consolidated their authority and realised their ambitions for economic and social transformation, they induced or forced millions more to make long journeys in the service of national development, while preventing other kinds of mobility.

A fourth driving force for Asia's mobility revolution – more speculative and less easy to demonstrate concretely – is a rise in environmental insecurity. In the second half of the nineteenth century, large parts of Asia suffered from cyclical climatic phenomena of unprecedented intensity: the 1870s and the 1890s experienced some of the most intensive El-Niño Southern Oscillations in a millennium. The pace of social and economic transformation increased communities' vulnerability to climatic shock, while also opening up migration as an avenue of escape. Tens of thousands of young Chinese and Indians sought security and survival overseas. Social networks, flows of information, and relations of credit turned migration into a viable means of escape from subsistence crises.

The rise of mass migration in the second half of the nineteenth century formed part of a process that made possible the twentieth-century 'tipping point' in anthropogenic climate change: a process of land clearance, intensified energy use, population concentration, and an increase in human productive (and destructive) capacity. This might well have caused a more lasting level of environmental instability, though it is difficult to make categorical statements. Later in the twentieth century, the development projects of post-colonial Asia often took the form of an assault on nature. These campaigns displaced millions directly – as refugees from dam-building projects – and indirectly – when those projects wreaked havoc with local environments. Scientists forecast that increasingly unpredictable monsoons, more frequent flooding, and an increased incidence of drought will produce a growing stream of 'climate refugees' from coastal areas of Asia.[3]

---

[3] Edmund Burke III and Kenneth Pomeranz (eds.), *The Environment and World History* (Berkeley: University of California Press, 2009).

Transport, Communications, and Ideas

Asia's mobility revolution after 1850 required a number of facilitating conditions. Foremost among them was the global revolution in transportation and communications. Mass migration overseas was made possible by the steamship, and later by air travel. Railways and later roads facilitated overland migration. As we shall see, once the opening of new transport links allowed an initial wave of migration, this often created a self-sustaining circuit of further migration.

Communications were almost as important. The telegraph, the international postal service, and the printing press allowed for the spread of knowledge and information about distant places, and allowed families to keep in touch over ever-longer distances. Transport and communications contracted people's sense of both time and space. This process by which the world has come to seem both smaller and more connected is, of course, what we mean by the term 'globalization', but globalization in Asia has a long history.[4]

Finally, a precondition for migration – which was itself a result of migration – was a subtle, sometimes imperceptible, shift in attitudes and social norms. 'Migration', the American demographer Kingsley Davis wrote, 'is the result of an idea – an idea of what lies somewhere else'.[5] Historically, there were political and cultural barriers to migration and mobility in many Asian societies. These eroded over time. Migration became a normal, even expected, experience for millions of Asian families. At some point in the second half of the twentieth century, many Asian societies (but by no means all of them) underwent a further change in attitudes, allowing many young women to undertake long-distance migration without a consequent loss in their families' public reputations. This shift was so sweeping that by the late twentieth century, 60 per cent of the world's international migrants were women, and a majority among them were Asians.

Periodization

A rough periodization of the history of migration in modern Asia encompasses four main phases, which correspond with the sequence of chapters in this book. The first phase (Chapters 1 and 2) is the period from 1850 to about 1930: these decades witnessed the beginnings, the

---

[4] A.G. Hopkins (ed.), *Globalization in World History* (London: Pimlico, 2001).
[5] Kingsley Davis, *The Population of India and Pakistan* (Princeton: Princeton University Press, 1951), 107.

rise, and the peak of mass migration in Asia, and involved millions of people in both short- and long-distance migration. The migrations of this period led to the formation of wholly new societies across Asia, in turn leading to a significant redistribution of population and the growth of settlement in areas that had, until the late nineteenth century, been sparsely populated.

The second period (Chapter 3) encompasses the middle decades of the twentieth century, from the economic depression of the 1930s to the aftermath of the Second World War and the crucial years of Asia's decolonization. These decades witnessed the disintegration of the system of inter-regional migration that had developed from 1850. Economic crises broke apart the connected markets that channelled young men from coastal India and China to Southeast Asia's frontiers. Migration became a political problem, as indigenous nationalist movements mobilized against migrants and outsiders. The Second World War broke the links of labour migration altogether, while stimulating the mass movement of refugees. The creation of new states after 1945 produced a further wave of forced migration.

The period from the 1950s to the 1970s (Chapter 4) marked the 'golden age' of the nation-state in Asia. This era saw a reduced level of international migration, as restrictions on entry and exit became widespread. For the first time, passports and visas began to govern the mobility of Asians across borders. Yet these years also saw very significant migration within national boundaries, stimulated (and often forced) by post-colonial development projects. The 1950s also saw an acceleration of Asia's urban growth. From this point on, movement from rural to urban areas has become the most common form of mobility in Asia.

The fourth phase in the modern history of Asian migration is the period since the early 1970s (Chapter 5): the era of contemporary globalization. This period has seen a further expansion in both internal and international migration, with the latter once again reaching the peak levels of the 1920s. Fundamental economic transformations underlie this renewed migration: the rise of flexible modes of mass production; the growth of the global service industry; the declining importance of agriculture to many Asian economies (with the significant exception of India); and the shift of the global economic center of gravity towards East Asia, Southeast Asia, and the oil economies of the Persian Gulf. These changes have been – and continue to be – accompanied by a further acceleration and cheapening of long-distance transport (notably air travel) and electronic and telephonic communications.

The Debates

The history of Asian migration has stimulated lively debate, even as migration has been under-emphasized in larger narratives of modern Asian history. Three problems have been at the root of historians' debates. The first concerns the causes of migration: historians have debated the relative weight of individual agency, family pressures, economic imperatives, and external coercion in shaping migration. Related to this is a deeper question: how free has Asian migration been in the modern world? Second, debate has focused on the cultural consequences of mass migration, and the formation of multiple Asian diasporas. Third, historians have focused on the changing regulation and government of migration over time. Each chapter of this book will consider these problems in more detail, but it is worth setting out their contours at the outset.

Freedom and Agency

For decades, scholars believed there was a categorical difference between European migration across the Atlantic in the nineteenth century and migration across the Indian Ocean and the China seas. The contrast turned on the question of freedom. One recent survey, for example, compares the 'voluntary and self-bound migrations in the Atlantic system' with Asian migration that 'involved a minority of free migrants, large numbers of self-bound migrants, and forced moves'.[6] Asian migration, on this view, was by and large a product of European imperial intervention and coercion. By contrast, scholars have argued recently that Asian and Atlantic systems of migration are broadly comparable, and that Asian and European migrants alike were responding to the underlying forces of globalization. Adam McKeown points out that indenture played a relatively insignificant role in Chinese migration overseas, and that the vast majority of Chinese migration remained under Chinese control. Alongside other historians of Chinese migration, McKeown emphasizes instead the power of family networks in channelling people from particular villages in China to distant but specific destinations overseas.[7]

By contrast, in the view of Jan Breman, the violence of European empires must remain a crucial part of the story. Asian labour in the

---

[6] Dirk Hoerder, *Cultures in Contact: World Migrations in the Second Millennium* (Durham, NC: Duke University Press, 2002).

[7] Adam McKeown, 'Global Migration, 1846–1940', *Journal of World History*, 15, 2, (2004), 155–189; Philip Kuhn, *Chinese Among Others: Emigration in Modern Times* (Singapore: Singapore University Press, 2008).

colonial era, he argues, was 'mobile but unfree'. Breman shows that colonial states and European capitalists used all of the means of coercion at their disposal, including the reinforcement of older indigenous forms of bondage, to uproot people and whole communities from the impoverished countryside in order to work in the modern plantation sector. Colonial stereotypes played their role, too: by representing migrants as 'the worst and weakest in society, human refuse for whom there was no place', colonial states ensured that 'the use of compulsion' to force people to move 'became not only acceptable, but even desirable'.[8]

The challenge for historians lies in specifying the nature of this coercion, while also identifying its limits, and looking for the many ways in which Asian migrants retained a margin of freedom in their journeys: freedom to choose their destinations and to make new lives for themselves. Under constraint, Asian migrants made sense of their journeys, sought to shape more secure futures for themselves and their families, and asserted claims to public respect and to specific rights. Migrants found a measure of freedom in their creation of sacred landscapes on the plantations and on the city streets. They could and did participate in the public sphere of print and performance; they mobilized politically; they asserted, in the smallest ways in everyday life, their autonomy and their identity.

At every stage, we need to ask very specific questions about coercion, constraint, and liberty: how were migrants recruited? Who paid for their passages? What kinds of powers were responsible for migrants and their welfare? How was the enforcement of debt obligations and contracts organized, and what were the consequences for breaching these obligations? Were they legal – enforceable by courts – or did they rely on forms of communal sanction?[9] These questions are as relevant to the study of contemporary migration in Asia as they are to that of the nineteenth century.

Diasporas and Cultural Change

As individuals they meet, but only in the marketplace, in buying and selling.

J.S. Furnivall

Migration is central to the cultural history of modern Asia. Migration allowed cultures, ideas, and institutions to travel across the continent.

[8] Jan Breman, *Labour Migration and Rural Transformation in Colonial Asia* (Amsterdam: Free University Press, 1990).
[9] Walton Look Lai, 'Asian Diasporas and Tropical Migration in the Age of Empire: A Comparative Overview', *Journal of Chinese Overseas*, 5 (2009), 28–54.

Migrants took with them religious practices and rituals, political ideas, social and family structures. But how did these change in the process of migration, and what effects did they have on the societies to which migrants moved?

On one side of the debate, historians have argued that although cultures travelled with migrants, they remained closed and static in the process. Far from being a process of cultural exchange and mixture, they argue, what emerged from Asia's age of mass migration was a culture of enclaves, segregated from one another. Some have argued that this was part of a conscious process of colonial 'divide and rule'. Others have opted for material explanations, highlighting the ways in which labour markets were ethnically segmented, reinforcing cultural separateness.

The most influential version of this thesis about the cultural effects of Asian migration emerged in the 1930s and 1940s in the work of the British colonial administrator and scholar J.S. Furnivall, who spent most of his career in Burma. Furnivall argued that the era of mass migration in Asia had everywhere created what he called 'plural societies'. 'The first thing that strikes the visitor', Furnivall wrote of Southeast Asia's port cities, 'is the medley of peoples – European, Chinese, Indian and native'. Crucially, Furnivall pointed out, 'it is in the strictest sense a medley, for they mix but do not combine. Each group holds by its own religion, its own culture and language, its own ideas and ways'.[10]

A contrary (and more recent) view holds that migration in Asia led to a process of cultural mixture and exchange, producing creative instances of cultural hybridity. Encountering each other for the first time in diverse metropolitan centres, Asian elites developed new ways of speaking to one another, leading to the development of new linguistic practices, and new cultural forms. The rise of the printing press in Asia's port cities – made possible by the migration of typesetters, intellectuals, and journalists – catered to the needs of a consuming public of migrants eager for news from distant homelands. The public spheres of the port cities allowed mobile peoples to communicate, debate, and argue with one another; often they argued in English, alongside other bridging *lingua francas*.[11]

Taking a broad view of migration, it is equally easy to find instances of cosmopolitanism and of segregation. Unsurprisingly, works on cosmopolitanism have focused on the literate elites of the port cities,

---

[10] J.S. Furnivall, *Colonial Policy and Practice: A Comparative Study of Burma and Netherlands India* (Cambridge: Cambridge University Press, 1948), 304.
[11] T.N. Harper, 'Empire, Diaspora and the Languages of Globalism, 1850–1914', in A.G. Hopkins (ed.), *Globalization in World History* (London: Pimlico, 2001), 141–166.

whereas work on cultural separation takes as its starting point the plantation economy and its practices of ethnic segmentation and spatial segregation. Historians of cosmopolitanism and cultural hybridity have focused their research on the sphere of civil society, whereas those who insist on the hardness of cultural and ethnic boundaries take the administrative categories of the state as their point of departure.

It is important to consider specific encounters and interactions between Asian migrants of diverse origins, and between more recent migrants and longer-settled groups. There is now a vast literature on the contact of cultures in the age of European imperialism, yet this work focuses almost exclusively on the encounters between Europeans and Asians. For most Asian migrants in the nineteenth and twentieth centuries, the 'others' they encountered were not primarily Europeans but other Asians. This is true, still, in the migrant societies of the contemporary Middle East and Southeast Asia. Looking at actual sites of interaction between diverse peoples in the age of migration, we will see that the outcomes of these interactions spanned a wide spectrum: from racism, prejudice, and violence at one end, to creative cultural accommodation and religious innovation at the other. The key question to ask is how mobile people made sense of their encounters with strangers, while retaining or even reinforcing their sense of cultural or linguistic distinctiveness. Today, as in the past, the process of inter-cultural communication in Asia's migrant worlds is fraught with risk, but it can also be empowering and enlightening, even entertaining.

Migration and the State

Migration has always had 'its enemies' in Asia.[12] Initially, the 'enemies of migration' in Asia were traditional imperial bureaucracies, a classic case being the Chinese state that evinced a deep (if intermittent) hostility to emigration before its reforms of the late nineteenth century. In time, this cast of enemies came to include nationalist political movements that championed the rights of 'sons of the soil' over 'immigrants', and the modern nation-states over which such movements established control in the second half of the twentieth century.

A central theme in recent work in the history of migration is the development and global extension of border controls in the twentieth century. Controlling migration – particularly immigration – became central to the sovereignty of modern nation-states in the twentieth

---

[12] Wang Gungwu, 'Migration and Its Enemies', in Bruce Mazlish and Ralph Buultjens (eds.), *Conceptualizing Global History* (Boulder, CO: Westview Press, 1993).

century. Many of the laws and techniques to control migration origi-
nated in the United States, Australia, Canada, and South Africa, and
many of these measures arose from the desire to exclude Asian immigrants.[13] However, the relationship between migration and citizenship
was complex in Asia, where the policing of borders and the restriction of human mobility were (and remain) difficult to imagine and even
more difficult to enforce.

In historical perspective, Asian states have shaped and constrained
the possibility of migration, unable ever fully to control it. Even as they
have exerted a serious cost on individuals and communities on the
move, successive colonial and post-colonial attempts to control migration in Asia have always been exceeded and undermined by ungoverned
migration along informal networks, many of them with deep historical
roots. The chapters that follow highlight the fragility of state control
over migration as often as its power. In the present day, Asia's 'migration industry' of private recruiters and agents, transporters and traffickers, is enormous. It has a long history.

The Archives of Migration

How do we study the history of migration in Asia? One reason that
history has reflected the perspectives of states and settled peoples is
that they dominate the written record. By the mid-twentieth century,
in most of the world, possessing a national archive was an indispensable
element of the identity of any sovereign state, a repository of its official
memory. Migrants appear in the archives through the eyes of the state;
that is to say, migrants appear as a problem to be solved by resettlement,
integration, segregation, or deportation.

The proliferation of censuses across Asia in the last quarter of the
nineteenth century exemplified the concern of expanding colonial
states to increase their knowledge of the populations over which they
ruled. Among the many ways in which they categorized people – by
race, ethnicity, religion, or caste – censuses began to count people who
resided outside their place of birth. In territories such as British Malaya
that witnessed significant immigration from overseas, censuses began
to distinguish 'immigrant' from 'indigenous races'.

Because states took an increasing interest in categorizing their populations, censuses remain an essential starting point for historians of migration. Most of the estimates we have of the scale of global migration come

---

[13] Adam McKeown, *Melancholy Order: Asian Migration and the Globalization of Borders*
(New York: Columbia University Press, 2008).

from census data. Censuses are problematic, however. They give a snap-shot of a population at the time they were undertaken. The proportion of foreign-born residents enumerated in a census gives little sense of the mobility of that population, which might not constitute a settled population so much as a constantly shifting pool of arrivals and departures. Where most migration was circular in nature, this presents a particular problem. For historians most interested in overseas migration, censuses can be supplemented by statistics on the numbers of arrivals and departures each year, of the kind that port authorities and customs officials began to compile with increasing rigour. Ships' logs and registers of passengers have long been valuable sources for historians of European migration. Although they are less easily available in Asian archives, such sources, where extant, are vital to studying flows of people.

Increasingly, historians are unsatisfied with studying migration solely from the perspective of the sending or the receiving country. Where older histories of immigration focused on the ways in which migrants underwent a process of settlement and assimilation in their new societies, historians now emphasize the vital connections that diasporas maintained between their homelands and their new homes. Studying migration from multiple perspectives necessitates using multiple archives, tracing migrants' journeys from their points of origin as well as at their destinations; it involves trying to chart the ways in which return journeys, financial remittances, and long-distance communication helped to maintain family relationships over long distances.

One important way historians have studied the complex relationships that migration brought is by focusing their attention on the level of the individual or the family. Narrowing the lens in this way, historians have written histories of migration that avoid turning migrants into statistical abstractions, paying attention to the intimate dimensions of the migrant experience.

The archival sources for this sort of micro-history of migration are considerable.[14] Across the British Empire, concern with documenting and identifying migrants, indentured labourers, and pilgrims led to an expansion in the state's surveillance over movement overseas, generating a vast archive of documentation. There is the prospect of using these sources to say something about the journeys of non-elite, even illiterate, people. Migrant registers, declarations of intent, court records, passports, and identity papers constitute the 'barely discernible traces that the humble and the ordinary leave upon the world' – traces of their

[14] Miles Ogborn, *Global Lives: Britain and the World, 1550–1800* (Cambridge: Cambridge University Press, 2008).

ordinary and extraordinary journeys across empires.[15] Here, though, we run into the problem that despite their concern with identifying people, colonial states placed little store on the individuality of Asians. Millions of Asian migrants remained, quite literally, nameless. The archival trail very often runs cold.

Within the ranks of Asia's migrants were journalists, poets, and writers who left rich accounts of their experiences of mobility and of their encounters with other Asian migrants. In studying the cultural consequences of migration, many historians have turned to the archive of print that spanned Asia's migrant worlds. The last quarter of the nineteenth century saw the expansion of what Mark Frost has called an 'empire of letters', drawing together the port cities of the Indian Ocean and the China Sea. The spread of the printing press allowed for an expansion in publishing; the international postal service and the telegraph allowed news, information, and print to circulate with unprecedented speed. Through translation and re-publication, literate elites and intellectuals across Asia and beyond were in constant communication with one another.[16]

The study of print culture provides an illuminating window into the movement of ideas through Asia's migrant worlds, but it is also socially limited to a segment of the migrant population: the literate. What of the experiences of Asia's unlettered, working class migrants, past and present?

Here, the importance of oral history, and the use of ethnographic methods in historical research, become paramount. Oral history provides insight into the ways in which those who do not leave written records make sense of their migrant journeys. By collecting oral testimonies, by being alert to the humble importance of storytelling, historians can gain some insight into intimate experiences of migration: experiences of terror and excitement, of expectations frustrated and dreams realized. Oral histories reveal that more people have experiences of migration than censuses, statistics, or even newspapers would suggest. Even when memories are not strictly accurate – misremembered dates, exaggerations, and omissions are common features of individual and collective memory – they can be valuable for the sense of change over time that they convey. Sometimes this might involve a sense of nostalgia for an earlier,

[15] Amitav Ghosh, 'The Slave of MS. H. 6', in Partha Chatterjee and Gyanendra Pandey (eds.), *Subaltern Studies VII: Writings on South Asian History and Society* (New Delhi: Oxford University Press, 1992), 159–220: 161.
[16] Mark Ravinder Frost, '"Wider Opportunities": Religious Revival, Nationalist Awakening and the Global Dimension in Colombo, 1870–1920', *Modern Asian Studies*, 36, 4, (2002), 936–967.

more mobile world, a world before the nation-state. In other cases, what emerges is lasting relief that the trauma of migration is over, and the hope that the same would not lie in store for one's kin in the future.

One striking shift in recent times lies in the power of electronic communications, and the power of the internet in particular, to generate narratives of migration. Today, migrants are writing their own stories and their own histories: on blogs, in chat-rooms, on social networking sites, and other on-line forums. What implications will this have for historians of the future? What sort of archive will this multiplication of narratives produce? Are these on-line conversations about the migrant experience any less evanescent than the coffeeshop conversations of the early twentieth century? As the work of a historian reflecting on the present, this book can do no more than raise these questions.

Finally, historians find a valuable archive of migration in the landscape, in architecture, and in material culture. Everywhere, scattered across Asia, are material traces of migration. In the circulation of architectural forms, of particular methods of decoration or ornamentation, in the colour and textures of cloth and modes of clothing, historians can look for stories of migration that might be invisible to the archival eye. Attention to the ways in which histories of migration are embedded in everyday life might be particularly important in settings where migration has been stigmatized by official ideologies, where groups with long-distance connections have had to downplay or even to forget them.

A Note on 'Asia'

Asia is an abstract geographical term, with arbitrary boundaries. From the dawn of Europe's imperial expansion overseas, 'Asia' has gained its definition relationally: as that space that began where 'Europe' ended. Notwithstanding these origins, Asia has acquired a wide range of meanings, both scholarly and popular, in the modern world. Courses in Asian History remain standard fare in university curricula around the world. Asian Studies remains a vibrant academic field. Most people who inhabit the area labelled 'Asia' on a map have their own sense of what (and *where*) Asia is, what its boundaries are, and perhaps even an idea of what Asians might have in common. Politically, Asia has continued to have resonance into the late-twentieth and early-twenty-first centuries, with frequent invocations of 'Asian values', 'Asian culture', and even an 'Asian century'.

This book suggests that the history of migration provides a tool for thinking about Asia in new ways. Asia may well be an abstraction, but it took on real meaning from concrete journeys such as those described in this book. In a sense, this book is about many Asias: the Asian world of Islam, tying Indonesia to West Asia through pilgrimage and circulation, and stretching out to Cairo; the Asian world of migrant labour, linked by the flow of workers, traders and capital from the heartlands of India and China to Southeast Asia; the Asia of urban corridors and mega-cities stretching from Dubai to Shanghai, which today mobilises tens of millions of migrants. Where maps of migration represent migration as lines crossing stable territorial boundaries, a migrant's eye view of space might look quite different from those of states and cartographers. Asia is a mobile region. Its boundaries shift along with the connections that weave it together. The oil-rich cities of the Gulf, for instance, rose from obscurity to a place of centrality in so many Asian networks – migratory, familial, and financial – by the late twentieth century.

Writing of the Indian Ocean world, Sugata Bose argues that 'the human history of the Indian Ocean is strung together at a higher level of intensity in the inter-regional arena while contributing to and being affected by structures, processes, and events of global significance'.[17] Similarly, this book takes Asia – on land as well as at sea – as a particu-larly dense space of interaction rather than as a politically defined entity. Asia is a space linked together by the journeys of millions of people. At every stage, migration within Asia was always linked to global eco-nomic and political shifts, and Asians migrated to the farthest reaches of the world in the nineteenth and twentieth centuries. But the intensity of this connectedness was greater within Asia than beyond it.

I have, inevitably, made my own choices about the Asia I cover in this book. Admittedly I use phrases such as 'Asian migrants' as shorthand, sometimes with a generality that will make many scholars of particular regions uncomfortable. The book emphasizes those parts of Asia where flows of migration were greatest and that were most deeply shaped by migration: for that reason, it focuses especially on India, China, and the lands of Southeast Asia, where vast streams of Indian and Chinese migration converged with each other, and with many others. Some case studies have been chosen on the basis of what I know best, as a histo-rian of South and Southeast Asia; others seemed to me to exemplify the particular process or experience under discussion.

I hope, nevertheless, that readers with a special interest in those parts of Asia less extensively dealt with in the book will still find something of interest and relevance in the arguments, themes, and narratives in the pages that follow – some new questions to ask, if nothing more.

[17] Sugata Bose, *A Hundred Horizons: The Indian Ocean in an Age of Global Empire* (Cambridge, MA: Harvard University Press, 2006), 3.

1   Asia's Great Migrations, 1850–1930

Between 1850 and 1930, migration in Asia reached massive and unprecedented proportions. This expansion of migration took place amid widespread political and economic transformations. In these decades, most of Asia came under the domination, if not the direct control, of European empires. Asian peasant producers were more closely integrated – or subordinated – to world markets. Human migration and intensified production brought about fundamental ecological change. Many parts of Asia remained frontiers in the mid-nineteenth century: they were lightly populated, inhabited by shifting cultivators, and covered by jungle. Less than a century later, there were few Asian frontiers left.

At the same time, historical change in Asia became ever more closely connected with change on a global scale. From the middle of the nineteenth century, C.A. Bayly wrote, 'contemporary changes were so rapid and interacted with each other so profoundly, that this period could reasonably be described as the "birth of the modern world"'. Imperial states grew in power and capacity, and made greater demands on their subjects; ideas travelled around the world more rapidly and spread more widely than ever before; industrialization began to connect markets around the world more closely together. There was a 'step change in human social organization'.[1] Asia's great migrations were both a result and a driver of such changes. Migration facilitated the integration of large parts of Asia within an expanding global economy. But the vast majority of Asian migrants travelled elsewhere in Asia, and not beyond: as such, they created an even more intensive set of inter-regional connections within Asia.

This chapter focuses on the three most significant flows of migration across Asia between 1850 and 1930: the movement of up to 30 million people from India to present-day Sri Lanka, Burma, and Malaysia; about 19 million people from China to Southeast Asia (present-day Malaysia,

---

[1] C.A. Bayly, *The Birth of the Modern World, 1780–1914: Global Connections and Comparisons* (Oxford: Blackwell, 2004), 11.

Thailand, Vietnam, Indonesia and the Philippines); and more than 30 million people from northern China to the north-western region of Manchuria. A defining feature of Asia's great migrations was their temporary nature: in total, only 6 million Indians and 7 million Chinese settled permanently in Southeast Asia, and between 8 and 10 million Chinese in Manchuria. Even allowing for high rates of mortality, this suggests that most long-distance migrants eventually returned home. Asia's long-distance migrations were accompanied by an even greater number of movements over shorter distances.[2]

Around the middle of the nineteenth century, a conjunction of factors making migration possible came together: a revolution in transport; political crises in India and China; the expansion of imperial control and capitalist investment into the frontier regions of Southeast Asia and Manchuria. Migration to Southeast Asia really soared in the 1870s, with the advent of regular steamer services across the China Sea and the Bay of Bengal; the railway permitted the expansion of migration to Manchuria somewhat later, in the 1890s. In each case, the early twentieth century saw the first peak of migrant flows, followed by a second and even greater peak in the 1920s, after a slight fall-off after the First World War. The global economic depression of the 1930s saw a reversal of migrant flows across Asia, but migration recovered to high levels by the late 1930s, only to come to a crushing halt with the outbreak of a global war (Chapter 3).

Mobility in Early Modern Asia

Indian society has no history at all, at least no known history. What we call its history, is but the history of successive intruders who founded their empires.

Karl Marx, 1853

Most of early modern Asia was ruled by land-based empires of great reach and considerable longevity. Three great Muslim Empires – the Ottoman Empire (c. 1299–1923), the Safavid Dynasty (1501–1722), and the Mughal Empire (1526–1858), based, respectively, in present-day Turkey, Iran, and India – controlled the Eurasian landmass from the Mediterranean to the Bay of Bengal. The Qing (or Manchu) Dynasty

---

[2] Walton Look Lai, 'Asian Diasporas and Tropical Migration in the Age of Empire: A Comparative Overview', *Journal of the Chinese Overseas*, 5 (2009), 28–54; Adam McKeown, 'Global Migration, 1846–1940', *Journal of World History*, 15, 2 (2004), 155–89; Adam McKeown, 'Chinese Emigration in Global Context, 1850–1940', *Journal of Global History*, 5 (2010), 95–124.

ruled over a territory that more or less corresponds to the boundaries of modern China, between 1644 and 1912, succeeding the Ming Dynasty that had ruled since the fourteenth century. The Russian empire expanded steadily across Eurasia, east into Siberia.[3]

The image of Asia as static and agrarian, common to European writings on Asia over many centuries, was only part of the story. Agriculture played a dominant role in Asia's great land-based empires, but they sustained traditions of movement and circulation with deep roots. Writing of an even earlier period, between 500 and 1500 C.E., Stuart Gordon argues that 'it was its networks that made the great Asian world unique'; 'bureaucrats, scholars, slaves, ideas, religions, and plants moved along its intersecting networks'.[4]

For centuries, Asian merchants, bankers, and traders had participated in a sophisticated world of commerce across the Indian Ocean and the South China Sea. Asian networks of mercantile migration and exchange persisted through the experience of European conquest. From the beginning of the second millennium C.E., Jewish bankers based in Baghdad directed a commercial empire that stretched from Cairo to western India. Bankers from western India controlled a network of credit that reached as far as the Philippines in the east and the Red Sea in the west. Asian banking firms despatched both ships and agents across the Indian Ocean, leading to the development of cosmopolitan settlements of traders in port cities throughout the Ocean's littorals. Migration for military service was common, sometimes over long distances. Throughout South and Southeast Asia, the early modern period saw the intensification of elite circulation over long distances – the circulation of administrators, military experts, religious specialists, and those skilled in commerce.[5]

Until the nineteenth century, the most powerful mover of men and women was slavery. As Richard Eaton has argued, 'the interregional movement of slaves helped integrate peoples, economies, and cultures of South Asia with those of Central Asia and the Indian Ocean rim'. Similarly, in Southeast Asia, the 'movement of captive peoples and slaves was the primary source of labour mobility' before the nineteenth

[3] Stephen F. Dale, *The Muslim Empires of the Ottomans, Safavids, and Mughals* (Cambridge: Cambridge University Press, 2010); Jonathan D. Spence, *Search for Modern China* (New York: W.W. Norton, 1990); Dominic Lieven, *Empire: The Russian Empire and Its Rivals* (London: John Murray, 2000).
[4] Stuart Gordon, *When Asia Was the World* (New Haven: Yale University Press, 2008), 177.
[5] Sanjay Subrahmanyam, 'Connected Histories: Notes Towards a Reconfiguration of Early Modern Eurasia', *Modern Asian Studies*, 31, 3 (1997), 735–762.

century. Over centuries, most slaves in South Asia were war captives: many of the soldiers serving sultanates in north India were slaves captured in Central Asia, even as far away as Ethiopia. Burma's borderlands provided another major source of slaves. Slaves were used as soldiers, as cultivators, as domestic servants, or as mothers of future soldiers. Slave status was not always fixed in perpetuity; it was common for slaves to assimilate into local families, even elite families, over time. In Southeast Asia, slaves tended to come from weak or fragmented societies; often they were captured in border raids by forces from wet rice-cultivating zones. Broadly, they moved from east to west, and from non-Muslim societies practising shifting cultivation to settled, more powerful Muslim societies. Until 1820, the majority of residents in Southeast Asia's urban centres were captives or slaves.[6]

European Expansion and Asian Mobility

From the dawn of the sixteenth century, European trading companies loomed large as players in Asia's commercial networks, and as military powers in their own right. The commercial dynamism of Asian trade attracted European adventurers. Chartered private companies – the Portuguese, Dutch, French and English East India Companies – used force to secure trading monopolies in the Indian Ocean, but they depended heavily on Asian intermediaries. From their foothold on India's south-western coast, Portuguese power expanded across the Bay of Bengal, capturing the great Malay entrepôt of Melaka in 1511. The Dutch East India Company staked its claim to the lucrative spice markets of Indonesia from a base in Batavia (Jakarta), established in 1619 on the island of Java. Victory in the Battle of Plassey in 1757 gave the English East India Company control over Bengal, from where it expanded across the Indian subcontinent – and east, across the Bay of Bengal. These chartered companies began to exercise the power of states. In every case, the lucrative China trade – Chinese markets in luxury goods, and in tea – provided the main impetus for European commercial and maritime expansion in Asia.

European expansion in Asia depended on (and in turn stimulated) slavery and other forms of coerced migration. European trading companies used slaves to construct their fortresses and to work in the

[6] Anthony Reid (ed.), *Slavery, Bondage and Dependency in Southeast Asia* (St. Lucia, Queensland: Queensland University Press, 1983), 27; Indrani Chatterjee and Richard M. Eaton (eds.), *Slavery and South Asian History* (Bloomington: Indiana University Press, 2006), 11.

households of their officials. Rising European demand for local products provided an impetus for the expansion of pre-existing, indigenous patterns of slavery and bonded labour, especially in labour-scarce regions. The warfare provoked by European military intrusion produced thousands of new captives to be sold on as slaves.

The Dutch East India Company thrived on multiple circuits of forced labour, taking slaves from Bengal, Burma, the eastern coast of India, and the segmented or stateless societies of the Indonesian Archipelago. The slaves went to Batavia, to Ceylon, and to the southern tip of Africa to the Dutch settlement at the Cape Colony. Between 1659 and 1661 alone, the Dutch transported between 8,000 and 10,000 slaves each year from south India, exploiting a period of political violence and consequent famine. The Indonesian island of Bali emerged as a major regional centre for the slave trade, exporting over 100,000 slaves in the eighteenth and nineteenth centuries. Slaves from diverse origins worked on Batavia's docks and repaired ships. They worked as fishermen and cultivators, and as domestic servants.

By the late-eighteenth century, the European demand for Southeast Asian products to trade in exchange for Chinese tea stimulated indigenous slave-raiding in the 'Sulu Zone' – the region encompassing Borneo, the southern Philippine archipelago, and the outer islands of Indonesia. Indigenous raiders, from communities known as the Iranun and Balangingi, took up to 300,000 captives between 1770 and 1870. In time, as metropolitan attitudes towards slavery changed in Europe, Dutch authorities would attempt to suppress this trade, but it lasted well into the nineteenth century. So, too, did the slave trade in the north-western Indian Ocean, where as late as 1923, most of the boatmen and porters in Jeddah harbour – gateway to the Muslim holy cities of Mecca and Medina – were slaves.[7]

Chinese Sojourners

Wherever European adventurers went in Asia, they found that thriving communities of Chinese sojourners had either already established

[7] Markus Vink, '"The World's Oldest Trade": Dutch Slavery and Slave Trade in the Indian Ocean in the Seventeenth Century', *Journal of World History*, 14, 2 (2003), 131–77; James Warren, 'The Iranun and Balangingi Slaving Voyage: Middle Passages in the Sulu Zone', in Emma Christopher, Cassandra Pybus, and Marcus Rediker (eds.), *Many Middle Passages: Forced Migration and the Making of the Modern World* (Berkeley, 2007), 52–71; Janet J. Ewald, 'Crossers of the Sea: Slaves, Freedmen and Other Migrants in the Northwestern Indian Ocean, c. 1750–1914', *American Historical Review*, 105, 1 (2000), 69–91.

themselves, or followed soon in their train. The commercial and migratory links between southern China and the South Seas were of long standing. Between 1405 and 1433, Chinese maritime expeditions led by the Muslim admiral Zheng He (1371–1435) traversed Southeast Asia and crossed the Indian Ocean to Africa. The Chinese state soon turned its back on overseas adventuring, but Zheng He's voyages left small communities of Chinese en route, as 'precursors of China's modern emigration history'.[8]

Early European settlements in Southeast Asia and many indigenous principalities had significant Chinese populations. From the time of its founding until the notorious 'Chinese massacre' of 1740, the Dutch East India Company's base at Batavia was 'basically a Chinese colonial town under Dutch protection'.[9] Throughout the seventeenth century, an average of 1,000 Chinese each year arrived in Batavia, and a similar number departed for China. Portuguese-controlled Melaka and Spanish Manila also had large resident Chinese populations, occupying a pivotal role in their commercial life. In Manila, as in Batavia, the Chinese faced periodic persecution, and brutal massacres on several occasions – in 1603, in 1639, and in 1662. The entry of the British Empire into Southeast Asia's seas at the end of the eighteenth century expanded the commercial opportunities open to Chinese merchants, as Penang and then Singapore were declared 'free' ports: free from the monopolies and exactions of the Dutch and Portuguese regimes, and so particularly attractive to Chinese traders.

The relatively slow pace of Chinese immigration, and the total ban on the departure of women from China, led to the establishment of mixed, or creole, communities in all of these colonial settlements. Chinese traders took indigenous women as second wives. The communities they formed were known as Mestizos in the Philippines, Peranakan in the Indies, and Baba in Malaya. In each case, Chinese and indigenous customs and cultures melded to create distinctive new forms of dress, speech, cuisine, and comportment (Chapter 2). The eighteenth century also saw the first settlements of Chinese in Southeast Asia specializing in primary production. Chinese brotherhoods, known as *kongsi*, established settlements just east of Sumatra in 1720, and on the island of Borneo in 1740, mining – on a cooperative basis – for export to the Chinese market.[10]

[8] Philip A. Kuhn, *Chinese Among Others: Emigration in Modern Times* (Singapore: NUS Press, 2008), 8.
[9] Leonard Blussé, 'Batavia, 1619–1740: The Rise and Fall of a Chinese Colonial Town', *Journal of Southeast Asian Studies*, 12, 1 (1981), 159–178.
[10] Carl A. Trocki, *Opium and Empire: Chinese Society in Colonial Singapore, 1800–1910* (Ithaca: Cornell University Press, 1990).

The 'Last Great Enclosure'

Against these traditions of mobility (which depended, often, on slavery), countervailing pressures towards settlement and immobilization were intense. Throughout the early modern world, centralizing imperial states pressed hard on their frontiers. A gradual process of peasant colonization of lands for permanent, irrigated cultivation sharpened the divide between settled societies and shifting cultivators. In many places, this closing agrarian frontier constituted also a religious frontier: in the Bengal Delta, for example, the boundaries of settled cultivation were also the boundaries of the spread of Islam.

States sought to confine their subjects with fixed identities and places of permanent residence. Maps, censuses, and cadastral surveys made territory more 'legible', and populations easier to tax or to conscript for military service. States – European colonial states and Asian imperial states alike – made claims on the forest resources within their territory. In South Asia in the eighteenth century, a significant proportion of the overall population consisted of mobile artisans and workers, agricultural colonists, soldiers, service workers, refugees, nomadic peoples, and shifting cultivators. By the turn of the nineteenth century, an India of settled, arable farming – dominated by caste Hindus – had come into being.[11]

In South Asia and elsewhere, the greatest losers from this process of settlement and immobilization were nomadic peoples: pastoralists, forest peoples, and shifting cultivators. Historian Peter Perdue has argued that throughout Eurasia, expanding imperial states 'drew fixed lines through the steppes, deserts, and oases, leaving no refuge for the mobile peoples of the frontier'. Perdue describes this as the 'closing of the frontier' on a global scale, which 'eliminated permanently as a major actor on the historical stage the nomadic pastoralists'. Writing of the same process in Southeast Asia, the political anthropologist James Scott has called it 'the last great enclosure movement': a long process of settlement that provoked, over centuries, the formation of multiple 'maroon communities' in Asia's highlands, beyond the reach of valley-based states that drew their power from irrigated rice cultivation.[12]

[11] David Ludden, 'Presidential Address: Maps in the Mind and the Mobility of Asia', *Journal of Asian Studies*, 62, 4 (2003), 1057–1078: 1063.
[12] Peter Perdue, *China Marches West: The Qing Conquest of Central Eurasia* (Cambridge, MA: Harvard University Press, 2005), 10–11; James C. Scott, *The Art of Not Being*

A Mobility Revolution?

Migration within Asia underwent a dramatic change in scale after 1850. New routes and new kinds of migration emerged. Older forms of movement reinvented themselves under new conditions. This step change in the scale of migration was made possible by a revolution in transportation and technology; migrants were enticed and forced towards the frontier regions by the expansion of capital investment backed by the armed force of empires.

The railway and the steamship made long-distance travel easier, faster, and cheaper than previously imaginable. Breakthroughs in shipping and in the railways both came around mid-century. In 1845, the Peninsular & Oriental Mail service first crossed the Indian Ocean to Singapore and on to Hong Kong. With the opening of the Suez Canal in 1869, transit and trade between Europe, South and Southeast Asia, and from there to the China Sea, became more rapid. By the 1880s, steamships such as the one pictured in Plate 1.1 carried thousands of people each week across the Indian Ocean and the China Sea. Railway construction advanced at the same time, beginning in India with the construction of the Great Indian Peninsular Railway in 1853. Information travelled more swiftly. By 1870, the British India Submarine Telegraph Company connected Bombay with the Red Sea. A year later, telegraph connections spanned the Bay of Bengal: from Singapore, the line reached through Saigon, Hong Kong, Shanghai, Nagasaki, and up to the Russian port of Vladivostok.[13]

The collapsing of distance coincided with significant political shifts across Asia. In India, the East India Company's territorial expansion over the first half of the nineteenth century had brought with it a more intrusive, confident, and racially arrogant imperialism. The use of Indian troops in wars at home and abroad caused particular tensions within the Company's army. The East India Company's state intervened more deeply in the economy and in society. China, too, experienced an intensification of external pressure. The clash between British traders and the Chinese state came to a head in the 1830s. Concerned about the effects of the opium trade – both on Chinese society and on their authority – China's rulers attempted to ban it. Claiming to defend the principle of free trade, British forces intervened to protect their most

---

Governed: An Anarchist History of Upland Southeast Asia (New Haven: Yale University Press, 2009).

[13] Howard K. Dick and Peter Rimmer, *Cities, Transport and Communication: The Integration of Southeast Asia Since 1850* (Basingstoke: Palgrave, 2003).

Plate 1.1 **The SS 'Benalder' (1880), a 2,054 tons steamship owned by WM Thomson & Company. The steamship revolution ushered in a transformation in the scale of migration in Asia starting about 1870: the number of Indian and Chinese migrants making the journey to Southeast Asia jumped from thousands, to tens of thousands, and then to hundreds of thousands each year.**
Source: National Archives of Singapore, 128553. Used with permission.

valuable item of commerce, resulting in the First Opium War (1839–42). The Qing state's defeat opened the door to deeper Western penetration of the coastal ports, under a series of 'unequal treaties' granting them special privileges, and eroding the Chinese state's control – including, significantly, its control over Chinese emigration. The post-war settlement gave the English control over Hong Kong, which would become the largest port of overseas emigration from China.

Resulting from the tensions accumulating from English imperial expansion, the 1850s saw the outbreak of two of the greatest political revolts of the nineteenth century: the Taiping Rebellion in China (1851–64), propelled by Christian and Buddhist millenarianism, and the Indian Rebellion (1857), which began with a mutiny in the Indian Army. The social disruption caused by the Taiping Rebellion, led by Hong Xuiquan, who claimed to be the younger brother of Jesus Christ, was catastrophic. Perhaps 20 million people were killed over fifteen years of fighting. Warfare displaced millions more from their homes. Jonathan Spence's evocative account describes 'the masses of refugees and homeless villagers who wander in the area, displaced again and again by fighting that seems to have no end'. These refugees were faced with 'at least eight different kinds of troops who march and counter-march around their former homes'.[14] The disruption of local economies had millions on the move. The most vulnerable among them were the first to fall victim to press-gangs, labour recruiters, and kidnappers. Their journeys could, and often did, take them to the far corners of the world.

The Indian Rebellion brought to the fore social tensions that had accumulated in north India over a century of British expansion, and manifested itself in a widespread revolt by sections of the peasantry, artisans, and deposed aristocracies. The social upheaval that both rebellions caused led directly to an increase in migration: much of this was the internal migration of refugees in flight from conflict, but the general unmooring of the population, in both cases, mobilized a labour force that could be persuaded or coerced into making longer journeys.

The defeat of both rebellions served to consolidate British control over India, and weakened the Chinese state enough to permit the expansion of European influence over China. Through the force of the lethal military technologies that the foundries and shipyards of industrial Europe churned out, a renewed thrust of aggressive expansion brought almost all of Southeast Asia, with the exception of Thailand, under European control by the 1870s. Lower Burma had come under British control after the Anglo-Burmese war of 1852; the French began to assume direct control in Indochina, piecemeal, after 1862; the 1870s saw the British 'forward movement' in the Malay Peninsula, suborning Malay sultans in a series of treaties. Dutch expansion into the outer islands of Indonesia was more protracted, provoking a bloody war of resistance in the region of Aceh (in northern Sumatra) that lasted from 1873 to 1908. By 1885, British expansion in Burma was complete. Japan, too, began its rise to prominence as a colonial power in Asia, taking control of Taiwan in 1895 and Korea in 1910. In the same period, Japanese commercial interests in China expanded significantly.

The iron fist of imperial power opened Southeast Asia's frontiers to European and Asian capital investment. Globalizing capitalism, its search for new resources and new markets, provided the essential spark that moved millions. Asia's frontiers were opened by the search of

[14] Jonathan D. Spence, *God's Chinese Son: The Taiping Heavenly Kingdom of Hong Xiquan* (New York: Norton, 1996), 303.

capitalists for new lands on which to grow crops to feed Europe's burgeoning industrialization, and to satisfy the taste for sweetness and spice
sweeping Europe's consuming public. As European control expanded,
the sparsely populated frontier zones of Asia – the Malay Peninsula;
southern Thailand and Burma; the outer islands of Indonesia; eastern
India – attracted land-hungry investors. In Northeast Asia, it was not
Europeans but private interests within the Qing state that chased frontier lands in Manchuria; German, Russian, and Japanese investment
soon followed.

The opening of new frontiers of cultivation produced an insistent
demand for labour. This, more than anything, was the engine of Asia's
mass migrations. Asia's frontier regions had very low population den-
sities. Local peasantries in frontier areas did not find wage labour on
plantations attractive. Many fought stubbornly for their independence,
and opted for the freedom of subsistence production or shifting cultivation. They were put under inordinate pressure by the expansion of
industrial capitalism and modern states, but many refused to succumb.
The structures and precedents were in place to draw labour, instead,
from the densely populated heartlands of coastal southern China
and the eastern seaboard of the Indian subcontinent: the revolutions
in transport made this prospect a reality. The aftermath of slavery's
abolition in the British Empire in 1837 had provided the first experience of the large-scale export of Indian labour overseas – to the sugar
plantations of the Atlantic and Indian Oceans – under conditions of
indenture. The prior existence across Southeast Asia of small settlements of Chinese merchants, and even cultivators and miners, meant
that the initial spark of demand for labour led quickly to a rapid expansion in migration.

Under these circumstances, pressures within Indian and Chinese
society compelled large numbers of people to seek their fortunes far
from home. Population growth in both India and China began to put
strain on the most fertile lands. Agricultural yields began to decline as
a result. In China, a long-term drift of population towards the coastal
areas of the south led to tensions between (relative) newcomers and
longer-settled populations. Land pressure was exacerbated by ecological catastrophe. The second half of the nineteenth century witnessed
periods of exceptionally severe drought, which historians have traced to
severe El-Niño events, leading twice (1876–79; 1896–1902) to devastating famines. These killed tens of millions; during and after the famines
there were surges in internal and overseas migration.

The revolution in the mobility of Asian labour that began in the 1850s,
and accelerated after 1870, happened concurrently with a process that

is much better known to historians: the consolidation of a settled, sedentary peasantry across agrarian Asia. In permitting, even forcing, millions of Asians to move over long distances, colonial states and Asian elites ensured that others stayed firmly in place. British India is a case in point. As the quantity of Indian emigration overseas increased, the colonial state and its intermediaries cemented their legal and political control over a settled peasantry. Changing systems of land tenure and customary authority, enforced by the colonial courts; new demands of taxation; new systems of survey and registration; the further decline of the indigenous artisan economy: all of these forced immobilization upon many groups in India that had previously enjoyed greater mobility. Dutch authorities in Indonesia, while encouraging the movement of indentured labour to the plantation belt of Sumatra, ensured that 'traditional' local authorities, propped up by the state, would keep 'village Java' static. As later chapters will show, the conflict between indigenous peasantries tied to the land and enclaves of migrant workers from distant shores would develop over the twentieth century, with serious and sometimes tragic political consequences.

Asia's Age of Migration, 1850–1930

By the 1870s, plantation-based production of commodities for export was well established on Asia's frontiers. The Malay Peninsula produced tin, sugar, pepper, gambier, and – around the turn of the twentieth century – rubber. Sumatra specialized in tobacco; Java in sugar; the outer islands of the Indonesia in spices. Ceylon and parts of south India produced tea and coffee; the north-eastern Indian region of Assam became a growing frontier of tea plantation. As rubber emerged as one of Asia's most valuable commodities, it was grown on a smaller scale in French-controlled Vietnam. The expanding labour force of the plantation zones needed to be fed. Rice, the essential article of subsistence across large areas of Asia, came initially from the traditional rice-producing regions: the river deltas of southern India and southern China. Stretched to capacity, these regions were unable to supply rising demand. New regions of rice production opened up, in Burma, Thailand, and Indochina, attracting another wave of migration to the great river deltas of mainland Southeast Asia: the Irrawaddy, Chao Phraya, and Mekong basins. Over the second half of the nineteenth century, more than 14 million acres of land had been newly planted with rice in these regions.

To these frontiers of production and cultivation, and to the port cities that swelled with the expansion in trade, millions of Asian migrants

Table 1.1 *Indian and Chinese Migration to Southeast Asia, 1891–1938*

Period	Indians	Indians	Chinese	Chinese
	Entering Southeast Asia	Departing Southeast Asia	Entering Southeast Asia	Departing Southeast Asia
1891–1900	1,423,756	1,064,070	1,875,423	1,419,603
1901–10	2,836,691	2,434,993	2,500,000	1,908,045
1911–20	3,795,985	3,145,913	2,465,449	1,901,023
1921–30	4,851,130	4,093,655	3,818,103	2,860,811
1931–38	2,651,139	2,524,491	1,805,510	1,982,054
Total	15,558,701	13,263,122	12,465,283	10,071,536

Source: Kaoru Sugihara, 'Patterns of Chinese Emigration to Southeast Asia, 1869–1939', in Kaoru Sugihara (ed.), *Japan, China, and the Growth of the Asian International Economy, 1850–1949* (Oxford: Oxford University Press, 2005), 244–274: 246. Figures for Indian migration include Malaya and Burma only.

moved. They moved to work as tin miners and rubber tappers; they grew rice and harvested tobacco; they worked as petty shopkeepers and wholesalers; they provided the credit to local cultivators; they worked on the docks and in the restaurants of the cities; they pulled rickshaws, built railways, and, in time, drove buses and taxis. Some of them were under contracts of indenture. The most unfortunate migrants were coerced or deceived into signing such contracts; others viewed them as an unfortunate compromise, or as the lesser of two evils. The majority, however, raised funds for their journeys from family members and local creditors, or from professional labour recruiters and migration agents, in the hope of a handsome return.

As the scale of Asian migration assumed unprecedented dimensions, multiple and dispersed currents of human movement became linked inextricably, constituting an interconnected system. At the core of this system were the two largest streams of movement: from southern India and southern China to the lands of Southeast Asia (Table 1.1). Indian migration remained within the British Empire, confined to three major destinations: Burma, Ceylon, and Malaya. Chinese emigrants travelled more widely: to Thailand and the Philippines, right across Indonesia, and to Vietnam. The Malay Peninsula was where these two great migrations met: Malaya received more Chinese emigrants than any other single destination, and a large flow of south Indian migrants. Concurrent with Indian and southern Chinese migration to Southeast Asia, the

migration from north China to Manchuria assumed great and growing significance, attracting millions from then northern provinces of
Shandong and Hebei.

These major overseas and overland migrations from India and China
stimulated many smaller streams of migration. The increased demand for
rice that growing agglomerations of migrant labour demanded spurred
a process of peasant colonization that had begun on a small scale centuries earlier. Asia's great river deltas underwent a process of peasant
migration and settlement as rice cultivation expanded. Vietnamese peasants from the Red River Delta and coastal areas moved to the Mekong
Delta. Burmese peasants migrated to the Irrawaddy Delta. Thai cultivators from the country's Central Plains settled on the banks of the Chao
Phraya River. To provide these areas of expanding cultivation with
credit, services, and infrastructure, millions more Indians and Chinese
moved, as bankers and railway workers, sanitation workers and shopkeepers. Thousands of Koreans moved to Manchuria's towns and frontiers in search of opportunity, as did poorer Japanese colonists. These
connected processes of migration gave rise to entirely new societies with
highly mixed populations in both urban and rural areas.

Each of these flows of migration experienced vicissitudes shaped by
local conflicts and regional ecologies, but on a broad scale, the chronology of Asian migration is clear and convergent. Almost everywhere, the
1870s marked the decade of rapid acceleration, with a steady and rapid
growth of migration to a peak in the early twentieth century. After a
brief dip in the 1910s, migration resumed to an even greater peak in the
1920s: 1927 was the single greatest year of migration. That year, nearly
300,000 people journeyed from India to Burma and Malaya; well over
half a million Chinese travelled to Southeast Asia, and close to 1 million
to Manchuria. Almost everywhere, the economic depression of the 1930s
saw this trend reversed, with a net reduction in migration: a period of
repatriation and retreat, when mobility became more difficult.

The chronology of Asian migration, then, is the chronology of economic development and capitalist transformation – the chronology of
boom and slump – punctuated in specific cases by political and climatic
interruptions or accelerations. The great challenge in writing the history of Asian (or any) migration is to show how this periodization on a
large scale maps onto the micro-chronologies of individuals' and families' life-cycles, or the seasonal rhythms of agrarian economies.

Between the 1870s and the 1930s, diverse strands of migration in
Asia exhibited similar patterns. Circular migration – sojourning – was
a dominant and distinctive feature of both Indian and Chinese migrations, underpinned by a more permanent process of peasant colonization

in frontier regions. These patterns began to shift in the 1920s: in most of Asia, the proportion of women undertaking long-distance migrations increased. The introduction of controls over migration provided another kind of force for convergence in the options that opened and closed for people on the move. Using a number of case studies, the next section of this chapter examines Asia's age of migration in detail.

Indian Migration, 1850–1940

Between 1834 – when the first Indian indentured workers journeyed to sugar plantations in the Caribbean and Mauritius in the wake of the abolition of slavery in the British Empire – and 1940, over 28 million people left India's shores. Most of this migration occurred after 1870. Most migrants returned to India in time; many others died along the way. The demographer Kingsley Davis reflected, in 1951, that 'unusually small' numbers of Indian emigrants had settled overseas. On Davis's estimate, which remains the best available, between 6 million and 7 million people of Indian origin had settled overseas by the end of the 1930s: Davis contrasted this with the 85 million people of British origin who settled outside the British Isles in the same period.

The overwhelming majority of India's overseas migrants travelled to Southeast Asia. This might surprise anyone familiar with the recent literature on Indian emigration, which has focused disproportionately on regions to which relatively few Indians travelled (South Africa, North America, the Caribbean). The figures, however, tell a striking story. Of approximately 28 million people who emigrated from India up to 1940, close to 27 million went to just three destinations in Southeast Asia: Burma, Ceylon, and Malaya. About 4 million Indians journeyed to Malaya (mostly from coastal Tamil districts), 8 million to Ceylon (primarily from the Tamil region of the far south), and between 12 million and 15 million to Burma (mainly from the Telugu districts of the east coast). The picture is as clear if we look to the number of people of Indian origin who settled permanently overseas: most of the 6 million who did not return to India settled in Southeast Asia, the majority of them in Malaysia and Sri Lanka, which to this day have the largest populations outside India of people of Indian descent. A further notable characteristic of Indian overseas migration (in contrast with Chinese migration) is that virtually all of it was to destinations within the British Empire.[15]

---

[15] Kingsley Davis, *The Population of India and Pakistan* (Princeton: Princeton University Press, 1951).

Regional Migration

Overseas migration took place amid multiple circuits of local and regional mobility over shorter distances. Different kinds of mobility – the movement of women to their husbands' villages on marriage, and their return 'home' for the birth of their children; the mass movement of people to festivals and pilgrimage sites – were woven into the fabric of everyday life in South Asia. There was no overall trend towards increasing internal migration in India in the nineteenth century.

But specific kinds of internal migration increased unequivocally. Above all, the second half of the nineteenth century saw the rapid growth in migration to frontier regions that instituted forms of plantation agriculture for export production. Kingsley Davis called 'commercial agriculture of the estate type' the 'greatest magnet' for internal migration in India: largest among these magnets were the tea plantations of Assam in the north-east, the coffee and tea plantations of the Western Ghats in India's south-west, and the newly-irrigated and fertile lands of the Punjab. The forces compelling Indian labour migrants to these destinations were precisely those that stimulated overseas migration for plantation labour. Methods of recruitment, too, were similar. In time, plantation agriculture within India would compete directly for migrant labour with plantations overseas.[16]

Malaya, Ceylon, and Burma

The draw of Southeast Asia for Indian migrant labour had deep roots. Parts of India's eastern coast had long been integrated into a regional economy spanning the Bay of Bengal, with a correspondingly long history of cultural contact. Tamil Muslim merchants had had close and longstanding links with the Malay world. From the time of their founding as British settlements, Penang (1786) and Singapore (1819) attracted a large and mixed South Asian population. East India Company soldiers, transported convict workers from Bengal, Hindu and Muslim merchants, and an increasing number of labourers arrived in Singapore and Penang each year from the 1820s. Labour circulation between south India and Ceylon was even more intensive, and dated back centuries. For generations there had been a circular or seasonal flow of labour from eastern India to Burma, over land, and using the multiple waterways of the Bengal Delta.

[16] Anang A. Yang, 'Peasants on the Move: A Study of Internal Migration in India', *Journal of Interdisciplinary History*, 10, 1 (1979), 37–58.

The growth of plantation agriculture stimulated demand for Indian labour, and saw it swell in magnitude after 1870. The search for Indian plantation labour began in Ceylon in the 1840s, with British attempts to exploit more intensively the island's natural riches. With the decline in the value of areca and cinnamon, Ceylon's traditional products, British administrators and planters decided to stake their fortunes on coffee. In Malaysia, the development of plantation agriculture began in the 1840s, with halting attempts to exploit the hinterlands of Penang by planting sugar and coffee. It was not until the 1870s, when most of the Malay Peninsula came under British control, that its interior opened to Western capital investment. Coffee and sugar soon made way for more lucrative plantations of tea (in Ceylon) and rubber (in Malaya), and the pace of migration increased, reaching a peak in the 1920s. Plantations needed to be fed, and neither Malaya nor Ceylon could produce enough rice for their needs. Correspondingly, the expansion of rice production in Burma set in train an even larger stream of migration, mostly from the Telugu-speaking districts and from Orissa.

The systems of labour recruitment that developed for the plantations of Ceylon and Malaya had similarities, although they were not identical. Older indigenous networks of labour recruitment were yoked to the power of the colonial state in order to secure a steady flow of labour. Initially, the system of indenture was used in both Malaya and Ceylon. Indian labour recruiters played a central role in the working of the indenture system. Recruiters would receive a fixed payment for each batch of workers they delivered to the emigration depots. Sometimes they did this on speculation, trusting that demand for labour was strong enough that there would be willing takers for the workers they had persuaded, deceived, or coerced into making the journey to the port. By the last quarter of the nineteenth century, planters found that the system of indenture simply failed to secure a large or steady enough supply of workers.

The system of recruitment that emerged to replace indenture came to be known as the *kangany* system (and in Burma as the *maistry* system). Under this arrangement, which had taken south Indian labour to Ceylon on a small scale for centuries, Tamil foremen working on a plantation were sent back to their villages in India by the planters to recruit their kinsmen. Rather than relying on labour recruiters, planters turned to trusted workers, usually workers who had done well for themselves. Debt remained central to the system. *Kanganies* could advance relatively large sums of money to the families of potential recruits. In other cases, they would pay the masters of tied farm servants in order to free them. More subtle forms of attachment could work even more powerfully. The *kangany* was usually linked to his recruits by caste or

Plate 1.2 **Two Tamil women with large pots on their heads at the well of the Maria Watta Tea Estate (1895). From the 1840s, South Indian plantation labourers moved to Ceylon in large numbers, including many women and families, to work on the tea plantations.**
Source: Library of Congress Prints and Photographs Division, Washington D.C., LC-D4271–237. Used with permission.

even kinship, leaving the recruits' families responsible for any debts they left unpaid.

It is difficult to generalize about the social composition of the labour force recruited by the *kanganies*. Low-caste and *dalit* communities were heavily represented among the emigrants, but not exclusively so. Members of higher agricultural castes, too, migrated in large numbers. Few, if any, Muslims from south India undertook migration for plantation labour, though Muslims were very well represented among those travelling to work in the cities of Southeast Asia. There were differences between Malaya and Ceylon in terms of the gender composition of the migrant labour force. Most of the emigrants to Malaya were young men; at most, 30 per cent of the Tamil plantation workforce in Malaya consisted of women. In Ceylon – partly again because of its proximity to India – family migration was the norm (Plate 1.2). The latter was also true of migration to the tea plantations of Assam.

The plantations that emerged in Southeast Asia were the result of centuries of experimentation around the Atlantic world with how to extract maximum value from human labour. Plantations were isolated and enclosed worlds. Workers remained closely under the surveillance and supervision of foremen and plantation managers who were often fellow South Asians, though sometimes of different caste or regional origins from the labour force. Conditions on the plantations were notoriously harsh. Mortality rates were high, as a result of poor sanitary facilities and environmental conditions. Workers were often beaten, even tortured. Examining the condition of migrants repatriated to India from Malaya when they were no longer fit to labour, an experienced British port surgeon declared that the returned migrants were 'in a worse state than the famine-stricken and diseased creatures I have seen in the hospitals of famine camps'. Harsh punishment met any purported violation of the terms of employment, as stipulated by the punitive labour code.[17]

Migration from south India to Southeast Asia was not confined to plantation workers. There was a steady flow of people to the cities and towns. South Indians moved to Malaya as administrators in the colonial service. Many higher-level administrators were Tamils from Ceylon, migrating for the second time in their families' histories. Merchant bankers of the Tamil-speaking Chettiar community played an important intermediary role in financing the expansion of plantation production, often providing the main source of credit for smaller Indian firms involved in the business of migration, and that could not access credit from European banks. Burma proved the most fertile territory for Chettiar businesses, which played a leading role in extending credit to indigenous Burmese cultivators (Chapter 3).

Working-class south Indian migrants travelled in large numbers to Singapore, Penang, Colombo, Rangoon, and smaller towns in Southeast Asia. They worked on the railways, in the Public Works Department, laying cables and building roads. The majority of Colombo's and Rangoon's rickshaw pullers and dockworkers were migrants from India. Migrants to the cities came from a wider region than the plantation workers, including many Malayalis from south-western India (Kerala); Punjabi Sikhs, many of whom worked as policemen, and Hindi-speakers from northern India, prominent in Singapore's milk trade. Like their counterparts headed for the plantations, urban workers invariably used family networks to find jobs, and as a means of social security.

[17] Sunil S. Amrith, 'Indians Overseas? Governing Tamil Migration to Malaya, 1870–1941', *Past and Present*, 208 (2010), 231–261.

A defining feature of Indian migration overseas was the dominant role of British Imperial authorities in every part of the process, from recruitment to transportation. Indian emigrants around the world travelled almost exclusively within the bounds of the British Empire. The British India Steam Navigation Company consolidated its monopoly over passenger routes, squeezing out the indigenous shipping merchants who had once played a central role.

The British Indian government proclaimed its humanitarian intent, arguing that only by overseeing the whole process of migration could it prevent the 'abuses' so widely prevalent under the system of indenture. The system of indentured labour across the British Empire was outlawed gradually between 1910 and 1917; by that time, though, the majority of South Asian migrants were already being recruited by more informal means.

An End to Circulation

Circular migration between India and Southeast Asia persisted until the 1930s. As the scale of migration increased, censuses in Southeast Asian colonies recorded a growing South Indian population. The Malayan census, for instance, counted around 30,000 Indians in 1870, 120,000 by 1901, and 275,000 by 1911: these figures 'represent a virtual population, constantly depleted and renewed by migratory flows, rather than a settled, self-renewing population'.[18] That pattern began to shift in the 1920s and accelerated in the 1930s. An increasingly settled and permanent South Indian population established itself in Malaysia and Sri Lanka. This was an unexpected result of the global economic depression of the 1930s. While many Indian workers were repatriated during the Depression (Chapter 3), others refused to return to India. They demanded instead that they be given small subsistence plots to cultivate on the fringes of plantation lands, until they could be re-employed on the estates.

Legal changes had an even more significant effect. As demand slumped, the Malayan government for the first time introduced restrictions on the entry of new migrant workers (the Chinese were most directly affected). For its part, the Government of India proved more reluctant to allow Indian workers to emigrate, worried that there was little it could do to protect their wages and conditions. Since women and children were exempt from these immigration as well as emigration

---

[18] Christophe Z. Guilmoto, 'The Tamil Migration Cycle, 1830–1950', *Economic and Political Weekly*, 28, 3–4 (1993), 111–120.

restrictions, the 1930s saw a significant rise in the number of women migrating to Malaya. Families divided across the Bay of Bengal reunited, as they realised that the old circular patterns of migration were now subject to arbitrary restrictions and reversals.

Chinese Migration to Southeast Asia

The second major stream of Asian overseas migration took millions of people from coastal southern China – primarily from coastal Guangdong and southern Fujian – to the 'south seas' (*nanyang*). The majority of Chinese emigrants departed from Hong Kong, Xiamen (known by Europeans as Amoy), Shantou (Swatow) and Hainan Island. Up to 20 million Chinese migrants travelled to Southeast Asia between 1850 and 1940: a total of 11 million to Singapore and Malaysia, about 3 million of whom were shipped on to Indonesia; another 1 million travelled directly from China to Indonesia; 4 million to Thailand; and another 3 or 4 million to Indochina, the Philippines, and other parts of the Pacific. As with Indian emigrants, the majority of those Chinese who settled permanently abroad settled in Southeast Asia: 6.5 million of a total net emigration of 7.5 million. This trend sharpened over time. Whereas 40 per cent of Chinese emigrants in the 1850s travelled beyond Asia, between the 1880s and 1930, 96 per cent of Chinese emigrants remained *within* Asia.[19]

The shifting flows of Chinese migration over time illustrate clearly that the 1920s marked the high point of emigration. The peak year of Chinese emigration to Southeast Asia was 1927, and the route most travelled that year took migrants from Shantou via Singapore to Indonesia, and back via Singapore and Hong Kong.

Pressure and opportunity, desperation and ambition – all came together in the middle of the nineteenth century to spark a vast expansion in Chinese migration to Southeast Asia. The two decades of conflict between the Chinese State and the Western powers, framed by the First and Second Opium Wars (1839–42; 1856–60) forced the Qing state into extensive juridical and commercial concessions. The foundation of the treaty port system – where European powers could trade free from restrictions, and live under their own laws – allowed European powers to recruit labour for their colonies free from Chinese legal restraints. European intrusion served as a catalyst for ideological ferment and economic dislocation, coming together with conflicts and tensions internal to Chinese society. Advances in shipping technology brought Southeast

---

[19] McKeown, 'Chinese Emigration in Global Context'; Look Lai, 'Asian Diasporas'.

Plate 1.3 **Looking down the Chukiang River into the houses of the 400,000 boat population of Canton, China (1900). The photograph shows Guangzhou's bustling waterfront around the turn of the twentieth century. Many Chinese emigrants set out on their journeys from Guangzhou: from there, they would often travel via Hong Kong.**
Source: Library of Congress Prints and Photographs Division, Washington D.C., LC-USZ61–937. Used with permission.

Asia within closer reach: European square-rigged sailing vessels, clippers, and ultimately steamships put pressure on the Chinese junk trade, while facilitating a rapid increase in passenger traffic (Plate 1.3). The prior establishment of brotherhoods and settlements in Southeast Asia provided a ready set of institutions and networks to facilitate migration on a much larger scale. Finally, particular episodes of natural disaster could accelerate the exodus quite dramatically. The protracted drought of the late 1870s produced one of the worst famines of the millennium. Unsurprisingly, those years saw a spike in migration. Migration was a natural but not an inevitable response to subsistence crises: it took the opportunities provided by the new ease of mobility to make emigration a viable option for escape.

Migrant Networks

In the era of mass migration after 1870, Chinese travelled to Southeast Asia under a wide range of arrangements. What unites them is the cardinal importance of social networks and intermediary institutions in making migration possible. Some of these networks and institutions were rooted in the family and kinship. Other common forms included native-place and surname associations and, on a wider scale, dialect-group and regional associations. Through these networks moved information about job opportunities, credit for the passage out, availability of berths on ships, connections with employers, housing, social security, and even armed protection. These institutions also hosted the religious and cultural rituals that made long-distance migration less traumatic and new destinations more familiar. The importance of social networks was such that where one village had intensive emigrant connections, its neighbours might have none.

The most fortunate of the emigrants financed their own passages with family resources. Since many families viewed emigration as an investment, those with assets were willing to sell or mortgage them, in the expectation that the fruits of emigration would prove worthwhile. Next, on the spectrum between freedom and constraint, was recruitment by an 'old hand' – a system almost identical to the *kangany* system, where workers would return to their villages to recruit more men, on commission. Here, the recruiter would advance the cost of the passage, and often a recruitment bonus, to the emigrants' families: the emigrants were bound to work off these debts.

More common still was migration through what was known as the 'credit ticket' system, which was equally common in the recruitment of Chinese migrants to North America. An intermediary took on the migrant's debt of passage: intermediaries included professional labour brokers, regional lodges, brotherhoods, and shipping agents, often closely integrated with one other. Labour brokers in Singapore or Penang worked directly with boardinghouse keepers in Chinese ports, based on the rapid transfer of information about job openings and labour demand. Either on embarkation or on arrival, the migrant would contract himself to an employer, at least until he had worked off his debts. Labour brokers often worked directly for the Chinese brotherhoods that controlled migrant labour in Southeast Asia. The brotherhoods' command of armed force ensured that the migrants did not escape their control. Historian Kaoru Sugihara has shown in fine detail how networks of lodging houses, remittance agencies, and Chinese merchants worked in interaction: 'the brokers remitted money; remittance houses put the capital for remittance into exchange or commodity speculation; general stores combined with remittance houses; lodging houses were involved in commerce'.[20]

Migrants under the 'credit ticket' system suffered many kinds of abuse and exploitation, but the most unfortunate were those who had signed formal contracts of indenture directly with European employers. Chinese labour brokers, again, made these transactions possible. Labourers under indenture tended to come from the most disadvantaged backgrounds; they had least access to the social networks that made 'free' migration possible. In all, something close to 750,000 Chinese signed contracts of indenture in the late-nineteenth and early-twentieth centuries. This represents a small proportion of Chinese migrants overall. Approximately 250,000 of the indentured migrants went to the Caribbean and Latin America, where they suffered the most brutal conditions faced by Chinese migrants anywhere, conditions in some cases very close to enslavement.

Within Asia, the plantations of Sumatra were the main destination for Chinese indentured workers: approximately 250,000 made the journey between 1880 and 1910. Conditions on the tobacco plantations in Sumatra's Deli region, where most Chinese workers were under indenture, were most severe. Sanitary conditions were poor. Infectious diseases were rife. Up to a quarter of the Chinese migrant workers to Sumatra's plantation belt died before working out their contracts. Malaria, malnutrition, frequent injuries, and a high rate of suicide made Sumatra lethal for plantation workers. Until the turn of the twentieth century, it proved cheaper for planters to import new labourers from overseas than to care for the welfare of those already in Sumatra: in this sense, conditions in Sumatra were little different from those prevailing in the first phase of plantation slavery in the Caribbean. In general, indentured labour recruitment only flourished for destinations that

[20] Kaoru Sugihara, 'Patterns of Chinese Emigration to Southeast Asia, 1869–1939', in Kaoru Sugihara (ed.), *Japan, China and the Growth of the Asian International Economy, 1850–1949* (Oxford: Oxford University Press, 2005), 244–274, 268.

were particularly distant or unattractive, or where Chinese social networks were especially thin.[21]

Chinese Society Overseas

The range of destinations to which Chinese emigrants travelled, and the occupations they pursued, were notably diverse, particularly in comparison with Indian migrants. At the apex of Overseas Chinese society in the Nanyang were the long-settled creolized elites: the Peranakan in Java, the Baba in Singapore and Malaya, and Mestizo and Sino-Thai families in the Philippines and Thailand. Their wealth and power came from their success as intermediaries between colonial authorities and European capital, on the one hand, and the world of Chinese brotherhoods and labourers, on the other. Over time, local Chinese elites absorbed the wealthiest and most ambitious newcomers from China, often marrying their daughters to them. Some merchants were directly involved with the brotherhoods; others kept the brotherhoods at arm's length. By the end of the nineteenth century, as the scale of Chinese migration increased, the old elites began to face direct competition from merchants more recently arrived from China.

The distinctive institution of the opium farm – a monopoly concession on the sale of opium in a specific area, in exchange for delivering up lucrative opium duties to the state – underpinned the power of the Chinese elite. In Java, the primary consumers of opium were Javanese peasants, while in Malaya, the demand came from Chinese migrant workers. In both cases, the opium farmers had a captive market. They used their control over opium supplies to establish themselves as the crucial link between the products of the interior – rice, in Java; pepper, gambier, and tin in Malaya – and the markets of the city. They controlled credit, marketing, transportation, and distribution. Their authority came also from their control over public institutions. In Singapore and Penang, the British saw the Baba as key allies, and began to incorporate them into structures of rule: as Justices of the Peace, as members of the Grand Jury and, eventually, in the Legislative Council. In Indonesia, Peranakan elites gained control over the Chinese Councils that the Dutch established in all centres of Chinese settlement. Everywhere, competition for wealth and power within Chinese society multiplied in the later nineteenth century. As colonial states became intolerant of competing structures of authority, and as a moral crusade against opium swept both European and Chinese social reformers around the turn of

[21] McKeown, 'Global Migration'.

the twentieth century, the Chinese elite had to diversify their portfolios, investing in transport, urban real-estate, tin mining, and rubber.[22]

The middle rung of Chinese society in Southeast Asia, perhaps the largest segment, consisted of those involved in the retail trade, which migrant Chinese came to dominate almost everywhere. According to one Japanese study in 1939, about 2.7 million of the 6 million or so Chinese settled in Southeast Asia worked in the retail trade; in Thailand, 70 per cent of the Chinese population was in this sector.[23] In many cases, Chinese migrants had little option but to find a niche in the retail trade, as colonial laws favouring indigenous settlers barred the Chinese from landholding. In Java, small Chinese traders were widely dispersed in rural areas. They worked as transport contractors or salt distributors, they ran general stores, they acted as small creditors to Javanese cultivators. They played a crucial role in the monetization of the Javanese agrarian economy, taking Javanese rice to the market, and allowing European (and later Japanese) manufactured goods to penetrate rural Java.[24]

Participation in the retail trade was the fastest route to economic and social mobility for Chinese emigrants. This sense of potential comes through in the story of a Chinese shopkeeper in Manila, interviewed in the 1920s by a research student at the University of the Philippines. The shopkeeper arrived in the Philippines 'penniless'. He worked as a storeroom assistant in a Chinese shop, subsisting only on 'cold rice which was hard to swallow as iron bullets'. He observed his boss at work and learned the ways of trade. He learned, first, to speak colloquial 'Chinese Tagalog', and eventually a little English and Spanish also. He learned to use the abacus. He saved his meagre but growing earnings, sending a portion back to his family in China. Eventually, he saved enough to invest in a small shop in a rural area, serving the local peasantry. 'Among the reasons for this success', he reflected, 'I would place first in importance honesty'.[25] This reads as a quintessential rags-to-riches story of migration, complete with a moral lesson on the virtues of thrift and industry. This man's fortune was exceptionally good, but his tale is not exceptional. Of course, for every success, there were cases of failure, disappointment, and bankruptcy.

---

[22] Trocki, *Opium and Empire*; James R. Rush, *Opium to Java: Revenue Farming and Chinese Enterprise in Colonial Indonesia* (Ithaca: Cornell University Press, 1990).

[23] Sugihara, 'Patterns of Chinese Emigration', 269.

[24] Rush, *Opium to Java*.

[25] Siy Ka Bio, 'Chinese Retailing in Manila', unpublished thesis, University of the Philippines, Manila, 1924: cited in Chen, *Emigrant Communities*, 61–62.

Among the migrant Chinese who worked in agriculture and mining, the greatest number went to the tin mines of Malaya, followed by Sumatra's tobacco plantations. Spurred by investment from Chinese capitalists (many of them opium farmers) and burgeoning demand from European markets, Malaya's tin production soared in the last quarter of the nineteenth century. Malaya's tin mining had been pioneered in the eighteenth century by small bands of Chinese settlers. They were capitalized by *kongsis*, with each of their members receiving a share of the profits. Even after the infusion of large capital investment from urban merchants, small mines remained the norm, with an average of seventy miners per digging by the late nineteenth century. By this point, however, their egalitarian ethos was under pressure, as Chinese capitalists struggled for control over the mining industry. In British Malaya, the worst conditions were encountered by those Chinese miners in remote areas, without the protection either of brotherhoods or the colonial state. On the admission of a Malayan official commission of inquiry, Chinese miners working under such conditions were treated with 'a severity (it might even in some instance be termed ferocity) which would be impossible on estates less difficult of access'.[26]

The 'Traffic' in Women

Until the 1920s, migration between China and Southeast Asia was overwhelmingly male. As migration expanded, so too did the (licensed and unlicensed) traffic in women to work in the brothels that flourished in Southeast Asia's port cities and frontier regions. James Warren's groundbreaking work has shown that the demand from Southeast Asia for young women from China was so great by the turn of the twentieth century that it could not be met. The same poverty that drove young men to seek their fortunes overseas impelled desperate parents to send their daughters away – often for a price – with recruiters who roamed the countryside. Most of the recruiters were women: some claimed to be nurses or seamstresses, while others were more straightforward about their intentions. Deception and coercion were widespread; the possibility of escape from poverty and hunger drew many young women to venture far beyond the worlds they knew.

Like their male counterparts, young women destined for Southeast Asia found themselves under close control at every stage of their journeys; they were much more likely to travel under physical restraint.

---

[26] Philip Kuhn, *Chinese Among Others: Emigration in Modern Times* (Singapore, 2008), 190.

Because the trade in women was increasingly illicit, as both Chinese and British authorities started to take an interest in the issue, the risks of the journey were correspondingly greater. Like male labourers, women passed through the hands of a network of brokers, intermediaries, and creditors. The majority of them ended up in the brothels of Singapore, from where many went on to other destinations in the region. The brothel keepers, too, tended to be Chinese women. Making imaginative use of coroner's court records, Warren depicts the harsh life of women who suffered the worst forms of violence and abuse, and a complete lack of freedom; yet he shows, too, the small ways in which young Chinese prostitutes could resist, even escape, the conditions they faced.

Between 1887 and 1894, more than 7,600 young women arrived in Singapore to work in brothels: most of them came from Shantou and Hong Kong. Migrant (or trafficked) women in Singapore were exceptionally mobile, though rarely of their own will: as with plantation labourers, so with sex workers – Singapore was a centre for transshipment throughout the region. Chinese girls were a majority among the young women brought to Singapore for sex work, but there was also a growing traffic in Japanese girls: from Singapore, the Japanese women went all over Southeast Asia. Only in the 1920s, when Japanese authorities banned the further migration of Japanese prostitutes, did this movement fall into decline.[27]

Controlling Chinese Migration

Chinese migration to Southeast Asia reached its peak in the 1920s. Shipping became cheaper and faster, and migrant networks reached the point where they were self-perpetuating, channelling cousins, sons, daughters, and uncles back and forth across the South China Sea. By this point, however, political, social, and economic conditions had changed significantly.

Politically, colonial states extended their bureaucratic reach, and sought to control Chinese labour more directly. The early twentieth century saw the proliferation of paternalistic colonial schemes to protect indigenous agrarian populations from over-rapid change, including the reformist 'Ethical Policy' of the Dutch in Indonesia and the British policy to reserve agricultural land for Malay peasants. In Indonesia, pass laws and residence restrictions on the Chinese tightened. In British Malaya, the popular brotherhoods were suppressed and criminalized

---

[27] James Francis Warren, *Ah Ku and Karayuki San: Prostitution in Singapore, 1870–1940* (Singapore: Oxford University Press, 1993).

as 'secret societies', driving them underground and limiting their influence. When the economic tide turned in the 1930s, the stage was already set for colonial regimes to introduce restrictions on the further migration of Chinese. Singapore and Malaya began in the 1930s to enforce, for the first time, legislation restricting fresh Chinese immigration.

Social and demographic change accompanied the political and economic shifts. Most significantly, the gender composition of Chinese migration began to change. Almost exclusively male in the pioneering years of the 1870s and 1880s, by the 1920s, a significant flow of Chinese women had set out for Southeast Asia. Where in some pioneer communities on the frontier there had been up to twelve Chinese men for every Chinese woman, the ratio was closer to 2 to 1 by the 1920s, and in some social and geographical settings it approached parity. The gradual process by which settled Chinese families constituted themselves in Southeast Asia had important consequences for the development of Chinese diasporic consciousness, as the next chapter (Chapter 2) will explain. As we have seen with respect to Indian migration, the instability of the Depression years in the 1930s hastened this process. Chinese women were exempt from the migration restrictions of the era, so that some of the continued migration across the China seas in the 1930s took the form of family reunification, even as Chinese women began to migrate as labourers of their own accord.

Because of the increase in 'free' migration by Chinese women to Southeast Asia, as wives or as labourers in their own right, the trade in Chinese girls and women began to decline. From the 1920s, the 'traffic in women and children' emerged as a subject for activism by abolitionists both in Europe and in Asia, with the support of international bodies such as the League of Nations. Identifying the prevalence of 'child slavery' in Southeast Asia involved a complicated set of cultural negotiations. While international activism drew attention to the plight of women and children in the sex trade, it could also lead to conflict. Some Chinese elites in Southeast Asia backed the abolitionist campaign against the institution of *mui tsai*, a form of bond service that shaded uneasily into adoption, and in which young girls from China worked as unpaid servants in the households of wealthier patrons in Singapore or Hong Kong. Others saw it as an undue intrusion upon Chinese cultural practices and an inhibition on the formation of settled Chinese families.

Indian and Chinese Migration Compared

Indian and Chinese migration overseas were linked in the European imagination, and in the language of the time. Working-class migrants from China and India alike became known as 'coolies', in North America and the Caribbean as much as in Asia. Some linguists argue that the term 'coolie' originates in Tamil *kuli* (denoting payment for menial work, *kuli-al* or *kuli-karan* being the term for a day labourer). On another view, it comes via the Urdu *quli* (again denoting labour or service); still others suggest that 'coolie' is a Portuguese rendering of the name for the indigenous Koli people of Gujarat, whom early European observers associated with hard labour. Finally, some scholars believe 'coolie' comes from the Chinese *ku-li*: bitter labour. Whatever its origins, the term served to reduce the social and political lives of Chinese and Indian workers to their labour power alone; it was a term of denigration, even dehumanization. The term expressed the racist assumptions prevalent at the time: that Indian and Chinese 'coolies' were constitutionally suited for hard labour in the tropics, and that – in contrast to free white 'workers' – they needed coercion to make them work.

Indian and Chinese migration to Southeast Asia arose from a shared set of initial stimuli. They were a result of the demand for labour that emerged from the expansion of European imperialism and global capitalism. They were made possible by a revolution in transportation that made both the Bay of Bengal and the South China Sea easier, faster, and cheaper to cross. Their lands of origin shared demographic and economic characteristics. Both were regions of intensive rice cultivation. Both were densely populated, in sharp contrast with Southeast Asia's very low population density. Politically, India and China experienced European imperialism in different ways, yet both societies were sufficiently destabilized to give rise to large-scale uprisings in the 1850s. The connected nature of climatic events came together with the integration of food markets to produce severe drought and devastating famines in both India and China in the 1870s and the 1890s, leading millions of young men from both societies to make the journey overseas. Only gradually, in both cases, did women begin to migrate, and until the 1930s, gender ratios were very unbalanced.

Most observers at the time, and since, have emphasized the contrasts between Indian and Chinese migration. Colonial officials thought Tamils in Malaya were 'not nearly so capable of taking care of themselves as are the Chinese clans'.[28] 'There is a vast difference', one Indian

---

[28] Letter from F.H. Gottlieb, Magistrate of Province Wellesley to the Lieutenant-Governor of Penang, 16 November 1873: National Archives of India, New Delhi. Department of Revenue Agriculture and Commerce, Emigration Branch, Proceedings 10–13, June 1874.

journalist in Malaya wrote, 'between the methods by which the Chinese and Indian labour reaches Malaya ... the Chinese labour movement is free and voluntary'.[29] The sharpest contrast between the two experiences is that Indian migration from the 1870s took place under the closer control of the colonial state. Indian labourers travelled on British ships. Colonial magistrates oversaw their journeys. They worked on European-owned plantations. Most Chinese migrant labour, by contrast, was destined for work in Chinese-owned enterprises. Chinese migration was much more autonomous of the colonial state, which is not to say that it was any less exploitative of labourers.

Chinese and Indian migrants filled different niches in the Malayan economy. The urban economy of the port cities drew in both Chinese and Indian labour, but in the Malaysian hinterland, Indian workers went largely to the rubber plantations, Chinese labourers to the tin mines. At the same time, the economic opportunities open to Chinese labourers in Malaya were wider. There were plenty of 'rags to riches' stories of impoverished Chinese labourers who succeeded as merchants, virtually none in the case of Indian labourers. British (and elite Indian) observers put this down to the Indian migrants' lack of initiative. A more convincing explanation lies in the fact that Indian migrants were much more closely tied to the world of plantation production, which was designed to prevent social mobility. As Kaoru Sugihara has argued, the Chinese system of recruitment through lodging houses allowed for greater social and geographical mobility than the *kangany* system, since 'the sense of "trust" was apparently transferable from the broker to the lodging house, and then from the lodging house to the employer or foreman'.[30]

In their brotherhoods (*kongsis*), the Chinese had a much denser web of social institutions than Indian labourers in Southeast Asia. The British allowed Chinese society significantly more scope for self-government than they allowed to Indian migrants, a result of the much weaker political hold that the British Empire had over China compared with India, and the greater opacity – to the British – of Chinese social networks. Chinese social institutions allowed for closer links between urban Chinese merchants and labourers in the hinterland than in the case of the Indian communities, where a gulf remained between plantation labour and the small world of urban intellectuals and merchants. In part, this may be explained by the longer history of Chinese labour migration and agricultural settlement in Southeast Asia. It owes much

[29] K.A. Neelakandha Aiyar, *Indian Problems in Malaya* (Kuala Lumpur, 1938), 14.
[30] Sugihara, 'Patterns of Chinese Emigration', 260.

more to differences in social structure between southern China and south India.

Similarities between Indian and Chinese migration to Southeast Asia are equally notable. Indian and Chinese patterns of migration to Southeast Asia were both circular: Indians and Chinese alike were 'sojourners' in the Southeast Asia. Both streams of migration changed over time: initially, overwhelmingly male and with a gradual turn towards family migration and the migration of women in the twentieth century. Despite the greater involvement of the colonial state in recruiting Indian labour, it is clear that informal social networks – based on kinship and locality – were significant at every stage of the migration process in the case of both Indian and Chinese labour. Debt played a central role in the journeys of most Chinese and Tamil workers to Southeast Asia, and the varieties of indebtedness bear many similarities. Finally, the fact that most Indian migration was under colonial control did not wholly prevent a steady and continuing stream of 'illegal' migration from south India under the control of Indian shipping merchants and recruiters, and much more akin to the patterns of Chinese migration.

Indian and Chinese experiences of migration to Southeast Asia did not simply bear similarities. There were significant connections between them. In Malaya in particular, Indians and Chinese laboured under a shared legal regime that cast them as temporary 'immigrant races' and differentiated them from the 'indigenous' Malays. The next chapter will examine the ways in which the interaction between Indian and Chinese diasporas created diverse political and cultural connections between them. On the fringes of plantation lands, and above all in urban areas, Indian and Chinese cultural worlds came into contact, collision, and interaction. Recognizing themselves (and each other) as diasporas, Indian and Chinese political and cultural leaders learned from one another, even as they competed with each other to claim that their respective communities were modern, and fit for citizenship.

Migration to Manchuria

The magnitude of this migration [is] perhaps unprecedented in modern history and assuredly unparalleled today.

C. Walter Young

Migration from coastal China to Southeast Asia has played a central role in our story so far. But China's own land frontiers attracted an even greater number of migrants from the northern provinces of Shandong and Hebei. Chinese migration to Manchuria, between 1890 and the 1940s, constituted one of the largest migrations in modern history. Between 28 and 33 million Chinese migrants moved to Manchuria after 1850, together with approximately 2 million Koreans and 500,000 Japanese. If we include migration from Russia into Siberia, a further 13 million people can be added to this migration to Asia's far north-east. Between 8 and 10 million of the Chinese migrants to Manchuria settled there permanently.

Overland migration to Manchuria and overseas migration to Southeast Asia shared similar underlying causes, and similar conditions of possibility. They followed similarly circulatory paths; the majority of migrants to Manchuria, as to Southeast Asia, eventually returned home. The history of migration to Manchuria links the smallest family decisions to large shifts in international and imperial politics. In contrast with migrants to Southeast Asia, Chinese migrants soon constituted an overwhelming numerical majority in Manchuria; they had fewer encounters with indigenous people, or with migrants from other parts of Asia.

China's frontiers had expanded throughout the early modern period. In keeping with a broader pattern across Eurasia, the centralizing, militarized Chinese imperial state pushed outwards, conquering Mongolia and Xinjiang, subjugating the nomadic inhabitants of those lands. The Miao people of Guizhou were subject to a particularly relentless assault by the Qing state and the Han Chinese settlers who followed in its train. Conquest was not achieved without protracted struggle, which persisted through the eighteenth century. Through the process of conquest, migration, and settlement, these frontier areas had become more clearly 'Chinese' by the beginning of the nineteenth century. New lands provided an outlet for a fast-growing population. The population of China, estimated at 75 million in 1400, had grown to 320 million by 1800, and about 420 million by the middle of the nineteenth century. By 1850, lands to the west had been exhausted, and only one frontier remained: Manchuria, the vast expanses that lay north of the Great Wall.[31]

Until the mid-nineteenth century, Manchuria remained very sparsely populated. Its population consisted of Manchus, Tungus, and other

---

[31] The following section on Manchuria is based on Thomas R. Gottschang and Diana Lary, *Swallows and Settlers: The Great Migration from North China to Manchuria* (Ann Arbor: University of Michigan Press, 2000), and James Reardon-Anderson, *Reluctant Pioneers: China's Expansion Northward, 1644–1937* (Stanford: Stanford University Press, 2005).

communities that lived from shifting cultivation, hunting, fishing, and trade in forest produce. Russian encroachment in the far north of Manchuria proved the catalyst for a concerted attempt to consolidate Chinese authority over Manchuria. The Qing state did this initially by granting large plots of land to Manchu noblemen, who then required Chinese migrant labour for the purpose of cultivation. It was only in the second half of the nineteenth century that mass migration north began, reaching a peak in the 1920s.

The coming of the railway transformed the scale of migration to Manchuria. Railway construction began in 1898. The Chinese state granted to the Russians a lease on land to construct the China Eastern railway line across Manchuria to the port of Vladivostok, and a lease over the Liaodong Peninsula for the construction of the South Manchurian Railway. When Japanese forces prevailed in the Russo-Japanese War in 1905 – marking Japan's rise as a major military power in the world – the Japanese assumed the Liaodong lease as part of the post-war settlement. Railway construction absorbed masses of Chinese migrant labour. Once the railway opened, in 1902, migrants could travel easily, and relatively cheaply, from the port of Dairen to Heilongjiang and Jilin. From the late 1890s until 1940, about 500,000 migrants a year made the journey to Manchuria. The growth of Jilin provides an example of this expansion: from about 327,000 in 1850, the population of Jilin had grown to nearly 4 million by 1910.

The 1920s were a time of political upheaval and experiment in China. Nationalist forces sought to unite the country under their leadership, first cooperating with and then confronting the rising Chinese Communist Party; confronting or absorbing a myriad of local military leaders (commonly referred to as 'warlords') with widely differing goals and tactics. In these conditions of uncertainty, a fresh wave of migrants and refugees streamed into Manchuria, fleeing the widespread armed conflict that destabilized north China – and the ever-present risk, for young men, of conscription – exacerbated by further episodes of ecological disaster. From 1926, there was a significant increase in the magnitude of migration: that year, 600,000 Chinese arrived in Manchuria, and up to 1 million in 1927. By this stage, three-quarters of the migrants to Manchuria were arriving by steamship in the port of Dairen. From there they travelled north by railway, but also by all manner of local transport: on carts, on pack animals, on sampans and – in many cases – on foot.

The Japanese takeover of Manchuria in 1931 marked a new phase in the region's political history. Restive elements of Japan's Kwantung Army orchestrated an explosion on the railway as a pretext to force authorities in Tokyo to annex Manchuria; this was a long-held dream among Japanese nationalist groups, who saw Manchuria's expanses as a solution to poverty and population growth at home. Renamed 'Manchukuo', it was ruled as an ostensibly autonomous territory under the restored Manchu emperor Puyi, but with the Japanese military firmly in control. Notwithstanding Japanese occupation, migration from north China continued apace – even after the outbreak of all-out war between Japan and China in 1937 – as massive Japanese investment ushered in an industrial revolution in Manchuria. Like the other command economies, Manchuria weathered the global economic depression relatively well, with a continued and expanding infusion of Japanese capital investment.

The pattern of migration to Manchuria, for most of the period in question, remained circular. Like their counterparts travelling to Southeast Asia, migrants were sojourners – 'swallows', in local terminology – more often than they were settlers. Between 1890 and 1940, only about 8 million Chinese settled in Manchuria, though this was, in the end, greater than the number of Chinese who settled in Southeast Asia. Migration followed the seasons. Most voyagers from north China made the journey to Manchuria in March or April each year; after the New Year festivities in their home villages, they returned after an average sojourn of between two and four years. From the late 1920s, however, there was an increasing tendency towards Chinese settlement in Manchuria. The American observer C. Walter Young estimated that between 1925 and 1930 alone, more than 2 million Chinese had settled in Manchuria.

The mining and railway industries recruited heavily, but most Chinese migrants to Manchuria went as cultivators. A relatively small proportion of the migrants owned land on a freehold basis, of widely varying size. Many more leased their land, or worked as sharecroppers. Large parts of Manchuria were owned by Chinese official organizations, private or semi-private companies, and by large landowners. A Western observer travelling through Manchuria in the 1920s and early 1930s observed 'several land companies in Harbin, formed principally of officials and ex-officials, each of which held virgin cultivable land in Heilungking (Heilongjiang) province in as many as ten separate estates, the estates varying from 100 to 10,000 acres'.[32] By this stage, the soya bean had

---

[32] C. Walter Young, 'Chinese Immigration and Colonization in Manchuria', in W.L.G. Joerg (ed.), *Pioneer Settlement: Cooperative Studies by Twenty-Six Authors* (New York: American Geographical Society, 1932), 330–359.

emerged as Manchuria's most important cash crop, accounting for 80 per cent of the region's exports; Manchuria accounted for nearly 60 per cent of the world's production of soya beans by the late 1920s.

Family was the 'engine of migration' to Manchuria; migration was 'governed by the needs of the family'.[33] In interviews with men and families in Shandong who had spent periods of their lives working in Manchuria, Diana Lary found that by far the most common response to the question of who made the decision to go to Manchuria was that 'it was decided in the family'. Between 1890 and 1940, families in Shandong and Hebei sent young men to Manchuria as part of a diversified strategy for family survival. One son, chosen by the family for his aptitude and initiative, or alternatively because he was less essential to the homestead, would be sent north, while the others remained at home or migrated seasonally within north China. The expectation of return was universal. After a sojourn in Manchuria, young men would, if they were fortunate, return with enough money to marry. Often this began a process of chain migration, as one of the returned migrant's brothers would take his turn to journey beyond the Wall.

Family pressures have emerged throughout this chapter as a crucial motivation for migration. In the case of Chinese migration to Manchuria, the social structure of north China explains the expectations and obligations on the part of migrants and the families they left behind. Most migrants to Manchuria came from small landowning families in north China, and the system of inheritance gave equal shares to each son. This had two implications as far as migration was concerned: First, it meant that young men left home for Manchuria confident that they would have land to return to after their sacrifices for the family. Second, and paradoxically, however, the tendency for landholdings to fragment, if the family decided to 'go their separate ways' rather than farm the land together, meant that an increasing number of households had plots too small to be viable. This made the promise of Manchuria's abundance all the more attractive.

Professional recruiters played some role in attracting men to Manchuria. Local labour contractors recruited groups of men in Shandong and Hebei on order from their counterparts in Manchuria. They paid advances to the families of the recruits. Large mining companies sent their own recruiting agents, opening offices in the major towns and cities of north China. But most Chinese migrants to Manchuria were 'self-starters' (*zifa*). They migrated in small groups, as kinsmen or fellow

---

[33] Gottschang and Lary, *Swallows and Settlers*; Reardon-Anderson, *Reluctant Pioneers*.

villagers, and they moved along existing family networks to destinations where uncles, cousins, or other local people had preceded them. When this happened on a large enough scale, whole 'villages across the sea' emerged, akin to branches of the original north China village, in Manchuria. Families exploited each other as much as they provided mutual support. Tales abound of young men taking up jobs with their uncles, or even their own fathers in Manchuria, and receiving nothing after years of labour.

Until the 1930s, Manchuria remained an overwhelmingly male migrant society. Few women migrated to a frontier that many considered dangerous, rough, and uncivilized. Young bachelors left north China, returning in time to marry; others left their wives and children behind. One story told by Thomas Gottschang and Diana Lary relates the experience of a man who left for Manchuria in 1927, fleeing from creditors to whom he owed a considerable sum. He was away for twelve years, during which time his family heard nothing from him; his wife returned to her own family. Suddenly, 'he returned one day without warning, and the family went back to the life it had lead before, as if the twelve-year hiatus had not occurred'.[34] Many were less fortunate. Families were shattered by long separation, abandoned wives driven to despair and even suicide. Countless men lived with the shame of failure in Manchuria, returning home defeated.

In death, migrants to Manchuria marked most visibly their abiding connections with their homes in north China. In the early decades of settlement in Manchuria, most bodies were conveyed back for burial in the ancestral homeland, as Walter Young observed:

Grim evidence of this very consequential attachment to the ancestral soil may be seen in the slow-moving stream of wooden carts, drawn by horses, mules and oxen in tandem and abreast, southward bound through the Great Wall at Shanhaikwan from Manchuria, each cart piled high with plain wooden coffins lashed together. These are the remains of the pioneers who have died in the 'foreign land' of Manchuria.[35]

The construction of local burial grounds in Manchuria was the most symbolic indication of the gradual shift from sojourning to settlement.

The long-term effects of Chinese migration to Manchuria were pivotal. Prasenjit Duara has argued that only the mass migration of the period after 1890 made Manchuria 'unalterably Chinese'.[36] This

---

[34] Gottschang and Lary, *Swallows and Settlers*, 85.
[35] Young, cited in Gottschang and Lary, *Swallows and Settlers*, 104.
[36] Prasenjit Duara, *Sovereignty and Authenticity: Manchukuo and the East Asian Modern* (Lanham: Rowman & Littlefield, 2003), 41.

reminds us that putting migration at the heart of the narrative can make us re-think national and regional boundaries that seem natural or taken for granted in state-centred histories. Migrants made Manchuria Chinese, even as they served the interests of an expanding Chinese state. Migrants re-shaped regional geographies. They transformed perceptions of core and periphery, frontiers and borderlands.

Conclusion

In this chapter, I have shown that there was a wide spectrum – from near-slavery to relative freedom – within which Asian migrations took place. There was no straight line leading from slavery to indentured labour, and eventually to free labour. Slavery persisted, in places intensified, in the Asian world. In parts of the Indian Ocean and the China Sea, it lasted into the twentieth century. Indentured labour covered a wide spectrum of experience. At one end of this spectrum, conditions of indenture were virtually indistinguishable from slavery; at the other end, indentured labour migration owed much more to individual and family agency. Throughout its reign, indentured labour depended on existing social networks and systems of labour recruitment. Taking a broad view, only a minority of Asia's migrants in the nineteenth century signed contracts of indenture. Slave, indentured, and 'free' migrants worked alongside one another, or at least in close proximity.

'Free' migration was, in its own ways, highly constrained; it involved many kinds of coercion. Debt played a role almost everywhere. In some cases, official agencies were dominant; in others, informal and family networks played a greater role. Coercion could take the form of irresistible pressure from family to contribute by migrating for work, or the naked legal form of the 'coolie ordinances'. For free or unfree, violence was never far from the surface of the migrant experience. Migrant workers were subject to the naked violence of the planters in frontier areas. They experienced the quotidian violence of male migrant worlds: the violence of opium and gambling syndicates; the violence experienced by the women who were sent, often under duress, to 'serve the needs' of men on the frontier; the violence of hunger. Freedom of labour and freedom of migration could stand in tension with one another. By the twentieth century, attempts to free labourers from exploitation led to calls from colonial administrators and Asian nationalists for the restriction of freedom of emigration from India and China.

Through these shades of freedom and constraint, Asia's migrant worlds were worlds of adventure and self-realisation. In some fortunate cases, migration brought tremendous economic and social advancement, as in our case of the Chinese shopkeeper in the rural Philippines. Turning to the cultural history of migration, the next chapter will show that, even in the most difficult conditions, Asian migrants rendered new landscapes familiar by making them sacred, building shrines and temples to spirits and deities across the seas. They clubbed together for mutual support and protection; they often developed – or were forced to develop – openness to the world and to the ways of strangers. Another way to think about freedom and migration is to examine the ways in which the experience of migration stimulated new ideas and new debates about freedom, justice, and morality. Asian migrants travelled under varying degrees of liberty and constraint. Their experiences of doing so led many to question anew which freedoms they valued most.

2 The Making of Asian Diasporas, 1850–1930

diaspora noun *3. The dispersion or spread of any people from their original homeland; 4. People who have spread or been dispersed from their homeland* DERIVATES: *diasporic* adj. Oxford English Dictionary

Long used exclusively in relation to the Jewish Diaspora (and later encompassing the African experience of slavery), the term 'diaspora' has undergone a significant expansion in its usage and definition. At its most imprecise, diaspora has become synonymous with migration; almost any migrant group is now labelled a diaspora. The term is more useful, however, when it draws our attention specifically to the kinds of connections migrants maintain with their homelands and with others of shared origin dispersed around the world. 'Diaspora' can be used to describe a *process* of migration and dispersal, and also the *condition* of living in diaspora – that is to say, a form of consciousness that arises from the experience of migration and exile.

Contemporary discussions of diaspora draw heavily on the recent experience of diasporas in the multi-cultural democracies of Western Europe, and especially North America. This chapter shows that the formation of Asian diasporas *within* Asia developed from the distinctive characteristics of Asian migration in the nineteenth and early-twentieth centuries (Chapter 1): the relative proximity between homelands and destinations; the dominance of sojourning or circular migration; the relative absence of women; the sheer scale of the movement.

During Asia's age of migration, diasporas formed and unravelled alongside other more transient kinds of community. Diasporas emerged from the interaction between the large numbers of working-class migrants and smaller, but influential, communities of intellectuals, journalists, and teachers. In the port cities, many Asian diasporas encountered each other for the first time, and sought new ways to communicate across the divide of language and culture. Diasporas were both a source of and a conduit for modern ideas about nationality; yet the experience of migration complicated some of the certitudes of

57

nationalism. At the same time, Asia's mobility revolution reinvigorated much older forms of movement. Diasporic networks allowed religious ideas to travel quite as far and fast as secular ones. Old paths of pilgrimage, under modern conditions, gave rise to new forms of transnational community.

Central to the creation of diasporas was the relationship between new and old migrations, or between migrants and the descendents of migrants. They had different investments in maintaining ties with the homeland; for second- or third-generation descendents of migrants, the idea of 'return' was often metaphorical – for newer arrivals, it was very real. European authorities tended to treat old and new migrants collectively, on the basis of race – as 'Chinese', 'Indian', or 'Arab' – however different the nature of their overseas connections. As the flow of fresh arrivals declined – as in the 1930s – some diasporas cemented their boundaries through the construction of schools, social institutions, and more permanent places of worship; in other cases, the reduced flow of people and ideas across the seas, and the formation of locally settled families, led long-distance connections and affiliations to lapse.

This chapter shows that as millions of Asians moved between the 1870s and the 1930s, they took with them not only their skills, capital, or labour power, but ideas, cultural practices, sacred symbols, and ways of life; all of these changed in the process of migration, as they transformed the new lands where they took root.

Cities and Diasporas

The intellectual and political ferment caused by Asia's age of migration resulted from the intersection of different kinds of mobility, of which 'migration', properly speaking, was only one example. The mass migrations of the period between 1870 and 1940 (Chapter 1) were accompanied by many other kinds of movement, smaller in scale, but of great cultural and political significance. Just as labour and mercantile mobility had a long history in Asia, there was nothing new about these other kinds of mobility, which included pilgrimage, the circulation of monks and religious scholars, and the movement of students in search of knowledge. What changed were their scale, their pace, and the extent of their inter-connection. The movements of pilgrims, students, journalists, and political exiles across Asia were often peripatetic. They were crucially important in allowing the transmission of new ideas across the continent: ideas about empires and nations, ideas about political organization, ideas about modernity.

How did ideas travel across Asia? Historians of imperialism have recently begun to think in terms of the networks – of people, ideas, laws, institutions, goods, and guns – that bound large imperial systems together. These networks did not simply connect Asian or African colonies to European metropolitan centres; they also connected different dependent parts of these empires to each other. The concept of the network provides us with a helpful way of thinking about the ways in which Asia's migrant worlds functioned as circuits – intellectual and cultural as much as economic. The central nodes in the network, around which financial as well as cultural resources coalesced, were the port cities and other urban centres of Asia: Tokyo, Shanghai, Singapore, Jakarta, and Calcutta. Many of these were imperial capitals, which were thereby linked to the metropolitan heart of the European empires. Political power, financial institutions, printing presses, and educational institutions were concentrated in these cities. Each city, however, was connected in a myriad of ways with its hinterland, and with other Asian cities.

Tokyo: Metropolis of Asia

The rise of Japan as a regional and global power had a significant effect on the networks of ideas and people flowing across Asia. Japan underwent a political revolution, known as the Meiji Restoration, in 1867. Feudal–military rule gave way to a reforming government that invoked the authority of the newly restored Meiji Emperor (1852–1912). Japan opened itself to the world, seeking to adapt elements of Western political and military technology in order to preserve its autonomy. This led, in short order, to the development of constitutional government, widespread educational reforms, rapid economic advance, and rising military strength. After defeating Chinese forces in the Sino-Japanese War of 1895, Japan began a process of territorial acquisition in the region, including Korea and Taiwan, becoming an imperial power in its own right. The Japanese defeat of the Russian Empire in the war of 1904–05 cemented Japan's arrival as a power on the international stage, a victory that was watched and celebrated throughout the non-Western world.

Japanese connections with the region expanded rapidly, not least through large-scale Japanese migration to East and Southeast Asia. Hundreds of thousands of Japanese travelled to Korea, Manchuria, Singapore, and Indonesia as adventurers, labourers, industrialists, spies, and even prostitutes. In turn, Tokyo exerted a strong attraction for a new generation of young Asian students from across the continent.

Plate 2.1 **The Ginza (looking north), the most important thoroughfare in Tokyo (1904). Tokyo became a site of interaction for students, exiles, and revolutionaries from across Asia and the epitome of an Asian urban modernity.**
Source: Library of Congress Prints and Photographs Division, Washington D.C., LC-USZ62–125514. Used with permission.

For Asian travellers, Tokyo was the epitome of urban modernity. Its streets were bathed in electric light. Its places of leisure and entertainment offered the prospect of a new world of pleasure and consumption (Plate 2.1). Tokyo's monumental architecture, its tramcars, and its public spaces, as depicted in Plate 2.1, symbolized the spirit of the new age. Japanese migrants from rural areas and travellers from overseas experienced, for the first time, 'Western-style' restaurants, cafés where patrons could drink coffee and alcohol in stylish surroundings, and department stores such as Mitsukoshi, with desirable goods displayed behind class cases.

Tokyo became a place of political exile. From the late nineteenth century, Tokyo was a key meeting point for students and revolutionaries from across Asia and beyond. In 1896, the first thirteen Chinese students arrived in Tokyo on an official educational exchange programme. Seven of them lasted the course, to graduate in 1899. From then on, the number of Chinese students in Tokyo increased dramatically. By 1903, there were approximately 1,000 Chinese students in Tokyo, and, by 1905–06, anywhere between 8,000 and 20,000. As Paula Harrell points out, 'over five years, what had started as a government-sanctioned overseas study program, modest in size, had mushroomed in size into a large-scale and largely unregulated migration of students abroad'. Harrell argues, plausibly, that this represented 'the first such phenomenon anywhere in the world'.[1]

Chinese students in Tokyo led lives of intellectual ferment. Within a few years of their arrival, they had formed clubs and societies. They founded journals of translation and published political pamphlets. Chinese students organized protests, the first of which surrounded the depiction of Chinese as 'uncivilized' in the Osaka Exhibition in 1903. Within a few years, some Chinese students began to entertain ideas of revolution, forming anti-Manchu societies, and nourishing the revolutionary movement of Sun Yat-sen, who based himself in Tokyo after 1900.

Chinese students in Tokyo were not alone. In 1904, the Vietnamese revolutionary Phan Boi Chau (1867–1940) formed the Reformation Association, and travelled to Tokyo, where he met with Japanese and Chinese student groups. He spearheaded the Dong Du ('Journey to the East') movement, which brought Vietnamese students to Japan, funded surreptitiously by Vietnamese businessmen, and supported by sympathetic Chinese junk traders who would smuggle the students out from under the surveillance of the French authorities, through Hong Kong. On one estimate, there were at least 500 Vietnamese students in Japan by 1907.[2] The same year, Chinese, Vietnamese, and other students formed the East Asian Alliance.

Tokyo's world of sojourning exiles and political figures reached far beyond East Asia, and beyond the world of students. By 1908, Tokyo was also a haven for Muslim activists and Pan-Islamists 'seeking collaboration with Japan against Western powers'. Through a series of secretive alliances with Japanese intelligence figures, pan-Islamists exiled from the Russian, British and Ottoman Empires found refuge in Tokyo. They included the Indian Muslim Maulana Barakatullah (1856–1927), who taught Urdu at Tokyo University, Egyptian army officer Ahmad Fadzli Bey, and Abdüresid Ibrahim, a Russian Tartar journalist and major pan-Islamic figure in the Ottoman Empire. Between them, they began publishing *Islamic Fraternity*, an English-language newspaper that promoted a pan-Islamic revolt against European imperialism.[3] Barakatullah played a key role, too, in the establishment of Tokyo's

---

[1] Paula Harrell, *Sowing the Seeds of Change: Chinese Students, Japanese Teachers, 1895–1905* (Stanford: Stanford University Press, 1992), 2.

[2] Christopher E. Goscha, *Thailand and the Southeast Asian Networks of the Vietnamese Revolution, 1885–1954* (Richmond, UK: Curzon Press, 1999).

[3] Selçuk Esenbel, 'Japan's Global Claim to Asia and the World of Islam: Transnational nationalism and world power, 1900–45', *American Historical Review*, 109, 4 (2004), 1140–1170.

'India House', a meeting place for Indian students and a hotbed of political activity.

Tokyo was one point in a much larger network that linked disparate parts of Asia more closely together in a web of journeys, ideas, information, and political organizations. They reached far beyond Tokyo: the Vietnamese networks illustrate the expanse of the new political networks made possible by the age of migration. As Christopher Goscha shows, from the first decade of the twentieth century, Vietnamese Communist activists made use of a whole range of connections that linked Vietnam with both East and Southeast Asia, not least the extensive 'trans-border' community of ethnic Vietnamese who lived in northern Thailand and southern China. By the 1920s and 1930s, under the direction of Nguyen Ai Quoc (later to be known as Ho Chi Minh), Vietnamese revolutionaries made use of the very infrastructure that made Asia's great migrations possible, deploying as agents and informants a whole network of Chinese and Vietnamese sailors working on ships crossing the South China Sea. Goscha's conclusion is apt: 'militants were trying to place both age-old and colonial patterns of Chinese and Vietnamese immigration in Asia in the service of regional revolution'.[4]

Urban Publics

Tokyo exerted a particular force of attraction for students and political exiles because of its position as the capital of Asia's pre-eminent power. Throughout Asia, however, migrants encountered modernity in rapidly expanding cities. Cities, and particularly port cities, were the meeting point for different diasporas. Asia's metropolitan centres – Singapore, Shanghai, Guangzhou, Calcutta, Jakarta, Rangoon – were precociously cosmopolitan. Their populations were much more ethnically and culturally diverse, and much more mobile, than those of the European cities of that era. As Anthony King observed, 'the culture, society and space of early twentieth century Calcutta or Singapore prefigured the future in a much more accurate way than that of London or New York'.[5]

Singapore is a case in point. Singapore, Tim Harper argues, 'became a central locus of a number of overlapping diasporic worlds and was intersected by a series of information regimes'. By virtue of its importance

[4] Goscha, *Southeast Asian Networks of the Vietnamese Revolution*, 80.
[5] Anthony D. King, 'Introduction: Spaces of Culture, Spaces of Knowledge', in Anthony D. King (ed.), *Culture, Globalization and the World-System: Contemporary Conditions for the Representation of Identity* (London: Macmillan, 1991), 8.

as a port and a financial centre, Singapore became a place of transit or sojourn for people on the move. Singapore was a way station for thousands en route to perform the *hajj* or to study in Mecca; for merchants conducting business in Calcutta or Guangzhou; for labourers headed (willingly or not) to Sumatra and the outer islands of Indonesia. Consequently, Singapore also stood at the centre of Southeast Asia's world of print, through which dispersed migrant groups communicated with each other and with their distant homelands, and through which they received news, instructions, and new ideas from sites of political or spiritual importance. The humblest labourers used the services of Singapore's burgeoning cast of letter writers crouched over makeshift desks by the roadside.

Singapore formed part of an English-speaking, imperial chain of port cities around the Indian Ocean world, in constant communication with one another (as much as with London). This was a world of journals and debating societies, of intellectuals engaged in constant conversation about social and religious reform, about political legitimacy, about economic change, and about the condition of living in diaspora.[6] At the same time, a distinct circuit of reading, writing, and publishing in the Malay world – much older, yet facilitated by the transformation in transport and communications – made Singapore also the cultural centre of the Malay-speaking world. 'Students converged on Singapore', historian William C. Roff writes, 'where they met and sat at the feet of itinerant scholars from the Hadramaut, and from Patani, Acheh, Palembang, and Java – most of whom had themselves studied in Mecca'.[7] The rapid expansion of publishing was made possible by the circulation of a growing number of journalists, editors, printers, typesetters, and investors. New technologies of printing – presses, inks, and paper – moved rapidly across the Indian Ocean and the China seas.

The public sphere was never confined to the world of print culture. Popular culture, the culture of the street, stimulated the interaction of many migrant groups. They converged in the performance and observation of religious processions and rituals, or in places of popular entertainment. On the city streets, the mass migration considered in Chapter 1 came together with the migration of students and intellectuals that this chapter has introduced. On the street, 'high' and 'low' culture, the

---

[6] Mark Ravinder Frost, '"Wider Opportunities": Religious Revival, Nationalist Awakening and the Global Dimension in Colombo, 1872–1920', *Modern Asian Studies*, 36, 4 (2002), 937–967.

[7] William R. Roff, *The Origins of Malay Nationalism* (New Haven: Yale University Press, 1967), 43.

oral and the literate, blurred into one another: quotidian gatherings of large groups of (often illiterate) men to hear the daily newspaper being read aloud in coffee-shops exemplify this process.

It was the encounter between many different migrant worlds, for instance, that made Shanghai such a cosmopolitan city in the late nineteenth century. This transcended any distinction between internal and overseas migration. Recent scholarship has made clear that Shanghai's cosmopolitanism reached far beyond the confines of its international settlement.[8] Shanghai's urban culture was shaped by the arrival of successive waves of migrants, beginning after the cataclysm of the Taiping Rebellion (Chapter 1). The economic collapse of the surrounding region led thousands of performers and theatre troupes to find refuge in Shanghai, underpinning the efflorescence of Shanghai's cultural life, centred on the theatre district. By 1900, it had more than 100 opera houses. The flow of refugees, exiles, and migrants into Shanghai continued into the twentieth century, the evolving urban culture reflecting each new stream of arrivals: White Russians and Russian Jews, Koreans in flight from the Japanese, hundreds of thousands from north-eastern China seeking work in Shanghai's urban economy after the upheaval of the Boxer Rebellion.

Shanghai's urban culture was a potent mélange of influences, and reflected the convergence upon the city of both regional and international migrants. Native place associations flourished as migrants from other parts of China arrived. At the same time, the large cast of international characters that made their appearance on Shanghai's stage produced a heightened sense of globalism. In popular newspapers and magazines, in the bookshops, and in theatrical performances, the range of references expanded to encompass the struggles of Filipino revolutionaries, the fate of distant Poland, and the condition of African Americans.

This mobile world of entertainers and their equally transient publics met in what Meng Yue has likened to early shopping malls: plebeian pleasure palaces that combined shopping, entertainment, and exotic novelties. The most famous of them was 'Great World'. The Austrian film director Josef von Sternberg, visiting in 1931, regarded Great World with horrified fascination, and his vivid account gives a sense of life within the complex:

The establishment had six floors to provide distraction for the milling crowd, six floors that seethed with life and all the commotion and noise that go with it, studded with every variety of entertainment. When I had entered the hot

[8] The following account is based on Meng Yue, *Shanghai and the Edges of Empires* (Minneapolis: Minnesota Press, 2006).

stream of humanity, there was no turning back even had I wanted to. On the first floor were gambling tables, singsong girls, magicians, pick-pockets, slot machines, fireworks, bird cages, fans, stick incense, acrobats, and ginger. One flight up were the restaurants, a dozen different groups of actors, crickets in cages, pimps, midwives, barbers, and earwax extractors.[9]

In time, travelling entrepreneurs took this concept to Singapore, where they re-created Great World, and where the concept developed in equally cosmopolitan directions.

The next section of this chapter brings together some of these key themes – diasporas, networks, and cities – through a closer examination of two particular flows of people and ideas: the Islamic links of pilgrimage, migration, and scholarship linking Southeast Asia with the Middle East; and Chinese and Indian diasporic networks of Southeast Asia. In both cases, we will witness the vital connection between diasporas, cities, and the exchange of ideas in Asia.

Islam and Diaspora

The expansion in global migration from the mid-nineteenth century energized much older forms of human mobility. Spurred by capitalist globalization, facilitated by a revolution in transportation, Asia's age of migration also reinvigorated the movement of scholars and pilgrims. With the more rapid circulation of information and the expanding scale of movement, the nineteenth century witnessed the formation of multiple Muslim diasporas that connected Asia. Religious revival provided a new language in which to understand the rapid changes sweeping the world – including the change represented by mobility and migration.

An expanding and increasingly connected network of Muslim scholars and teachers cleared the way for the transmission of new ideas throughout the Muslim world. In their circulations, Muslim teachers and students facilitated the exchange of ideas between the Middle East and the wider world of Islam, fostering particularly close connections between the Middle East and Southeast Asia. Relatively small numbers of mobile people exercised significant cultural and political influence. Their conspicuous mobility fostered a revolution in ideas and religious practice.

The world of Islam was closely connected long before the nineteenth century. Diasporas played a central role in channelling these connections. For many centuries, wealthy merchants and notables from around the world made the journey to the Hijaz. But during the second half of

---

[9] Yue, *Shanghai*, 190.

the nineteenth century, and particularly after the opening of the Suez Canal in 1869, the *hajj* expanded in scale. Thousands of pilgrims of modest means began to make the journey. The technological transformations making the *hajj* more accessible to millions of Asian Muslims were, of course, precisely those that made possible the mobility of millions of labourers (Chapter 1): the steamship, the railway, motorized transport, and the increased circulation of information. The regulation and surveillance of the *hajj* by European and Ottoman imperial authorities presaged later efforts to regulate other kinds of migration. It was a modern movement, of a very old kind.

The changing scale and nature of the pilgrimage to Mecca from the Malay world exemplifies the broader transformation of the *hajj* in the later nineteenth century. In the middle of the nineteenth century, perhaps 2,000 pilgrims a year from Indonesia and Malaya performed the *hajj*, including many local sultans and princes. By the late nineteenth century, this number had risen to over 7,000 each year. Before the 1860s, most pilgrims embarked on their voyages on small vessels, from many small ports. After the opening of the Suez Canal, *hajj* shipping increasingly came under the monopoly control of large Dutch and British shipping lines, in part because of the implementation of new regulations governing the conditions on board pilgrim ships.[10] The fact that European captains might not pay more attention to their pilgrim passengers' safety than their indigenous counterparts provided the inciting incident for Joseph Conrad's influential novel *Lord Jim*, which opens with a vivid depiction of the sinking of a pilgrim ship, the *Patna*; the protagonist, Jim, spends the rest of the novel trying to expiate his guilt and shame at having abandoned the sinking ship.[11]

By the last decades of the nineteenth century, the pilgrimage from the Malay world was both more concentrated and more regulated. Where previously pilgrims would embark with others from their home regions on small vessels, now larger ships sailing from a restricted number of ports – Jakarta, Padang (in Sumatra), and Singapore – brought together pilgrims from across the Indonesian archipelago. One of the unintended consequences of this shift was to create among the voyagers a keener awareness of other peoples from distant parts of Indonesia, people who spoke different languages and had different customs, but who shared the faithfulness that compelled all on board towards Mecca. When they

[10] Roff, *The Origins of Malay Nationalism*; Michael Francis Laffan, *Islamic Nationhood and Colonial Indonesia: The* Umma *Below the Winds* (London and New York: Routledge, 2003).
[11] Joseph Conrad, *Lord Jim* [1900] (London: Penguin, 1988).

arrived in Mecca, pilgrims from different parts of the Indonesian archipelago were known, collectively, as 'Jawah', adding to their new sense of collective identity. Such experiences were at least as significant as Dutch educational and administrative policies in fostering Indonesian national consciousness.[12]

Colonial authorities sought to keep a close eye on the *hajj*, worried by the prospect of pan-Islamic political mobilization and by fears of infectious disease being transmitted by pilgrims. Dutch authorities introduced a pilgrim passport, which had to be stamped on exit and entry from the Indies, and at every Dutch consulate en route to Jeddah. The British, for their part, required less information to be furnished by prospective pilgrims for display on their passports. As a result, many pilgrims from the Indies chose to embark at Singapore, as a way of circumventing the Dutch regulations. Singapore became the premier port of embarkation for the *hajj* in all of Southeast Asia. Pilgrims' journeys were governed by the international sanitary agreements that came into force beginning in the 1850s. Many pilgrims' first stop, before arriving at Jeddah, was the quarantine station at Qamaran Island.

The *hajj* became a lucrative business, and spawned a whole industry of recruiters, agents, guides, financiers, and facilitators. In many ways, we can see this as part of a broader, global development of a 'migration industry' in the nineteenth century (Chapter 1). On the Southeast Asian side, the *hajj* had a direct connection with the world of migrant labour described in Chapter 1. Pilgrims from across the Indonesian archipelago contracted (or even indentured) themselves to work on plantations in Singapore and Malaya as a way of raising funds for their pilgrimage, or after their return, as a way of redeeming the debts they had incurred during the *hajj*. Prominent merchants in Singapore, who played a key role in financing the *hajj* for poorer pilgrims, made many returning *hajjis* undertake plantation labour to pay off their debts. Some prospective pilgrims never got any further than Singapore, failing to raise the requisite funds, or becoming ensnared by debts or contracts.

On the other end of the journey, there developed an extensive network of pilgrim guides (*shaykhs*) on whom pilgrims depended on their arrival at Jeddah. The guides organized transportation and accommodation, procured necessary supplies for the pilgrims, acted as translators, and guided them around the holy sites. The guides spoke the local and regional languages of their clients; some had agents who recruited directly from across the Malay world. To look after Malay and Indonesian pilgrims alone, there were over 180 guides by the 1880s.

---

[12] Laffan, *Islamic Nationhood*.

Many observers focused on the myriad of ways in which the *shaykhs* fleeced and cheated unsuspecting and naïve pilgrims. Mecca's growth depended on, and stimulated, flows of unfree migration across the north-western Indian Ocean. The populations of Mecca, Medina, and the port of Jeddah doubled in the nineteenth century. Slaves undertook most of the work of construction that allowed these cities to grow. They worked in Jeddah's port, and in the households of Mecca's notables.[13]

In the second half of the nineteenth century, Mecca was the great crossroads of the Muslim world, a site where Muslims of diverse origins encountered one another and developed a tangible sense of the global community of the faithful to which they belonged. Mecca was a place of pilgrims and transient travellers, of sojourners and long-term settlers. This complex, mixed, and shifting society gave rise to ideas and exchanges that reverberated far beyond Arabia.

The best evidence we have about the social world of Mecca comes from the writing of the Dutch scholar and Muslim convert C. Snouck Hurgronje, who spent a year in Mecca in 1884 and 1885. Hurgronje's testimony is problematic. He was, after all, an agent of the Dutch state. His observations are coloured always by his quest to reduce the potential for the *hajj* to produce politically radicalized opponents of Dutch imperialism. Questions have been raised, too, about whether his conversion to Islam was genuine. Nevertheless, Hurgronje produced the fullest account we have of everyday life in Mecca, and his experiences there introduced at least a note of ambivalence in his attitudes towards European imperialism.

Mecca in the Nineteenth Century

'As Mekka is partly a town of foreigners', Hurgronje wrote, 'the whole many-tongued mass of humanity ... feels itself there quite at home, but always as foreigners'. He used the language of race to describe the 'different types of inhabitants, from the fair-skinned Turks through all intervening shades to the pitchblack Nubians'. Hurgonje believed that 'the immigrants of different nationalities begin by forming separate societies', observing that 'though their dealings may bring them into contact with various circles, they have intimate intercourse with their own countrymen only'. Mecca was divided into quarters inhabited by pilgrims, sojourners, and longer-term migrants of common origin: residents from the Malay world, for instance, occupied the Jawah quarter. Hurgronje pointed out that Mecca attracted many long-term migrants

---

[13] Ewald, 'Crossers of the Sea', 78.

from around the world, as well as transient pilgrims. He described a process through which 'citizens' of Mecca constantly absorbed new-comers through marriage. Between 'Meccans' and 'foreigners', he argued, there was 'an endless series of gradations, but no sharp divid-ing line'. Very prominent, too, were Circassian and African ('Nubian') slaves, traded in the central slave market 'near the mosque gate, called Bab Dereybah'.

The interaction between pilgrims, sojourners – students, scholars, and teachers – and more permanent migrants to Mecca created a net-work that spanned the world of Islam and expanded its boundaries. The constant flow of people to and from Mecca provided a conduit for new forms of learning, new expressions of piety, new ways of living a good Muslim life. The 'very kernel' of the Jawah colony in Mecca, Snouck Hurgronje believed, 'are the teachers and students'.

New ideas took root. These were ideas not only about faith and reli-gious practice, but about politics; ideas about empires and justice; about the extent to which Muslims could live under the rule of non-Muslims. In the following extract, Snouck Hurgronje related a conversation he claims to have overheard. Even if we grant an element of embellishment or even invention in his reportage, we can imagine that conversations like these might well have been common on Mecca's streets and in its shaded courtyards.

In a very mixed Jawah society, one Javanese settled in Mekka will enquire of the Achehnese present, as to the progress of events in their home. The answer runs that they have nearly driven out the accursed Dutch, and one day will surely have done with them. One Javanese grown grey in Government service and pensioned considers the attitude of the Acheh is unreasonable. 'Europeans must govern us, that is God's will; why drive out the Dutch, throw away blood and money, finally to get instead of Dutch, English master'. The Achehnese answers scornfully, such cowardice on the part of the Javanese increases the arrogance of the kafirs; the Achehnese fight on the side of God, and despite the devilish war-machines of the Christians they have sent thousands of them to Hell. 'Just as the Sudanese are doing to the English', adds a Jawah settled in Mekka.[14]

The ideas of Mecca circulated through texts, and through the itin-eraries of individual teachers. Books and literary publications from Mecca travelled back to Southeast Asia with returning pilgrims and scholars. 'Among the merchandise exported out of Mekka', Hurgronje surmised, 'figure, above all, printed books the authors of which are either Jawah settled in Mekka, or Mekkan professors specially esteemed

---

[14] Hurgronje, *Mekka*, 245.

Plate 2.2 **Malayan pilgrims return from Mecca (1949). The photograph shows the bustling harbour-front in Singapore as a pilgrim ship returns from Mecca. When the photograph was taken, in 1949, the number of pilgrims making the journey was significantly reduced compared with the peak of the late 1920s.**
Source: National Archives of Singapore, 66237. Used with permission.

by the Jawah'. A stint in Mecca increased immeasurably the prestige of a religious scholar. Upon returning to the Malaya or Indonesia, he would assume a position as the local religious teacher or village head-man, extending his influence, and spreading the ideas he had gained from his time in Mecca.

The rhythms of the pilgrimage to Mecca from across the Indian Ocean followed the ebb and flow of migration more generally. The steam-ship – pictured in the background in Plate 2.2 in a photograph from the 1940s – revolutionised the *hajj*. The peak years of the pilgrimage before the Second World War coincided with the peak years of labour migration (Chapter 1), with 1927 as the single greatest year of pilgrim-age. That year, 132,109 pilgrims arrived by sea in Jeddah, including 39,157 from Indonesia, 26,089 from India, 29,604 from Malaya, and 18,876 from Egypt. The onset of the global economic depression in the

1930s led to a plunge in the numbers, down to a total of 84,821 in 1930, and just 20,705 in 1933.[15] The numbers increased thereafter, but never, until the 1950s or 1960s, did they reach the levels of the 1920s.

Where Mecca remained the traditional centre of learning, Cairo emerged, by the late-nineteenth century, as the home of Islamic modernism, centred particularly on the formidable community of scholars and teachers associated with al-Azhar mosque. Associated with the teachings of Muhammad Abduh and his disciple Rachid Rida, Muslim modernists sought to reconcile Islamic teachings with industrial modernity and modern ideas about nationality. They emphasized the importance of rigorous scriptural interpretation (*ijtihad*), and sought to rid Islamic practice of accumulated cultural traditions that departed from its fundamentals. These ideas had a great impact on Muslims from Southeast Asia, who imbibed them during their travels and through circulating texts. For a time, Cairo became a central nodal point in the Asian Muslim world.

The most direct way in which those who had travelled to Mecca and Cairo were able to shape the transmission of ideas in the Malay world was through the circulation of schoolteachers, and the establishment of modernist *madrasas* (as distinguished from the traditional village schools, known as *pondok*) across the Malay world. To take just one example, the Al-Diniah *madrasa* in the Malaysian state of Perak was founded in the 1930s by Shaykh Junid al-Tala, a Hadrami from Sumatra, who had travelled widely in the Middle East. Many of its teachers had been educated in Egypt, or at Malaysian or Sumatran institutions built on an Egyptian model. The founders of such institutions had usually studied in Cairo themselves. In this way, the intellectual and institutional innovations that arose from travel to the Middle East spread to those who had not travelled at all.

In his important work on the history of ideas in the modern Malay world, Joel S. Kahn writes that 'Islamic reformers in the Malay world from the early twentieth century imagined new forms of global community'. They imagined a 'trans-border' Malay world that transcended the territorial boundaries imposed by European empires.[16] The journeys of Malay (as also South Asian) pilgrims, scholars, and seekers to the Middle East and later to Cairo brought them into contact with a wider Muslim world. This led to a heightened awareness of their interconnectedness,

---

[15] Sugata Bose, *A Hundred Horizons: The Indian Ocean in an Age of Global Empire* (Cambridge, MA: Harvard University Press, 2006), 214–215.

[16] Joel S. Kahn, *Other Malays: Nationalism and Cosmopolitanism in the Modern Malay World* (Singapore: Singapore University Press, 2006), 92–93.

but also awareness, and even a sharpening, of difference and distinction. From these encounters came a vision of the Muslim world that was much less territorially specific, and at the same time a clearer vision of a Muslim world divided into nations.

The experience of mobility – mobility as travel, as pilgrimage, as migration – brought diverse people together in new ways, and spawned a range of networks that crossed Asia and connected Asia to the wider world. This encounter sparked a wide-ranging exchange of ideas about faith, nations, and empires. Putting mobility at the centre of our story can destabilize many of our received understandings about the source of the formative religious and political movements in modern Asian history.

Diasporas and Nationalisms

The travels of intellectuals, activists, and students played a foundational role in the development and the transmission of new political ideas across Asia. Nationalism, communism, pan-Islamism, pan-Asianism – regional and local expressions of identity – all clamoured for attention in the worlds of print and public debate that flourished in Asia's major urban centres.

Asia's literati was limited in size, but intersected with the much larger, and less literate, world of labour migrants. In some cases, the intellectual vanguard built direct connections with the migrant working class, as in the case of the Vietnamese Communist networks among sailors on the ships that crossed the South China Sea. Often it was when the diasporic elites of the cities encountered the working and living conditions of migrant labourers from their homelands that they intensified their political engagement. The process of migration grouped together, in the eyes of states and authorities, people who might previously have felt little in common. In Indonesia, urban intellectuals, traders, small shopkeepers, and contracted tin miners – many of them speaking mutually unintelligible dialects – were all, in the eyes of the Dutch authorities, 'Chinese'. More and more, they began to behave as such.

Consequently, one way in which mobility spurred political debate was to turn migration itself into the subject of a transnational debate and political mobilization. Political leaders in both India and China began to think anew about questions of sovereignty and nationality, faced with the question of who would be responsible for the lives of their diasporas overseas. Migrant groups facing insecurity abroad felt that only if their homelands became strong, respected nations could they intervene to protect their subjects overseas. Conversely, nationalist leaders in India and China felt that the poor treatment of their labour diasporas reflected badly on their nations' reputations in the world.

The ill-treatment of Indians abroad came to symbolize the subordination of India by the British. In the first decade of the twentieth century, a significant political mobilization in India highlighted the plight of Indian indentured workers shipped to other parts of the British Empire. As shown earlier (Chapter 1), most Indian indentured workers ended up in the distant sugar colonies of the Caribbean and the Indian Ocean, but Malaya, too, received a significant number of indentured Tamil workers. Addressing the imperial legislative council in 1912, the Indian liberal politician Gopal Krishna Gokhale spoke of the 'vast and terrible amount of suffering' caused by the system of indentured labour, the 'personal violence' and 'bitterness' that continued to be reported from all the regions of Indian settlement in the British Empire. Beyond suffering, 'disgrace' in the eyes of the world was the greatest concern of the Indian elites who condemned indentured labour. Indentured labour, Gokhale declared in 1912, was 'degrading from a national point of view', for 'wherever the system exists, there the Indian are only known as coolies, no matter what their position might be'.[17]

The suffering of Indians overseas stimulated fervent artistic responses, including a famous song about the suffering of indentured Indian women on the sugar plantations of Fiji, by the Tamil poet and nationalist, Subramania Bharati.[18]

> Do they dream of their native land?
> Of the day they will see it again?
> Does each think of her mother's house?
> Their crying voices wracked with sobs
> O wind, you would have heard them;
> in this well of pain, the cries of our women,
> will you not echo them again?
> In the cane sugar plantations, ah!
> In the cane sugar plantations!

The most famous of India's nationalist figures, Mohandas (Mahatma) Gandhi, was himself an itinerant imperial traveller, circulating between Gujarat, London, and South Africa, first as a student and then as a barrister. Historians of Indian nationalism are coming to realise how formative Gandhi's South African experience was in shaping his moral and political ideas and tactics. Gandhi's story reminds us that migration within Asia was always closely connected with broader imperial

---

[17] Cited in Amrith, 'Indians Overseas?'
[18] Subramania Bharati, 'Karambu Tottattilee' [my translation from the Tamil].

and global networks of mobility. While the political initiative within the *Indian* diaspora lay beyond Asia – in South Asian communities in South Africa, Britain, and North America – Southeast Asia was central to the development of *Chinese* nationalism.

Chinese Nationalism Overseas

The mutually reinforcing link between the diaspora and the Chinese national movement is illustrated by the 'first transnational pan-Chinese protest movement' in 1905. The protest revolved around opposition to the legislation restricting or excluding Chinese immigrants from the United States. It began when Chinese community leaders in San Francisco persuaded Shanghai merchants to boycott American goods. From Shanghai, the boycott spread to other Chinese coastal cities. A central figure in organizing the boycotts was a Hokkien merchant who had been raised in Singapore. Through his influence, the boycotts spread throughout Southeast Asia. The protestors depicted the poor treatment of Chinese migrants to the United States as a humiliating insult to the Chinese 'race' and nation, and to all Chinese overseas. 'We humbly hope that the Chinese merchants in Nanyang will promptly act and respond to this call', one appeal declared, for 'if we manage to boycott American goods, then we shall be regaining dignity for the four hundred million people of our race'.[19]

The circulation of ideas accompanied the movement of tens of millions of Chinese across the South Seas. At stake was the contention of different ways of being Chinese, and being modern, in a world of strangers. Underlying the different positions taken in this debate was the sheer diversity of the ways in which Chinese experienced travel and mobility, the richness and tension of their encounters with other Chinese, and with other peoples. Whatever else they were about, these arguments were also arguments about migration: about where migrants' loyalties should lie, the institutions through which they should be governed, and the broader question about whether, generations after their forefathers had left China, the Chinese overseas remained Chinese.

It is no coincidence that the mass migration of Chinese beyond their shores happened at the same time as Chinese politics underwent a period of intense ideological ferment. Both, in a sense, were responses to the decades of social upheaval and conflict that had followed the Western incursions into China in the nineteenth century. From the 1880s, Chinese politics – both reformist and revolutionary – forged closer links

---

[19] Kuhn, *Chinese Among Others*, 262–264.

with the Chinese overseas. Reforming Qing officials and anti-Manchu activists alike began to see the Overseas Chinese as a fruitful source of financial support and investment, with resources and expertise to contribute to their competing efforts to modernize China. For their part, many Chinese in the diaspora began to see that a strengthened, modernized China, with a stronger position in the world of nations, would improve their position as Chinese minorities in foreign lands.

Recognising the absurdity of the official ban on Chinese emigration, in place since the seventeenth century, and the alienating effect on returning migrants of the depredations of local officials, reformers within the Qing administration aimed to strengthen the relationship between the Chinese state and the Chinese diaspora. The Chinese government established its first overseas consulate, to defend the interests of Chinese overseas, in Singapore in 1878. Qing commissions of inquiry investigated the conditions of Chinese 'coolie' labour in Cuba, Peru, and Sumatra, and were appalled by their findings. In 1893, under pressure from reformers, the emigration ban was formally rescinded.

With China's humiliating military defeat by Japan in 1895, the project to 'save' China became more urgent. Within the Qing state, reformers temporarily gained the upper hand, and sought to implement a programme of 'self-strengthening', consisting of military and managerial modernization. Under the direction of reformer Kang Youwei (1858–1927) and his disciple Liang Qichao (1873–1929), the emperor issued a rapid series of reforming edicts, known collectively as the Hundred Days Reforms. Their defeat by a counter-revolution within the palace led to the exile or execution of many reformers. Kang and Liang fled to Tokyo. From Tokyo, Kang and Liang travelled extensively among Overseas Chinese communities in Southeast Asia, delivering lectures to large audiences, gaining financial support for their Emperor Protection Society, and raising awareness within the diaspora of China's dire predicament. Liang invoked the memory of a glorious past, when the Chinese themselves were intrepid explorers, and colonizers in Southeast Asia. He suggested that in the diaspora might lie the source of China's regeneration.

The frustrations faced by the reformists within China strengthened those who believed that only revolutionary transformation could rescue China. The Chinese diaspora proved a battleground of ideas. Reformers and revolutionaries competed for support, funding, and influence, in frequent journeys through the lands of Chinese overseas. Sun Yat-Sen (1866–1925), who would come to be known as the 'father of modern China', built his political movement from the support of overseas Chinese communities. Born near Guangzhou, educated in

Hawaii and Hong Kong, Sun first came to international prominence
when, on a visit to London in 1896, Chinese agents attempted to kid-
nap him. Combining republican activism with a career as a physi-
cian, Sun based himself in Tokyo from 1900. In 1905, he formed the
Tongmenghui (the Chinese Revolutionary League) with the support of
the radical Chinese student community based in Tokyo. Sun began to
travel more widely throughout Southeast Asia, and in 1906, he formed
the Singapore branch of the Tongmenghui; within the year, smaller
branches had been established in Malaya and in Vietnam.

The contacts and resources that Sun mobilized during his travels
provided the lifeblood of the Chinese revolutionary movement. After
failed uprisings in southern China in 1908, Sun and his supporters
were driven out of Vietnam by the French authorities, and many found
exile in Singapore. The lines of influence between Sun's movement
and Overseas Chinese communities did not run only in one direction; Chinese intellectuals in the diaspora had already been exposed
to a range of ideas about race and nationality – not least those of the
European powers under whose authority they lived – that shaped their
understanding of the Chinese revolutionary message. Overseas Chinese
support was crucial to several attempted uprisings in the southern provinces in the first decade of the twentieth century. The diaspora played
relatively little role, however, in the successful revolts of 1911 that ultimately brought an end to the Qing dynasty. The final fall of the Qing
dynasty came about through regional uprisings that precipitated, in late
1911, a series of provincial declarations of independence. Soon after
the revolution, however, Overseas Chinese began to contribute their
resources, finances, and skills to building a new China.

The debates that took place in the Chinese public spheres of Southeast
Asia outstripped the boundaries of nationalism, to encompass a much
broader range of questions and anxieties surrounding what it meant
to be Chinese in plural societies. Mobility brought with it encounters
with cultural difference; the confirmation, or the questioning of prejudice; the experience of exclusion and discrimination. A central point of
contention surrounded the position of culture, broadly speaking: how
far could (and should) Chinese culture adapt to being practised in a
world of non-Chinese, during a period of rapid political and economic
transformation?

The work of Dr Lim Boon Keng (1869–1957) is symptomatic of
a much wider trend within the Peranakan Chinese leadership in
Southeast Asia. Tim Harper has written of the 'ambiguous identifica-
tions and self-definitions' of Lim and his contemporaries. They were
'complex figures' that do not fit easily within conventional categories

distinguishing between nationalists and colonial compradors.[20] Lim was a third-generation Baba, and the beneficiary of a distinguished education at Raffles Institution, Singapore's elite English school. He studied medicine at Edinburgh University on a Queen's Scholarship. Lim's conversion to Christianity, and later apostasy, took place along-side his discovery of Confucianism, and his struggles to learn classical Chinese. Back in Singapore, Lim was a founder of the Straits Chinese Literary Association, dedicated to the revival and discussion of Chinese classics, and of the Straits Philosophical Society, where Singapore's lite-rati debated all manner of subjects, from the work of Herbert Spencer to doctrines of political liberalism and constitutional government. Lim's eloquence and influence were exceptional, but the breadth of politi-cal and intellectual influences that shaped his worldview was common among his community.

Diasporas and Institutions

The mass migration of Chinese overseas in the second half of the nine-teenth century produced institutions and organizations that helped Chinese migrants to maintain connections with their homes, and to build bonds of solidarity with one another. Through these organiza-tions, Chinese migrants overseas began to constitute themselves as a diaspora. Indian institutions overseas were less developed, because Indian migration remained under the closer control of the imperial authorities (Chapter 1). Nevertheless, there are similarities as well as contrasts between Indian and Chinese institutions overseas.

The Chinese diaspora was from the start a composite, built from a set of associations based on locality. Locality and region remained essential points of identification for Chinese overseas, even after more-encompassing ideas of race and nation had taken hold. The towns hosted the widest array of diasporic institutions, and became the centre of Chinese associational life: there, large numbers of Chinese laboured as traders and shopkeepers, rickshaw pullers and dockworkers. Singapore, in particular, hosted a proliferation of Chinese migrant institutions. Through these associations, Chinese overseas maintained connections with their home regions (*qiaoxiang*), while reinventing new bonds of solidarity in a world dominated by sojourning men.

Chinese institutions overseas were established along parallel lines, with overlapping bases of solidarity. Societies based on real or fictive

---

[20] T.N. Harper, 'Globalism and the Pursuit of Authenticity: The Making of a Diasporic Public Sphere in Singapore', *Sojourn*, 12 (1997), 261–292.

Plate 2.3 **The Khoo Kongsi in Penang (2008). Established in 1835, the Khoo Kongsi was a prominent surname association in Penang, bringing together a wide range of Chinese migrants who were not necessarily directly related to one another.** *Photograph by Sunil Amrith.*

kinship were also common, taking the form of surname associations, as in the case of Penang's Khoo Kongsi, depicted in Plate 2.3.

Surname associations undertook to provide a decent burial for their members, far from home, but also played a role in the organization of weddings, and even in support of legal proceedings by (or among) their members. Even more widespread, however, were societies formed on the basis of common local or regional origin in China (*huiguan*), dividing the Chinese migrant population by 'compatriot group' (*bang*). Such societies most often took the form of dialect groups.

The *huiguan* also played an important role in the contest for political and economic power and influence within the Chinese communities of Southeast Asia. Positions of leadership within the *huiguan* reflected, and in turn consolidated, wealth and prestige (Plate 2.4). The role of the *huiguan* in controlling the distribution of employment and patronage allowed them to consolidate the congruence between different *bang* and particular niches within the economy.

Plate 2.4 **The Ying Fo Hui Guan, Singapore (2010). The Ying Fo Hui Guan was one of the regional associations that provided social support and solidarity for Chinese migrants in the diaspora. The photograph shows the association's headquarters in Singapore; the front room serves as a museum.** *Photograph by Sunil Amrith.*

Participation in the associations and their rituals instilled in many members a sense of diasporic consciousness: a consciousness of living together with one's compatriots far from home, but with a commitment to maintaining connections across distance with homes left behind. They sought to reproduce familiar social structures from China, and at the same time adapted these structures to the demands of living as migrants in new societies. The connections that Chinese diasporic associations in Southeast Asia maintained with different regions in China meant that they could act very effectively as conduits for the transmission of ideas.

So, too, by the early twentieth century, could the Chinese newspapers and Chinese schools, which were spreading rapidly everywhere in Southeast Asia. Penang's first Chinese school opened in 1904. In Indonesia, there were 54 Mandarin schools across the East Indies by 1907, many of them built by newly arrived Chinese. By the late 1930s, there were more than 50 girls' schools across Malaya, with a total student

Plate 2.5 **Chinese girls' school, Singapore (undated, c. early 20th century). The early twentieth century saw a proliferation of Chinese schools across Southeast Asia, including schools for girls. The presence of teachers and textbooks from China led to a significant transmission of ideas between China and the diaspora in Southeast Asia.**
Source: Library of Congress Prints and Photographs Division, Washington D.C., LC-USZ62–84233. Used with permission.

body of over 10,000 (Plate 2.5). Chinese schools in Southeast Asia based their curricula on those of the Chinese mainland. They used textbooks from Shanghai publishers. Many of the teachers were from China, and they brought with them both Republican and Communist sympathies. In turn, successful emigrants returning to China established many new schools in their home regions. In an important study of Chinese emigration, undertaken in the 1930s, the American-trained Chinese sociologist Ta Chen concluded that the influence of returned emigrants on their local societies in China was 'exerted largely through the building of schools', arising from their 'profound faith in education'.[21]

With education came new ideas about citizenship and new expressions of personal and collective identity. A salesman for a Chinese rubber factory in Singapore declared that 'since I graduated from the Chinese school I have become more and more sympathetic towards China'. This man, who had lived in Singapore for 'many years', admired the colonial government 'for its ability to maintain peace and safety and to conduct clean politics', but looked forward to a future in which 'political stability will soon prevail in China'. Another of Chen's informants, a wealthy merchant in Singapore who had donated significant sums to education, put it simply: 'for me, education has a profound meaning. I firmly believe in national salvation through education'.

Throughout this period, a smaller but significant number of Overseas Chinese chose to educate their children in the schools (and in the languages) of their European colonial rulers. Admission to exclusive European schools was restricted to the Asian elite. Some mission schools, however, were more open to more Asian children from a wider range of backgrouds. Many Chinese parents embraced them with enthusiasm. Chen's research gives us a remarkable insight into the hopes and aspirations of Chinese who educated their children or their siblings in European schools. In the early 1930s, he was able to examine intimate letters received by a Chinese student at a French school in Vietnam, sent by the student's brother – a businessman – who had financed his education. Writing at the height of the 1930s' Depression, the elder brother wrote that 'to be able to attend school under these unfavourable conditions, you must work exceptionally hard'. The most important subjects, he insisted, were 'Chinese, English, French, and mathematics'. He enjoined his younger brother to 'obey the rules of the school and avoid frivolity, idleness and absence from classes'. Through the tumultuous politics of the period, his advice to his brother was emphatic: 'Don't permit yourself to be disturbed in your work by talk about communism and other unworthy subjects'. For some young Chinese migrants, education lived up to its promise of social mobility; for many others, it created a sense of frustrated expectations.[22]

---

21 Karen Teoh, 'A Girl Without Talent is Therefore Virtuous: Educating Chinese Women in British Malaya and Singapore, 1850s–1960s' (PhD Dissertation, Harvard University, June 2008).

22 Ta Chen, *Emigrant Communities in South China. A Study of Overseas Migration and its Influence on Standards of Living and Social Change*, ed. Bruno Lasker (London: Oxford University Press, 1939), 153–160.

If Indian institutions overseas were less extensive than their Chinese counterparts, they were not completely absent. Chettiar, Sindhi, and Tamil Muslim merchants established chambers of commerce throughout Southeast Asia to speak for the interests of their members in negotiations with the colonial authorities and with Chinese merchants. The Chettiar bankers had chambers of commerce in Rangoon, Singapore, and Penang by the turn of the twentieth century. Urban leaders in Singapore and Malaya began to establish Tamil schools, though not on anything like the scale of their Chinese counterparts. Working-class migrants, too, began to form associations to press their claims and to provide mutual security. To take just one example: the Kadayanallur Muslim Association was formed in the late 1930s, and brought together the large number of Muslim migrants in Singapore from the south Indian weaving village of the association's name.

Some might explain the greater density of Chinese associations compared with Indian associations in terms of the 'organizational genius' of the Chinese overseas. Social and political explanations for the contrast carry more weight. Distinctions of caste and faith – between Hindu and Muslim – made Indian associations smaller and more exclusive than their Chinese counterparts: dialect and regional associations were more open to incorporating a wider range of members. The lack of a direct relationship between employers and employees – most Tamil plantation workers laboured on European plantations – weakened the relationship between Indian labour and capital overseas. Finally, colonial authorities kept much closer watch on Indian associations; in comparison, they allowed significant leeway to Chinese organizations, at least until the turn of the twentieth century.

Rituals of Diaspora

Ritual binds diasporas together. The performance of familiar rituals can provide a sense of connection with a new land. Migrants often aim to recreate, as faithfully as possible, ritual practices from their homelands. This can lend diasporic rituals an antiquated air; they might appear frozen in time, even as the source culture in the homeland continues to change. Even where this is the case, we must be attentive to the inevitable process of transformation that underpins any movement of culture. In every performance in a new setting, often before an audience of strangers, migrants' rituals were subject to a constant process of transformation and translation.

In the evolution of rituals and the construction of temples, mosques, and shrines, we can trace the changing phases of migration: from

Plate 2.6 **Mariamman Temple, Penang (2009). The Mariamman Temple in Georgetown, Penang, was built by Tamil merchants about 1835. The construction of ornate places of worship was an indication of the establishment of a more permanent, settled diaspora overseas, and a common use of the wealth that emigration and trade had brought to the diaspora's elite.** *Photograph by Sunil Amrith.*

pioneer settlement through circular migration (sojourning), to community formation and stabilization. Throughout Asia's age of migration, migrants to new lands took with them sacred symbols. Within days or weeks of migration to a new and unfamiliar place, men and women built small shrines to distant gods. Often these would consist of little more than a mark or an image at the foot of a tree. As migration expanded, sacred symbols would circulate with increasing velocity. Ritual experts, craftsmen, performers, and priests travelled alongside labourers and merchants. They built larger and more lasting places of worship. They staked a firmer symbolic claim of belonging in their new lands. The development of the Hindu landscape of Singapore and Malaysia is a case in point. By the early twentieth century, there was a shift towards more settled patterns of temple construction and worship, as pictured in Plate 2.6, reflected in grander and more permanent buildings, the re-assertion of traditional patterns of ritual authority and, in a few cases, the installation of Brahmin priests.[23]

In mixed societies of migrants from across Asia, the public, performative aspect of ritual brought many forms of religious practice into direct contact with one another. Diverse Chinese, Hindu, and South Asian Muslim rituals involve annual public processions in commemoration of festivals. In Singapore and Malaya (as also in South Africa and Mauritius), the popular south Indian Hindu festival of Thaipusam gained a wide following – much wider, indeed, than it enjoyed in India. This annual procession in honour of the god Murugan continues to enjoy widespread popularity to this day. The festival culminates in an annual procession through the streets by devotees who bear heavy burdens as a form of thanksgiving: this involves the endurance of significant pain, as palanquins are attached to devotees' bodies with spears and rods. Chinese migrants across the Nanyang would hold similarly grand processions for the Festival of the Hungry Ghost and at Chinese New Year. These occurred alongside a myriad of smaller processions: the movement of funeral corteges through the cities was especially common.

Public ritual was the source of conflict between European colonial authorities and Asian diasporas. Colonial rulers sought to control the use of public space by Asians, and to restrict the public expression of religion. Health and sanitary regulations came into play, invoked by municipal authorities to refuse permission to a particular procession or performance. By contrast, the opportunity for processional celebration provided many working-class participants a possibility of release and liberation from the hardships of their daily lives. The ability to lay claim to public space, to move through it in a commanding fashion, stood in stark contrast to the immobility of plantation or factory life.

At times, different migrant groups came into conflict over the use of public space: processions sought to follow the same routes, or to move through the neighbourhood of another community. Yet the very public nature of so many diasporic rituals also led to an unplanned and informal process of cultural contact. Almost every contemporary account of diasporic rituals in the nineteenth and early twentieth centuries conveys a sense that large audiences made up of people of diverse origins witnessed them. Some of those audiences began, slowly, to participate in others' performances. In the nineteenth century, Penang

---

[23] Fred W. Clothey, *Ritualizing on the Boundaries: Continuity and Innovation in the Tamil Diaspora* (Columbia: University of South Carolina Press, 2007), 58–77.

Plate 2.7 **Image of Mazu, Temple of Heavenly Blessings, Singapore (2010). The deity Mazu (also known as Tianhou) was famous as the protector of seafarers; Chinese emigrants in Southeast Asia often invoked her to bless their journeys. The Temple of Heavenly Blessings, founded by Hokkien merchants who had moved to Singapore from Melaka, served as a centre for the community and incorporated Chinese of diverse backgrounds.** *Photograph by Sunil Amrith.*

developed a hybrid and unique version of the Shi'a Muslim celebration of Muharram: the festival began to incorporate Chinese, Tamil Hindu, and Sunni Muslim participants, and it turned into a burlesque popular carnival. By the early twentieth century, small numbers of Chinese in Singapore and Malaya began to participate in the Hindu festival of Thaipusam, lending it their own meanings and understanding it in terms of its similarities with their own rituals.

Control over ritual was a crucial element in the exercise of authority within diasporic communities (this remains true to this day, as Chapter 5 will discuss). In sponsoring the Thaipusam celebrations, Indian merchants and moneylenders in Southeast Asia sought to incorporate under their authority working-class and lower-caste labourers. Similarly, the cementing bonds of the Chinese *huiguan* often came from their important role in organizing religious worship (Plate 2.7).

The Quest for Reform

A laughable combination or mixing developed [as] not a few native customs slipped into the patterns and habits of the Chinese.

Kwee Tek Hoay, founder of the Chinese Association of Java

Diasporic rituals were far from static. Reforming and modernizing ritual became a key concern for Chinese and Indian elites throughout Southeast Asia – as it was for many Muslim intellectuals. Living under the rule of European empires almost everywhere they went, and involved in constant encounters with other Asians, diaspora elites began to compete with one another for respect and respectability.

The sense of religious competition that emerged in many plural societies in Asia was another factor underpinning religious revival and reform. One reason the Confucian revival movement that began with Kang Youwei in China was so influential and energetic among Chinese in Southeast Asia was that for Overseas Chinese, being able to lay claim to the heritage of Confucianism as a 'world religion' heightened their status in their exchanges with the European powers and with other Asians. With the expansion of opportunities for interaction, and the proliferation of conflicts and negotiations over the uses of public space, shared understandings or norms could emerge between religious leaders over how to manage religious diversity in public. Moreover, the cosmopolitan nature of public debate in a port city such as Singapore meant that, at times, a sense of a shared project of religious reform could emerge. Hindu, Muslim, and Chinese ('Confucian') reformists in Singapore all shared a concern with how to establish and maintain religious authority over a transient, mobile population.

The transformation of social customs and religious practices lay at the core of many of the projects of Chinese reformers. A series of interventions aimed to change the ways in which the Chinese poor overseas worshipped, dressed, conducted themselves in public, and carried out rites marking births and deaths. A central concern was to make the Chinese diaspora appear modern and 'civilized' in the eyes of colonial administrators, and other Asians. Similarly, in the 1920s and 1930s, Tamil intellectuals in Southeast Asia embarked on a crusade against 'superstition', caste, and 'backwardness', among Tamil migrants, inspired by the Self-Respect Movement of Madras that campaigned against caste discrimination. In 1929, the Self Respect leader, Periyar E.V. Ramasamy (1879–1973), visited Malaya and addressed large audiences with his message of reform. By the 1930s, 'self-respect' marriages, conducted simply and without Brahmin priests, began to be performed among the Tamil diaspora in Southeast Asia. Whereas at one stage, migrants sought to create overseas as faithful a replica of their home culture as possible, by the twentieth century, many diasporic leaders argued that migration was itself a process of modernization. The culture of the homeland, 'backward' and unreformed, belonged in the past; only the purest and most rational elements of that culture would be reproduced in the modern diaspora.

The quest for ritual reform emerged partly because of a fundamental demographic and cultural shift that began to characterize Indian and Chinese communities overseas from the early twentieth century. As we have seen (Chapter 1), an increasing number of Chinese and Indian women began to migrate overseas. With the establishment of conjugal families in the diaspora, the nature of diasporic consciousness shifted. No longer did young sojourning men look exclusively towards their homeland for the maintenance of family ties. With the establishment of families overseas, diasporic communities developed firmer internal and external boundaries. They became more concerned with developing appropriate standards of behaviour and respectability in a new setting, particularly in the definition of gender roles. With an increase in the number of local-born children, new diasporic institutions took hold – schools, in particular. Many parents of children born in the diaspora felt anxiety that their children would lose their cultural 'roots'; some children would, in time, make an active choice to move away from those roots. Conversely, for others – including many Indian families overseas – as local-born children sought marriage partners, an intensified set of connections between the homeland and the diaspora developed.

The last word on diasporic families belongs to a mother in South China with two sons in the Nanyang, interviewed by Chen in the early 1930s:

Life in the modern world is a complicated affair, living together in one large family as we did when I was young seems to be no longer practicable nowadays. With all the improved means of communication, railways, steamer and automobile, the members of the family are continually separated and brought together again, only to be again dispersed.[24]

The concern with separation and reunion, and the nagging fear that distance may break connections irreparably, are at the heart of the diasporic experience.

[24] Ta Chen, *Chinese Emigrant Communities*, 144.

Conclusion

In this chapter, I have argued that the expansion in human mobility around Asia, from the late nineteenth century, brought with it the transmission and exchange of new ideas, new cultural practices, and new institutions. Mobility of different kinds – travel, pilgrimage, migration – brought thousands into contact with new ways of living and with new forms of expression. Mobility brought a sense of openness and cultural innovation, and a hardening sense of difference and cultural, even national, distinctiveness. Diasporas, with their dense webs of long-distance connections, produced new forms of identity and consciousness. Yet they also had their identities ascribed to them by others: by the machinations of colonial authorities, by the injunctions of their home governments, or by the prejudice of indigenous communities.

In the early stages of mass migration, diasporas were in flux, infused with new ideas, institutions and, not least, new arrivals from their lands of origin. As the pace of migration began to decline, diasporas assumed a more stable character. They developed sharper internal and external boundaries, and more permanent institutions: schools, newspapers, chambers of commerce, and cultural associations. Sojourning turned gradually to settlement, and societies shaped by circulation coalesced into locally rooted diasporic cultures with firmer contours. In one sense, the development of a clear diasporic consciousness was often the result of immobilization, the attenuation of migration, rather than mobility.

In the next chapter, I will show that diasporic connections could break much more quickly than they formed.

3   War, Revolution, and Refugees, 1930–1950

Why should we expect that we're going to spend the rest of our lives here?
There are people who have the luck to end their lives where they began them.
But this is not something that is owed to us. On the contrary, we have to expect
that a time will come when we'll have to move on again. Rather than be swept
along by events, we should make plans and take control of our own fate.

Amitav Ghosh, *The Glass Palace*[1]

In the 1930s, patterns of inter-Asian migration broke down and went
into reverse. The middle decades of the twentieth century were a period
of disconnection, shattering many of the links between East, Southeast,
and South Asia. The 1920s marked the height of migration in Asia;
not until the 1990s would levels of migration in Asia reach the same
level. By the 1930s, and for the first time since the 1870s, the number of Indian and Chinese migrants returning home outstripped the
number of new arrivals in the ports and plantations of Southeast Asia.
Just as the circuits of migration began to reconstitute themselves with
the first signs of economic recovery, a new age of global warfare intervened, producing mass migration of an entirely different kind: the mass
migration of refugees, in flight from catastrophic violence and social
collapse. The mid-twentieth century, in Asia as elsewhere, was the age
of the refugee.

This chapter traces the three successive transformations that had
many millions of Asians on the move. First, a global economic crisis
broke apart the connected regional economy that had led so many millions of Chinese and Indian labourers – alongside many others – to
cross the seas in search of work. Thrown out of work by the collapse in
world markets for rubber, tin, and tobacco, millions of migrant workers were repatriated. Others eked out an existence as 'squatters' and
sharecroppers on the fringes of the formal economy. In the wake of the
economic crisis, migrant labourers, traders, and merchants also found
that they became the target of hostility from local populations.

[1] Amitav Ghosh, *The Glass Palace* (London: HarperCollins, 2000), 310.

In the second transformation, the reversal of migrant flows coincided, in the 1930s, with an intensification of the scale and destructiveness of warfare. Through the 1930s and 1940s, war displaced tens of millions of Asians. The era of total war began with Japanese aggression in China in the 1930s – starting with the annexation of Manchuria in 1931, followed by a series of local skirmishes, leading to all-out war in 1937 – and subsequently extended to most of Southeast Asia after the Japanese attack on Pearl Harbor and simultaneous attack on Malaya and Indonesia in December 1941. The Asian conflict became entwined in and central to a global war. Escaping mobile armies and aerial bombs, in search of bare subsistence, millions sought refuge in rural areas, and millions more crossed frontiers in search of security. Millions died in the process.

The third transformation was a direct consequence of warfare: the war fatally undermined European imperial rule in Asia. Between 1945 and 1950, the map of Asia was re-drawn. New states were established – India, Pakistan, Burma, Indonesia, Ceylon, the People's Republic of China, the Philippine Republic – sovereignty was claimed or conquered, new borders were drawn and enforced. This process sparked a further movement of refugees who found themselves on the 'wrong' side of the new borders, often accompanied by intensive inter-communal violence, epitomised by the massacres and the massive population transfers surrounding the Partition of India in 1947.

Many Asians in the 1930s and 1940s moved because of forces beyond their control. Their journeys were forced by the decisions of distant military commanders, by the lethal products of new munitions factories, or by the pens of cartographers. But just as in the age of indenture, migrants and refugees were never simply victims. Desperation brought out resilience and adaptation, stimulated ingenuity in pursuit of survival, and provoked new forms of social solidarity. Migrants were the agents of change as much as they were its victims. The vast armies of soldiers that set Asia ablaze in the 1930s and 1940s undertook, themselves, journeys of almost unimaginable proportions. Older traditions of mobility facilitated guerrilla warfare in the jungle. Labour migrants proved a fertile recruiting ground for both rebel and imperial armies. Without these military migrations, there would not have been the problem of refugees. Migration was central to cementing new borders and boundaries: it was often in an attempt to contain the movement of people that states enforced more firmly their internal and external boundaries. Finally, addressing the problem of refugees stimulated new approaches to welfare and to administration, in ways that shaped the ideas and practices of government in the post-war world (Chapter 4).

Economic Depression and Disconnection

Beginning in the late 1920s, economic depression transformed the opportunities for Asian migration. The webs of interdependence that linked the economies of South, Southeast, and East Asia broke apart under the pressure of declining prices, contracting markets, and inter-regional competition. The evidence of agricultural over-production and a slide in commodity prices was clear by the second half of the 1920s. With the catalyst of the Wall Street crash of 1929, Asian agrarian economies fell into deep depression. Western demand for Asian exports fell sharply. Investors panicked and began to withdraw their funds. The planters and miners of Asia's frontier regions responded by cutting back production and laying off workers. Bruno Lasker, an analyst at the Hawaii-based Institute of Pacific Relations, summarized the impact of the Depression succinctly, looking back at the end of the Second World War. He noted that in the 1930s, 'international migration in eastern Asia was to a large extent arrested and even reversed in its course. This was one of the results of the general trade congestion which stopped the wheels of industry and crammed the godowns (warehouses) with unsalable commodities. The world heard of the new immigration restrictions, of the repatriation of contract labourers, and other international aspects of the human situation'.[2]

The figures on the flow of migrants to Southeast Asia tell a revealing story. For the first time since the 1870s, the number of Indians departing both Burma and Malaya exceeded the number of arrivals between 1930 and 1933. The number of Indians leaving Malaya outstripped the number of arrivals by 66,079 in 1930, by 69,661 in 1931, and by 57,535 in 1932.[3] A similar picture emerges when it comes to Chinese migration to Southeast Asia. While in 1929, the number of Chinese arriving in Singapore exceeded the number departing by over 100,000, by 1931, departures exceeded arrivals by 134,000 in 1931, by 129,000 in 1932, and by 58,000 in 1933.[4] Up to 190,000 Tamil workers were repatriated from Malaya to India between 1930 and 1932. Few if any provisions were made for their welfare, and many of their families in south India, dependent on their earnings overseas, were scarcely in a position to support the repatriated migrants. One Indian observer in Malaya noted

---

[2] Bruno Lasker, *Asia on the Move: Population Pressure, Migration, and Resettlement in East Asia Under the Influence of Want and War,* published by American Council, Institute of Pacific Relations (New York: Henry Holt and Company, 1945), 23.
[3] Sandhu, *Indians in Malaya,* 314–317.
[4] Lasker, *Asia on the Move,* 78.

that repatriation to India in times of distress 'is proving less and less effective as a remedy against unemployment'; repatriation meant that 'no relief is thereby afforded' to Tamil workers, 'but that their suffering is merely transferred from Malaya to South India'.[5] Indian plantation workers who remained in Malaya had their wages cut unilaterally by the planters. Throughout Southeast Asia, Indian and Chinese workers who were not repatriated had to seek subsistence by moving onto marginal lands as 'squatters', ironically giving some of them their first measure of economic independence. Javanese migrant labourers in Sumatra, because they were given small subsistence plots of land, were in a more secure position.

New imperial laws restricted labour migration. We have seen in previous chapters that colonial states exercised a steadily increasing level of control and surveillance over migration from the late nineteenth century on. It was not until the Depression struck that formal migration restrictions were imposed for the first time. In this respect, Southeast Asia lagged behind other parts of the world – notably the United States, Canada, and Australia, which had legislated the exclusion of 'undesirable aliens' from early in the twentieth century. Legal controls over migration *within Asia* (as opposed to those against Asian migration in North America and Australia) were a novelty in the 1930s. Worried by the prospect of political unrest in the light of economic crisis, colonial states now began to exclude 'foreign' migrants, although restrictions were not always enforced. In Malaya and Singapore, legislation implemented in 1930 was designed to exclude fresh Chinese migration, targeting Chinese specifically since, unlike Indian migrants, they came from outside the British Empire. Indian migration to Malaya, too, came under restriction through more indirect means: the state in 1930 suspended the issuance of new *kangany* licences, and thus suspended directly recruited labour migration. In Indonesia, Dutch authorities introduced a tax on 'alien' labour, which ended the import of new Chinese labour for the plantations of the outer islands.

New legislation came into effect, too, to try to restrain some of the transformations in social relations that were an inevitable consequence of the changing relationship between creditors and debtors, landlords and tenants, as a result of the Depression. In Malaya, the colonial state tried to restrict the alienation of land held by indigenous Malay smallholders, providing them with a measure of protection from their creditors.

---

[5] Confidential letter from the Agent of the Government of India in British Malaya, 3 April 1933: National Archives of India, New Delhi. Department of Education, Health & Lands: Overseas Branch, File No. 206–2/32 – L&O.

In Burma, by contrast, intervention came too late to prevent one of the most far-reaching shifts in the balance of economic power between a migrant minority – Tamil Chettiar bankers – and the Burmese majority: this would have significant, and tragic, consequences.

The Chettiars are a caste of merchant bankers who began as salt traders, before expanding into the pearl fisheries of the Palk Strait between India and Ceylon. They followed the British flag to Southeast Asia, establishing operations from Vietnam to Malaya, where they played a role in financing the opium trade. Burma, however, became by far their largest area of investment. Significantly, it was in Burma that Chettiar bankers developed the most intensive involvement in financing indigenous agriculture. With branch offices distributed in even the smallest agricultural towns, Chettiar firms – staffed by 'agents' who would fulfil three-year stints overseas before returning home to south India – lent to Burmese cultivators who had no access to credit from European banking houses, and at lower rates of interest than indigenous Burmese moneylenders. With the growth of Burmese rice production (Chapter 1), the scale of Chettiar investments in Burma increased. By 1929, Chettiar firms had 110–112 million rupees in short-term loans in Burma, and a further 32–33 million rupees in medium- and long-term loans.[6]

When the bottom dropped out of the world market for rice, the web of indebtedness on which Chettiar fortunes were built went awry. Unable to recover loans, and with pressure being placed on them from the European banks from whom they had borrowed capital, Chettiar firms foreclosed on mortgages, and took over a significant proportion of Burma's agricultural land: in 1930, Chettiars held 6 per cent of all occupied land in Burma; by 1938, that figure was 25 per cent. The social consequences of this shift, expressed in the resentment of suffering local cultivators, were clear for all to see. In testimony to a colonial commission, one witness from the Karen community put it in the following terms:

Chettiar banks are fiery dragons that parch every land that has the misfortune of coming under their wicked creeping. They are a hard-hearted lot that will wring out every drop of blood from the victims without compunction for the sake of their own interest. ... [T]he swindling, cheating, deception and oppression of the Chettiars in the country, particularly among the ignorant folks, are well known and these are, to a large extent, responsible for the present impoverishment in the land.[7]

[6] David West Rudner, *Caste and Capitalism in Colonial India: The Nattukottai Chettiars* (Berkeley: University of California Press, 1994).
[7] Government of Burma, *Report of the Burma Provincial Banking Enquiry Committee, 1929–30*, vol. 2 (Rangoon, 1930).

In a climate of fear, some Burmese turned against not only their Chettiar creditors but against all 'immigrant' Indians in their land.

Violence Against Migrants and Minorities

With contracting economies came increasing competition for scarce jobs, and a rise in resentment directed against migrant workers and immigrant minorities in Southeast Asia: this meant, in most cases, resentment against Indians and the Chinese. In the 1930s, latent conflicts between indigenous and immigrant communities developed into full-blown political movements, and even episodes of violence. Colonial immigration restrictions and policies of repatriating unemployed migrant workers aimed to forestall tensions, but only went so far. Burma, where Indian workers dominated the urban economy of Rangoon and Indian moneylenders gained an increasing hold over the land, experienced some of the worst instances of conflict.

The first episode of violence came in May 1930, at a time when the global economic depression was beginning to put great strain on Rangoon's port. Protesting against a cut in their wages, migrant Indian dockworkers decided to strike. In response, the shipping company brought in a group of Burmese workers to replace the striking Indian dockers. Following negotiations, the Indian dockers returned to work, only to find that their Burmese counterparts were there too. A fight broke out between the two groups of workers, and quickly developed into a more serious conflict. Violence swept through Rangoon, with groups of Indians more or less randomly targeted by large Burmese mobs. At least 120 Indians were killed, and about 900 injured in the fighting. Narayana Rao, an Indian labour organizer and former member of the Rangoon Legislative Council, estimated that up to 25,000 Indian 'women, men and children left their homes and sought protection in public schools and buildings'; if his figure were perhaps an exaggeration, a similar picture nevertheless emerges from colonial reports. Since most of the city's sanitary workers were Indian migrants, 'sanitary service was paralysed, and the city was rotting in filth'.[8]

The violence in Rangoon was a portent of things to come. When a massive anti-colonial rebellion broke out in Burma in 1930, led by the charismatic monk and preacher Saya San, Indians found themselves targeted by rebels. One of the largest anti-colonial revolts in Asia during the 1930s, the Saya San rebellion began as a revolt against the oppressions of the colonial capitation tax, but quickly developed into a broader

---

[8] A. Narayana Rao, *Indian Labour in Burma* (Rangoon, 1931), 187.

millenarian movement. Attacks on Indian moneylenders and shops followed, particularly in the Lower Burma districts of Hanthawaddy, Insein, Pegu, Pyapon, and Myaungmya. A British administrator stationed in Lower Burma described the sporadic burning of Indians' houses and fields by rebels, and wrote to his masters in Rangoon that 'it is very difficult to prevent villagers from going out at night, one or two at a time, and setting fire to isolated huts where Indians are living alone in the fields'.[9]

As a result of the tensions engendered by the Depression of the 1930s, migration emerged as a political problem in many parts of Asia, with long-term consequences. What had seemed natural a generation earlier – the easy (if often unfree) movement of vast numbers of people between regions – was no longer so straightforward, as the desirability of Asia's circuits of migration and circulation came under question.

One of the questions that emerged was about the very definition of a 'migrant': For how many generations was one a 'migrant'? At what stage did sojourners become settlers? Who would decide whether and how they could make that transition? As long as inter-regional migration in Asia was primarily circular (Chapter 1), the question of settlement rarely arose. In the 1930s, when the links of migration began to break, the future of migrants who decided to stay on at their destinations had to be confronted. The 1930s was an era of colonial reform. From India to Malaya, colonial states opened themselves up – in a limited and grudging way – to a measure of Asian participation. The question of which groups could exercise those rights of representation was often the catalyst for a broader debate about the relative status – indeed the very definition – of 'indigenous' and 'immigrant' peoples. The distinctions between the two were by no means self-evident. Once Asians began to think in terms of the rights and responsibilities of citizenship, the future of migration emerged as a central political problem.

Burma was distinctive in the extent of inter-communal violence that it experienced in the 1930s, but the tensions between migrants and local populations were heightened everywhere. In Thailand, the 1930s saw an intensification of the kind of prejudice that had found earlier expression in King Rama IV's notorious 1914 tract calling the Chinese the 'Jews of the East'. The formal re-naming of Siam as Thailand in 1938 emphasized the ethnic identity of the kingdom. In Indonesia, too, anti-Chinese sentiment and politics had a long history. The early

[9] Report by the Government of Burma on Recent Rebellions in That Province, 8 May 1931: National Archives of India, New Delhi. Department of Education, Health and Lands, Overseas Section, File No. 92–1/38 – L&O.

rallies of the Sarekat Islam (the first mass-based political organization in Indonesia) in the 1910s culminated in attacks on local Chinese
businesses; in the 1930s, there continued to be sporadic episodes of
violence and confrontation. In Malaya, there was no violence, but a
distinct anti-immigrant sentiment emerged at the heart of a rising
Malay nationalism. Malay newspapers and periodicals – themselves
the product of an earlier kind of intellectual migration and exchange
(Chapter 2) – turned their fire on Indian and Chinese dominance of
Malaya's economy, and demanded that the colonial state act in defence
of 'indigenous' Malays. Colonial officials across Asia, too, began to
turn on 'foreign Asians', finding in Indian and Chinese middlemen an
easy scapegoat for the economic woes of the era, and subjecting them
to new restrictions.

The 1930s threw up problems that would remain unresolved. They
would, in time, shape the future of migration in Asia and the fate of
settled communities descended from those who moved during Asia's
great age of migration. But, first, Asia's patterns of human movement
were transformed by war, which produced a new generation of migrants
and refugees.

War and Refugees in China, 1937–1945

China experienced nearly forty years of continuous warfare between
1911 and 1949. From the 1920s, conflict between Nationalist and
Communist forces – interrupted by periods of cooperation – and
between the Nationalist forces and regional military leaders ('warlords') raged with varying intensity. The scale of conflict took a new
turn in the 1930s, as Japanese forces began to intervene in China.
In the 1930s, Japanese politics came under the control of powerful,
if divided, militarists. Many of them saw territorial expansion into
China as a solution to the economic and social challenges that Japan
faced: a fast-growing population; dependence on imported raw materials; an international climate of rising strategic tension and inter-
imperial competition in the Pacific. The conquest of Manchuria in
1931 was followed by periods of intermittent fighting; a skirmish at the
Marco Polo Bridge in the middle of 1937 turned low-intensity conflict
into a full-scale war. By the end of 1937, Japanese forces had captured
Shanghai and Nanjing, with huge losses on both sides. The Japanese
conquest of Nanjing, in particular, was accompanied by a campaign
of exceptional brutality, in which hundreds of thousands of Chinese
civilians died. Japanese forces tried to rule their occupied territories through Chinese intermediaries, most significantly through the

collaborationist government of Wang Jingwei (1883–1944). The conflict turned into a war of attrition, as Japanese forces proved unable
to overrun China. After the fall of their temporary headquarters at
Wuhan, Nationalist forces moved inland to Chongqing, where they
were able to regroup, and where they began receiving American and
British military support after 1941.

The true number of people killed, displaced, and uprooted by warfare may never be known; estimates vary from 30 million to over 100
million people. The intensity and destructiveness of conflict in China
increased significantly in the 1930s. Faced with a well-trained imperial
army equipped with the latest technologies of death, bombed from on
high by lethal aircraft, subject to repeated massacres, tens of millions of
Chinese fled the fighting.

The Japanese annexed Manchuria in 1931, following an explosion on
the South Manchurian Railway – the work of restive local officers of the
Kwantung Army looking to provoke Tokyo into action. The invasion
came at a time when internecine conflict was already rife in China. An
accord between the Guomindang (GMD) and the Communists (CCP)
had broken down in 1927, and conflict between each side and regional
and local 'warlords' raged. Many armies crossed China in the 1930s.
Some of their journeys were truly of epic proportions. When GMD
forces encircled the Communist base at Jiangxi in 1934, Communist
forces retreated in what would become known as the 'Long March'.
Leaving women and children behind to face the wrath of the GMD
armies, about 80,000 men set out from Jiangxi in October 1934; a year
later, they reached Shaanxi province, where they would set up a new
base. Only 8,000 or 9,000 of the initial 80,000 had survived the journey, which had taken them across 6,000 miles in 370 days. The soldiers
and camp followers fought their way through the most treacherous terrain, surviving on a bare minimum of supplies. From time to time, they
were able to replenish their stocks by raiding provincial towns on their
path. In time, the Long March would play a crucial role in the mythology of the Chinese Communist Party; his role in leading the forces on
the march also allowed Mao Zedong (1893–1976) to gain the upper
hand within the party's leadership.

The movement of soldiers across the land presaged an even greater
movement of civilians trapped by the expanding conflict. Full-scale
war broke out after an encounter between Chinese and Japanese
soldiers at the Marco Polo Bridge on 7 July 1937, leading immediately to a Japanese attack on Beijing and Tianjin, followed by an
invasion of the Chinese mainland. Before long, the brutality of the
fighting provoked what historian Stephen MacKinnon has called a

mass movement of people 'unprecedented, even for Chinese history'.[10] The destructiveness of aerial bombing, and the violence of Japanese forces as they moved through China, led initially to a movement of refugees from North China towards the south, and inland to the west. In the second half of 1937, urban dwellers from China's central coast began a massive flight up the Yangzi, towards the nationalist capital Nanjing. After the Japanese attack on Shanghai, around 600,000 civilians fled the city, and a further quarter of a million crowded into the enclave of the International Settlement. In the Settlement, 'tens of thousands of homeless clogged the streets and hundreds of thousands more slept in office corridors, stockrooms, temple guild halls, amusement parks and warehouses'.[11] The urban landscape that had been built by migrants into Shanghai from the late nineteenth century (Chapter 2) became a vast, squalid refugee camp. In December 1937 and January 1938, a further wave of millions fled Ningbo and the notorious Nanjing massacre. At times, the actions of Chinese forces made the situation worse: in May 1938, the destruction of the Yellow River dikes as a defensive measure generated massive flooding, and millions more refugees.

The American observers Theodore White and Annalee Jacoby witnessed the refugee flight, and give a powerful sense of the scale of the human movement in 1938:

Through the long months of 1938, as the Chinese armies were pressed slowly back through the interior, they found their way clogged by moving people. The breathing space of winter had given hundreds of thousands time to make their decision, and China was on the move in one of the greatest mass migrations in human history. It is curious that such a spectacle has not been adequately recorded by a Chinese writer or novelist. Certainly the long files of gaunt people who moved west across the roads and mountains must have presented a sight unmatched since the days of the nomad hordes; yet no record tells how many made the trek, where they came from, where they settled anew.

Combined with the powerful images of the Hungarian photographer Robert Capa, picturing refugees on the move – crowded onto the roofs of trains; in long, snaking lines on foot – we get some sense of the enormity of China's refugee flight in 1938, and an inkling of the human

---

[10] Stephen MacKinnon, 'Refugee Flight from the Outset of the Anti-Japanese War', in Diana Lary and Stephen MacKinnon (eds.), Scars of War: The Impact of Warfare on Modern China (Vancouver: University of British Columbia Press), 118–135.

[11] Frederick Wakeman, The Shanghai Badlands: Wartime Terrorism and Urban Crime, 1937–1941 (Cambridge: Cambridge University Press, 1996), 7.

suffering that lies beneath the statistics. White and Jacoby concluded that:

The migrations of factories and universities were the most spectacular. How many more millions of peasants and city-folk were set adrift by the Japanese invasion no one can guess – estimates run all the way from three to twenty-five million. The peasants fled from the Japanese; they fled from the great flood of the Yellow River, whose dykes had been opened to halt the Japanese armies; they fled out of fear of the unknown. The workers who accompanied the factories numbered perhaps no more than 10,000; they came because without them the machines would be useless. The restaurant keepers, singsong girls, adventurers, the little merchants who packed their cartons of cigarettes or folded their bolts of cloth to come on the march, probably numbered hundreds of thousands. The little people who accompanied the great organized movements travelled by foot, sampan, junk, railway, and ricksha. Thousands crusted the junks moving through the gorges; hundreds of thousands strung out over the mountain roads like files of ants winding endlessly westward. There is no estimate of the number who died of disease, exposure or hunger on the way; their bones are still whitening on the routes of the march.[12]

Many of the refugees ended up in the city of Wuhan, which in 1938 became the *de facto* capital of the Chinese resistance. Stephen MacKinnon has studied the social experiment that took place in this city full of refugees and exiles. He describes the desperate situation as acting as a 'great leveller'. Chinese of different social and economic backgrounds, and from many regions, ended up in Wuhan, and were forced to live together. Among the 1.5 million people who had converged upon Wuhan by 1938 was a significant proportion of urban intellectuals. They took their printing presses with them, and Wuhan became the centre of a great cultural renaissance. The 'heady' atmosphere of Wuhan in 1938 spurred collective action and voluntary activity to provide relief, shelter, and medical facilities to the refugees.[13]

The initial years of the war (1937–40) produced the largest and most rapid movement of refugees. Refugees, without the resources or the will to settle in new lands, sought the first possible opportunity to return to their homes, which often they found had been destroyed. The movement of people continued. Later in the war, the disastrous famine that swept over Honan in 1942 produced yet another 'mass exodus', this time towards the neighbouring province of Shensi. One official of the

---

[12] Theodore White and Annalee Jacoby, *Thunder Out of China* (New York: William Sloane, 1946), 55; 64–65.
[13] Stephen MacKinnon, *Wuhan, 1938: War, Refugees and the Making of Modern China* (Berkeley, 2008).

Table 3.1 *Wartime Refugees in China, 1937–1945*

Province or city	Number of refugees	Percentage of population
Anhui	2,688,242	12.23
Beijing (Hebei)	400,000	15.45
Chahar	225,673	11.08
Fujian	1,065,469	9.25
Guangdong	4,280,266	13.76
Guangxi	2,562,400	20.37
Hubei	7,690,000	30.13
Hebei	6,774,000	23.99
Henan	14,533,200	43.49
Hunan	13,037,209	42.73
Jiangsu	12,502,633	34.83
Jiangxi	1,360,045	9.55
Manchuria	4,297,100	12.12
Nanjing (Jiangsu)	335,634	32.90
Shandong	11,760,644	30.71
Shanghai (Jiangsu)	531,431	13.80
Shanxi	4,753,842	41.06
Suiyuan	695,715	38.20
Tianjin (Hebei)	200,000	10.00
Wuhan (Hubei)	534,040	43.56
Zhejiang	5,185,210	23.90
TOTAL	95,448,753	26.17

Source: From *Nanmin ji liuli renmin zongshu biao* (1946), cited in His-sheng Ch'i, 'The Military Dimension, 1942–1945', in James Hsiung and Stephen Levine (eds.), *China's Bitter Victory: The War with Japan, 1937–1945* (Armonk, NY: M.E. Sharpe, 1992), 180.

United China Relief Fund declared that 'close to a million refugees were gathered along the one railroad line in West Honan, waiting for a chance to travel farther west'. The famine produced over 9 million refugees in all, and an untold number of fatalities.[14]

Quantifying the refugee flight in China during the war is difficult. Statistics were flawed, where they were compiled at all. Estimates of the overall number of refugees range from 30 million to 100 million. Recently historians have given credence to the higher number, arguing that the war produced approximately 95 million refugees in China between 1937 and 1945. Table 3.1 is based on a 1946 study by the Guomindang, and needs to be treated with caution, but it highlights just how vast this forced migration really was.

[14] Lasker, *Asia on the Move*, 38.

Refugee flight was not the only kind of forced migration that China experienced during the war. Millions more were conscripted to work on Japanese construction projects in Manchuria, North China, Mongolia, and Tibet. In Manchuria, the Japanese initially utilized the existing infrastructure of labour recruitment from North China (Chapter 1), in particular the 'head coolie' system. The stream of voluntary migrants from North China continued after the Japanese takeover of Manchuria in 1931. Different factions of the Japanese administration came into conflict over whether to restrict Chinese immigration in favour of encouraging Japanese settlement in the territory. The numbers of labour migrants from North China into Manchuria remained high throughout the 1930s: 630,000 in 1933, dropping to 362,000 in 1937, and rising again to 1,123,663 in 1939, when the number of migrants crossed the million mark for the first time since the 1920s.[15] This still failed to meet Japanese needs. By 1941, the Japanese turned to more coercive means of labour recruitment from North China, and within Manchuria. The Japanese used compulsory labour service corps, labour from students, and forced labour from prisoners, prisoners of war, and the transient urban population. As they became more desperate, they conscripted the elderly and children. By 1944, Japanese authorities had conscripted around 3 million Chinese to build railways, roads, trenches, and fortifications. A further 400,000 labourers were forced to work in Mongolia and Tibet, where Japanese forces invested much in fortifying the border regions.[16]

The war made unwilling migrants of tens of millions of Chinese. It also, however, produced new connections and new solidarities between the suffering refugees of China and the diaspora of millions of Chinese who lived overseas. As fighting displaced millions of people within China, some Chinese overseas rallied to the cause. Tan Kah Kee's China Relief Fund, run from Singapore, was the most prominent example of this movement of diasporic solidarity with China. Plate 3.1 shows Tan with members of his organizing committee in Singapore.

Tan made use of the existing networks of surname and dialect associations that had such deep roots in Singapore, as well as Chinese schools, voluntary societies, and women's associations, in order to raise large sums of money. Divisions within the diaspora were equally clear. Unsurprisingly, not all Chinese merchants gave willingly. In some

[15] This discussion is based on David Tucker, 'Labor Policy and the Construction Industry in Manchukuo: Systems of Recruitment, Management and Control', in Paul H. Kratoska (ed.), *Asian Labour in the Wartime Japanese Empire: Unknown Histories* (Armonk, NY: M.E. Sharpe, 2005), 25–59.
[16] Ju Zhifen, 'Northern Chinese Labourers and Manchukuo', in Kratoska (ed.), *Asian Labour*, 61–78.

Plate 3.1 **Group photograph of Singapore Overseas Chinese Association for Raising Relief Funds for China, headed by Tan Kah Kee (1937). Under the leadership of the Singapore businessman Tan Kah Kee, the China Relief Fund raised significant sums of money in support of the anti-Japanese resistance in China.**
Source: National Archives of Singapore, 142502. Used with permission.

cases, the fundraisers threatened force or resorted to extortion. And what unity there was in the diasporic effort did not seem to be echoed within the Chinese resistance: Tan, for one, found himself unimpressed by what he perceived to be the Guomindang's inefficiency and authoritarianism, gravitating in his allegiance towards the Chinese Communists.[17] In all, between 1937 and 1939, the Chinese diaspora raised 213,500,000 Chinese dollars for war and relief efforts, and subsequently purchased at least one fifth of all the Nationalist government's National Salvation Bonds.[18]

Diasporas and Refugees in Southeast Asia, 1941–1945

The cost of war in China, and the increasingly hostile international climate, emboldened those within the Japanese military who favoured

---

[17] Kuhn, *Chinese Among Others*, 269–270.
[18] Lasker, *Asia on the Move*, 80.

further territorial expansion. Following the attack on Pearl Harbor on 7 December 1941, the Japanese military conquest of Southeast Asia proceeded rapidly. Japanese forces attacked Malaya, with a simultaneous attack on Hong Kong and the Philippines. By February 1942, Japanese forces had secured the surrender of British forces in Singapore, and proceeded to gain control over Indonesia, Burma, and the Andaman and Nicobar Islands, together with territories in the South Pacific.

The Japanese occupation of Southeast Asia had a fundamental impact on Southeast Asia's political future. In the eyes of many Asians, the rapidity of the Japanese military victory undermined fatally European imperial claims to political supremacy and cultural superiority. The unseemly haste with which European empires retreated, abandoning their Asian subjects to their fate, damaged their prestige irreparably. Politically, the Japanese brought disparate Southeast Asian territories – divided between Dutch, English, and French rule – under the same administration. Japanese forces armed and trained militias of young Asians, many of them from ethnic communities – Malays, Burmese, Javanese – that European imperial authorities had denigrated as lacking in martial valour. Japanese techniques of social and political mobilization had a lasting impact on Southeast Asian political culture, particularly on young people. Many young Asians were attracted to the Japanese rhetoric of pan-Asian solidarity in opposition to European imperialism. Undoubtedly, Japanese leaders used such political language in pursuit of their own ends; but so, too, did Asian nationalist groups that worked with the Japanese in Burma, Indonesia, and Malaya.

The sense of possibility that many Asians felt in the first flush of Japanese victory soon soured. Japanese military brutality too often undermined their promise of liberation. Tensions emerged between Japanese war aims and the goals of their Asian nationalist collaborators. Japanese occupying forces had to deal, like Europeans before them, with the challenge of Southeast Asia's cultural pluralism. Often it was migrant groups – or the descendents of migrants – who suffered most during the war. The impact of the war on Southeast Asian society was destabilizing: the war forced millions to move in search of shelter or security, and trapped others in immobility. Millions were forced to turn inward, seeking security and shelter in rural areas as the threat to shipping across the Bay of Bengal and the South China Sea almost completely disrupted the oceanic connections that were already beginning to crack during the Depression.

The large diasporic communities that lived throughout Southeast Asia, and lived by and from their constant connections with their homelands in India or China, now found themselves cut off and, in many cases, stranded. The war accentuated and exaggerated the dilemmas of political affiliation that diasporas faced (Chapter 2). Now their choices could have lethal consequences. Diasporas were caught in the maelstrom of international politics: their fortunes were, more than ever, tied to the position of their homelands in the international conflicts. As a result, many of Asia's diasporas found themselves on opposite sides of the battle lines of the war.

Diasporas cut off from external communications were in an acutely vulnerable position, none more so than the Chinese. Soon after their occupation of Malaya, the Japanese military pursued and made an example of thousands of Chinese suspected of having supported the China Relief Fund, and of other 'anti-Japanese' activity after 1937. The experience of the infamous *sook ching* massacres remains a powerful memory in Singapore and Malaysia to this day. Chinese in Singapore, and in smaller Malayan towns, were rounded up. Japanese forces singled out and summarily executed many young men. Particular targets were intellectuals, lawyers, suspected Communists and sympathizers, anyone born in China, and particularly those who had arrived recently in Malaya. The severed heads of some executed detainees were prominently displayed in public places in Singapore. Disciplining, indeed terrorizing, the Chinese diaspora within occupied Southeast Asia was a key initial aim of the Japanese military, fearing the potential of diasporic connections and solidarities to foment resistance to Japanese rule.[19] Japanese measures were never entirely successful, despite – or perhaps because of – their brutality. Malaya's Chinese formed the nucleus of a powerful mobile army of resistance that took to the jungles and waged a guerrilla war against Japanese forces, growing increasingly effective as they managed to link up with Allied forces.

The experience of the Indian diaspora within Japanese-occupied Southeast Asia was more ambivalent. From the outset, the Japanese aimed to court the support of local Indian leaders by professing support for India's independence. The Indian Independence League, under the leadership of the veteran Bengali radical Rash Behari Bose – himself an exile who had spent decades in Tokyo – acted as an umbrella organization for the government of the Indian diaspora. Its armed wing, the Indian National Army (INA), emerged from the efforts of British Indian soldiers who were held as prisoners of war, and who decided to accept Japanese support to raise an army to fight for India's freedom. The INA was initially weakened by conflicts between its leaders and the Japanese, but gained a new lease of life with the arrival in

---

[19] Christopher Bayly and Tim Harper, *Forgotten Armies: The Fall of British Asia, 1941–45* (London: Penguin, 2004).

Singapore of Subhas Chandra Bose – former president of the Indian National Congress, who had escaped detention in India and set out for Germany, via the Northwest Frontier and Afghanistan, to seek support for an armed uprising against British rule in India.

Sugata Bose has described what followed as a 'fascinating drama of diasporic patriotism', highlighting how under Subhas Chandra Bose's leadership, the INA attracted the enthusiastic participation of Indians of widely different class, caste, and religious backgrounds. Women played a central role in the INA, which had a women's regiment – the Rani of Jhansi regiment – named after the legendary heroine of the rebellion of 1857.[20] The INA included a significant number of Tamil plantation workers in Malaya, instilling in them an unprecedented level of political mobilization and commitment. Long excluded from the urban-based Indian diasporic institutions in Malaya, Tamil plantation workers who joined or supported the INA during the war felt a sense of citizenship for perhaps the first time, as citizens of the Provisional Government of Free India: Subhas Chandra Bose's government in exile. Up to 80 per cent of the teenage girls who volunteered for the Rani of Jhansi regiment, for example, came from Malaya's rubber estates. In the circumstances of war, willingness to sacrifice, and the ability to endure suffering, counted for more than education or wealth; life on the plantations had equipped the INA's Tamil soldiers well for this.

An even greater number of Tamil labourers in Malaya experienced the war not as soldiers fighting for India's freedom from imperialism, but through the trauma of refugee flight and forced labour. War laid bare the centrality of chance in determining where migrants' journeys would end: chance, as much as choice, governed who died on the battlefields of Burma, who died on the Burma–Thailand railway, and who survived.

Despite the pressures of immobilization that the war brought, hundreds of thousands in Southeast Asia attempted to escape the fighting. Among the greatest of these movements was the one that historian Hugh Tinker called the 'forgotten long march': the mass exodus of Indians from Burma as the Japanese approached, most of them on foot, through Arakan and over the mountain passes to Assam.[21] In the atmosphere of fear and panic that set in as Japanese aerial bombings intensified over Burma, a great movement of Burma's Indian residents began in search

---

[20] Sugata Bose, *A Hundred Horizons: The Indian Ocean in an Age of Global Empire* (Cambridge, MA: Harvard University Press, 2006), 122–192.

[21] Hugh Tinker, 'A Forgotten Long March: The Indian Exodus from Burma, 1942', *Journal of Southeast Asian Studies*, 6 (1975).

of safety. European residents fled, and kept for themselves most of the places on the ships out of Burma: the racial discrimination at the heart of colonial rule was laid bare.

In *The Glass Palace*, novelist Amitav Ghosh evokes the atmosphere of Rangoon as the great exodus began. 'At the port, ships were going up in flames, with their cargoes still intact in their holds. There were no stevedores left to do the unloading: they too were mainly Indians … There were looters everywhere, breaking into abandoned houses and apartments, carrying their trophies triumphantly through the streets'. The novel's protagonists, like most of Rangoon's Indian residents, set out from Rangoon and found that 'the roads became so thickly thronged that they could barely move. Everyone was heading in the same direction: towards the northern, landward passage to India – a distance of more than a thousand miles'. The column advanced towards the north; 'their feet had stirred up a long, snaking cloud of dust that hung above the road like a ribbon, pointing the way to the northern horizon'.[22] The Indian refugees who set out on the journey north numbered around 140,000. Trekking through treacherous conditions, beset by malaria, and subject to attacks by groups of Burmese armed by the advancing Japanese forces, perhaps 40,000 of the refugees never completed the journey out of Burma, dying along the way.[23]

The refugees that succeeded in reaching India were housed in makeshift refugee camps in Assam, aided by the Tea Planters' Association of Assam. Conditions in the camps were dire. There were shortages of rice and water. One camp official reported that 'sanitation was at a standstill at the outset, but a force of sanitary sweepers was obtained from the refugees' – many of whom had worked as sweepers and nightsoil removers in Burma before the war. Refugees died each day, 'people who died of exposure, undernourishment, and sheer exhaustion'.[24] The registers of 'evacuees' that survive in the National Archives of India give a poignant sense of how diverse the body of refugees was. The 'occupations' listed included fishermen and cloth merchants, sweepers and milkmen, 'coolies' and cultivators, boatmen and machinists; a 'spare motor driver', a *paan* (betel leaf) seller, and a postman. Their destinations in India included, overwhelmingly, towns in the Telugu-speaking districts of Madras and the Bengali-speaking regions bordering on Burma,

[22] Ghosh, *The Glass Palace*, 467.
[23] *Burma Evacuee Register*, Part 2, No. 403 (B), National Archives of India, New Delhi.
[24] National Archives of India, New Delhi, Commonwealth Relations Department, Overseas Section, File Number F. 45–21/44-OS (1944).

particularly Chittagong, but also included destinations throughout the Tamil south, and as far north as Lahore and Amritsar.[25]

Forced Labour in the Wartime Japanese Empire

Southeast Asia's raw materials were, from the outset, a crucial motivating force propelling the Japanese conquest of the region, and they became strategically more important as the war progressed and Japanese military fortunes reversed. As in Manchuria and North China, securing an adequate supply of labour to mobilize resources for the prosecution of war proved a challenge for Japanese planners. Like any colonizing power, the Japanese attempted wherever possible to use existing structures and networks, but these proved insufficient to mobilize labour on the scale required. The Japanese authorities established 'patriotic associations' and communal organizations to act as intermediaries. These organizations were charged with recruiting labour for the war effort. In Malaya, such institutions included the Indian Independence League and Malay Welfare Association, as well as the Labour Service Corps, the Free Labour Corps, and the Chinese Labour Service Corps.

It was in Java, however, that close to half of the overall population of Japanese-occupied Southeast Asia resided. From Java, the Japanese conscripted labour for work throughout the region. By 1944, Java's railways were transporting close to 15 million passengers each month, the vast majority of them were labourers, known as *romusha* ('economic soldiers'). Even more common were shorter journeys undertaken on foot, for labour in neighbouring districts and villages. The *romusha* forced to leave Java's shores faced the worst conditions of all. About 300,000 Javanese *romusha* were conscripted to work outside Java: 120,000 were sent to Sumatra, 48,700 to South Borneo, and a further 31,000 to Malaya. They built roads, airfields, and railways; they cleared jungle, and worked underground, mining coal and bauxite. They died in huge numbers. Among the *romusha* sent overseas, well over 200,000 died – a mortality rate of nearly 75 per cent. At first, the recruitment of *romusha* was based on attraction and inducement, in the pattern of so much labour migration in modern Asia. Workers were offered high wages, recruitment bonuses, and a means of support for their families left behind. As it became clear that these promises were hollow, recruitment slowed down, and the Japanese resorted to coercion.

Particularly notorious as 'death traps' were the large construction projects that, between them, mobilized hundreds of thousands of labourers.

[25] *Burma Evacuee Register*, Part 2, No. 403 (B).

In Java, the largest such project was the construction of a railway line from Saketi to Bayah. It is difficult to estimate just how many *romusha* died in building it. Tan Malaka, the Indonesian Communist who had spent the 1930s travelling throughout Southeast Asia, 'from jail to jail', gave a harrowing account of the toll that the railway took.

The construction of the Saketi-Bayah road devoured the energy and lives of thousands of unpaid romusha. There were no provisions made for the housing, feeding, or health of the romusha, who were forced to work in a previously uninhabitable area infested with malarial mosquitoes. As a result of the hard work, lack of food and medicines, and the ever-present Japanese whip, the romusha fell like rice stalks before a scythe... Every day along the road from Pulau Manuk to Bayah one could see romusha covered with festering lesions struggling to reach a marketplace or an empty building where they could stretch themselves out to await death. In all the towns along the road from Saketi to Jakarta the markets, roadsides, and empty yards were filled with living corpses. Sometimes in the Bayah area up to ten corpses were buried in a single grave, because of official indifference and the lack of grave diggers. In the rainy season corpses were piled into graves half filled with water.[26]

Most lethal of all, perhaps, was the largest Japanese construction project in Southeast Asia: the Thailand–Burma railway, which was built on the blood of forced migrant labourers. The railway was built by about 62,000 Allied prisoners of war, and a further 200,000 Asian labourers from Thailand, Burma, Malaya, Indochina, and Indonesia. The story of the Allied prisoners of war is well known in all its details, thanks to the rich seam of memoirs and first-hand accounts that emerged. By contrast, the fate of the Asian 'coolie' labour that built the railway, and suffered much more, has remained largely unknown. Recent research has begun to enrich our understanding of their experiences.

From Malaya, Java, Burma, and Thailand, tens of thousands of workers converged upon the site of the railway's construction. They came by train, packed into freight carriages, and they came by foot, through dense jungle. Recruitment offices were established in Singapore and throughout Malaya in Spring 1943. At first, they used familiar methods: a recruitment bonus of ten dollars and a promised wage of a dollar a day. Japanese recruiters worked through foremen on Malaya's plantations, who persuaded, coerced, or deceived their workers into signing on for the journey north. As Japanese authorities grew increasingly desperate, and failed to meet their quotas, they turned to more coercive methods of recruitment. They announced the screening of free motion

---

[26] Tan Malaka, *From Jail to Jail*, trans. Helen Jarvis (Athens, OH: Ohio University Center for International Studies, 1991), 156–157.

picture shows, and rounded up all of the men who attended; they literally picked people off the streets, from restaurants and amusement
arcades. The experience of one survivor of the railway, interviewed in
1991 by historian Nakahara Michiko, was not uncommon.[27]

I was working on Kuala Selangor Estate. One day I was walking along the road
towards Bukit Rotan near my house. A Japanese military lorry stopped, and the
soldiers said something to me in Japanese. I could not understand them. The
soldiers forced me to get into the lorry. There were already thirty other people
there. I was wearing only a pair of shorts and sandals. I begged them to let me
go home to put on a proper shirt and pick up a blanket. The Japanese soldiers
did not allow me to go home; instead they sent me directly to KL and loaded
me onto a freight train for Siam. There we started by cutting dense jungle.
The Japanese did not give me a proper shirt or blanket for seven months. I had
to work in the jungle and sleep on the bamboo floor in a hut, half naked and
without any blanket.

Once they reached the labour camps along the railway lines, conditions
were appalling: the labourers were forced to work for long hours, were
given inadequate food, and were housed in cramped quarters with poor
sanitary conditions.

Immediately after the war, Allied forces estimated that 182,496 Asian
labourers had been put to work on the Thailand–Burma railway; of
these, only 21,445 were repatriated at the end of the war; 74,025 died,
and the rest were unaccounted for. These figures produce a mortality
rate of 41 per cent. Nakahara Michiko argues, based on extensive interviews with survivors, that this is surely an underestimate. She estimates
that the death rate was higher, and that the overall number of labourers
forced to migrate for work on the railway, too, was higher, since the
Allied figures did not take into account the large number of people who
deserted along the way (and many of whom died).

Towards the end of the war, the Japanese initiated another organized
movement of population, involving the resettlement of civilians from
Singapore and Malayan towns to rural areas, as part of an attempt to
solve the very serious food shortages that had plagued the Japanese
administration of Malaya. The plan was initially to resettle 300,000 people from Singapore in rural areas; in practice, a much smaller number
of people moved. Two Japanese relocation schemes were implemented,
with very mixed results. The Endau settlement in northeastern Johor
was designed for Chinese from Singapore. It was nominally outside the
control of the Japanese authorities, and was run and financed by the

---

[27] Nakahara Michiko, 'Malayan Labour on the Thailand–Burma Railway', in Kratoska
(ed.), *Asian Labor in the Wartime Japanese Empire*.

Overseas Chinese Association. Few of the settlers knew anything about growing rice, and the settlement failed to meet its agricultural objectives, yet it provided some freedom, and a lessening of direct Japanese control. By the end of 1944, about 12,000 settlers were recorded as living in Endau, far fewer than the Japanese had initially intended. The other main settlement was established as a Roman Catholic resettlement colony in Bahau, populated mostly by Eurasians and Chinese Catholics from Singapore – about 5,000 by the middle of 1945. Their experience was characterized by extremely high rates of death and illness from infectious disease, and a high rate of child mortality: malaria, above all, was responsible for this.[28] Alongside these organized movements of population were countless informal, and often surreptitious, movements, by family groups who sought subsistence and survival by moving into Malaya's forest frontier.

War and Migration

There can be no adequate measure of the sheer number of people that *moved* during the war. China alone saw anywhere up to 100 million people displaced during the war. On one estimate, 24 million people died in Southeast Asia alone.[29] Asia in 1945 was a continent ravaged.

At first glance, the scale and the nature of the wartime experience of forced displacement and refugee movement appear *sui generis*. On closer examination, however, important connections emerge, linking wartime migration back to the great age of Asian migration that began in the 1870s, and forward to the experience of migration in Asia in the second half of the twentieth century.

First, the war cemented structural shifts in Asian migration that had begun during the Depression. Mobility within Asia came under increasing control and restraint in the 1930s: inter-regional connections were broken, and patterns of movement were reversed. In this sense, the impact of the war on restraining movement across imperial and national frontiers, while sparking mass movement within them, hardened the boundaries that would govern migration in the post-war world. At the same time, however, the societies that earlier patterns of migration had produced – including diasporic societies of many kinds – were key actors in the conflict. Diasporas mobilized support for political struggles: the Chinese diaspora in the Nanyang raised funds for China's defence; members of the Indian diaspora in Malaya and

---

[28] Bayly and Harper, *Forgotten Armies*, 411–414.
[29] Bayly and Harper, *Forgotten Armies*.

Burma took up arms with the Indian National Army. And diasporas suffered, too, for the connections they had maintained and the solidarities they had expressed with their homelands. Few experienced this more sharply than the Chinese diaspora in Southeast Asia, singled out by the Japanese for persecution.

A second connecting force, making the wartime experience of migration pivotal to longer-term shifts, was that it was during the war that states began to take a greater interest and involvement in controlling migration. States and militaries mobilized and forced migration during the war, to serve the war machine, and to expand their productive capacities. States also found themselves forced to manage migrations that were beyond their control: caring for, feeding, and housing refugees; resettling displaced people; controlling the movement of people across frontiers. The wartime experience of state-engineered migration opened new possibilities, and pointed the way to the future. After 1945, many newly independent Asian states would (more or less explicitly) draw on wartime precedents to plan new migrations in the service of their national development.

Third, we can see the wartime experience of forced labour as part of an intensified and violent assault on Asia's frontier regions, in search of materials to keep the war machine going. We might see this as a final phase of the process that began in the second half of the nineteenth century (Chapter 1). Like their indentured forebears in the 1870s, the labourers in the war cleared jungle, brought new lands into production, and mined the earth for resources. This required the forced movement of human labour, at enormous cost in lives. For the Japanese, the assault on the frontiers ultimately failed. But it gave new ideas to the new states forged out of the war; many would try it again.

Displacement and a World of Nations, 1945–1949

The old is dying and the new cannot be born; in this interregnum there arises a great diversity of morbid symptoms.

Antonio Gramsci's *Prison Notebooks*

The war had undermined Western imperial rule in Southeast Asia. European powers emerged from the war fully committed to the maintenance of their overseas empires, but circumstances had changed more rapidly than their wartime planners could have predicted. Asian leaders were quick to point out the irony of a 'war for democracy' being fought to preserve imperial domination. Coercion, the ultimate backstop of imperial power, appeared more costly and less desirable in the post-war world. Asian leaders and intellectuals played an important role in shaping the new international language of human rights. At the same time, Allied forces had prevailed in part because they were able to persuade enough Asians to support their war effort; these collaborators began to call in their favours at the end of the war.

The abruptness of the Japanese military collapse in 1945 was a further factor allowing for political transformation in Southeast Asia. The interregnum in 1945 had allowed Indonesian nationalists and Vietnamese Communists to declare independence. The Dutch and the French waged bloody campaigns to reassert control over their former colonies, but both failed: the Dutch by 1949, and the French after the military defeat at Dien Bien Phu in 1954. The British were able to reoccupy Malaya, but at the cost of waging war against a Communist insurgency that erupted in 1948 (Chapter 4).

The years between 1945 and 1950 are foundational in almost every national historiography of Asia. Asian nations were born in this period. These are, perhaps, the years most familiar to any student of modern Asian history. Yet in the focus on struggles for sovereignty, the making of national heroes, and the path of armed conflict, it is often forgotten that, for millions of Asians, the upheaval and uncertainty of war did not end in 1945. The flow of refugees, displaced peoples, and migrants across the new political borders continued, and in some places accelerated. In the next chapter, we will examine how migrants in Asia experienced the political transitions of decolonization and revolution; how they became, or failed to become, new national citizens. First, however, the last section of this chapter turns to the final wave of displacements that were a central product of Asia's age of national revolution.

When the war came to a sudden end in August 1945, there were millions of people displaced across Asia. Writing in August 1945, the U.S. General Albert Wedemeyer correctly predicted that 'if peace comes suddenly, it is reasonable to expect widespread confusion and disorder. The Chinese have no plans for rehabilitation, prevention of epidemics, restoration of utilities, establishment of balanced economy and redisposition of millions of refugees'.[30] Everywhere in Asia, dazed and desperate people uprooted from their homes made their way to the cities, in search of survival and refuge. In his first novel, *The Fugitive*, set in the dying days of the war, the Indonesian writer Pramoedya Ananta Toer (1925–2006) evoked the atmosphere of Jakarta at the time, filled with people with little hope and nowhere else to go. 'When you go to

[30] Cited in Jonathan D. Spence, *The Search for Modern China* (New York: W.W. Norton, 1990), 484.

the city', the story's narrator observed, 'you see children sprawled life-less at the side of the road. In front of the market and the stores, down beneath the bridge, on top of garbage heaps and in the gutters there are corpses. Nothing but corpses. The place is filled with the dead – children and the old people'.[31] Similar scenes were in evidence across Asia: in Singapore and Rangoon, Shanghai, and Hong Kong.

The greatest movement of population, however, came in the region of Asia that had been least directly affected by the war: the Indian subcontinent. British rule in India had emerged from the war fatally weakened; the Indian National Army experience, by casting doubt on the future loyalty of the British Indian Army, was an important contributing factor to the changed balance of power. By 1947, India's post-colonial future was looking, increasingly, like a divided one. Divisions between the Congress Party and the Muslim League hard-ened, fuelled by, and at the same time exacerbating, the increasingly brutal inter-communal violence on the streets. The British were keen to quit India as quickly as possible. On 3 June 1947, British Prime Minister Clement Attlee announced the plan to partition the subcontinent into India and Pakistan.

There is a vast historical literature on Partition, much of it concerned with the high political machinations and calculations that produced such a catastrophic outcome. Only recently, however, have historians begun to examine the human dimensions of the tragedy, and in partic-ular, one of its defining features: the mass migration of refugees across the new international borders between India and Pakistan. Those migrations were accompanied by violence on a scale, and of a brutality, that shocked observers on all sides. Rape was used, on both sides, as a weapon of war: it was the most blatant expression of hatred, power, and the will to subjugate and humiliate the 'other' community. The history of rape in the violence surrounding Partition is, as Yasmin Khan has written in her sensitive account, a story of 'broken bodies and broken lives'.[32]

The movement of refugees began before independence, as violence, rumour, and fear compelled people to leave their homes and seek safety. Neighbours turned on one another after years of living in close proxim-ity. The borders between India and Pakistan – the infamous 'Radcliffe Line', drawn by a British civil servant who had never previously set

---

[31] Pramoedya Ananta Toer, *The Fugitive*, trans. Willem Samuels (New York: Penguin, 1990), 33.
[32] Yasmin Khan, *The Great Partition: The Making of India and Pakistan* (New Haven: Yale University Press, 2007), 133.

foot in South Asia – were announced the day after India and Pakistan gained independence. From then on, the flow of refugees turned into a flood.

Between 18 September and 29 October 1947, more than 849,000 refugees entered India on foot; between August and November 1947, a further 2.3 million crossed the Punjab by train. From September, the Punjab witnessed an organized 'population transfer': hundreds of military and other vehicles transported people across the border in armed convoys. In many cases, this proved a kind of 'ethnic cleansing', as local leaders drove out members of minority communities on both sides of the divide. Refugees were resettled in 'evacuee property'. The contingency of so many of the journeys that people made – seeking temporary refuge in the hope of return – was made permanent by bureaucratic procedures designating them 'evacuees', and deeming their houses and properties 'abandoned', and available for redistribution.[33]

People fled, most immediately and most commonly, in search of refuge. They fled in terror. Others made more protracted and painful calculations. Families split up, seeking to keep their options open, many of them in the belief that their displacements – and, indeed, the Partition – would be temporary. Damyanti Sahgal, interviewed by the writer and activist Urvashi Butalia in the 1990s, made the decision to leave her father behind and move from her village, near Lahore, to India. Her testimony evokes very powerfully the uncertainty and fear of those months, and the pain of separation faced by so many millions of families in South Asia.

My father said ... how can we leave everything and just go? I have so many men, they will protect me. There'll be some noise for a few days and then everything will come back to normal. So he refused to go. Then a second message came ... my uncle said your father is stubborn, so you should go. At the most he will be killed, but you, you will be gutted ... and this is very difficult for us to tolerate. You will be gutted ... so you should leave.

Father didn't agree ... the workers in his factory were mixed: Jats, Hindus, but on the whole it was a Muslim village so most of the workers were Musalmaans ... at the time they were respectful and humble. They seemed safe ...

When I tried to persuade my father he said, well if you feel scared you go. I said but bauji, he said, no bibi, if you feel scared you go. But where do I go? Then I came to Lahore. I remember asking what I should do, where I should go, my father was refusing to go. And they said the safest Hindu area is – now what is it called? Kamla, what is that, just north of Beasa ....

[33] Vazira Fazila-Yacoobali Zamindar, *The Long Partition and the Making of Modern South Asia: Refugees, Boundaries, Histories* (New York: Columbia University Press, 2007).

Saghal left Lahore by train for Amritsar. Few images of Partition are more deeply seared in popular memory in South Asia than the image of trainloads of refugees crossing the border in either direction. Indian writer Khushwant Singh's novel *Train to Pakistan* remains one of the most powerful pieces of writing about Partition. Many trainloads of refugees never reached their destinations. They were intercepted and set upon by armed mobs, their residents massacred or set ablaze. 'Train, train', Sahgal recalled, 'everyone was full of fear ... they kept saying put your windows up, put your windows up. Amritsar is coming and they're cutting people down there. We put our windows up ...'.

The majority of refugees, however, walked. They walked in columns of up to thirty or forty thousand people, stretching for miles on end. The story of Rajinder Singh, another of Urvashi Butalia's interviewees, gives a moving sense not only of the privations of the journey, but of the sense of thousands of people on the move, with no clear destination in mind.

Gradually, daylight came. This was the first night, and then it became morning and as the sun rose, it began to rain. It rained so much and our clothes became so heavy ... we could not even lift them. Our clothes got more and more wet, and people just left them there. Our stomachs were empty, we were hungry, our clothes were wet and sodden, our hearts were full of fear – where were we headed? Where would we end up? Our hearts were full of grief: what will happen? Where will we go? It's like when you started from home today, you knew you were going to Gandhi Nagar. We did not even know this. Which nagar, which side, which direction....[34]

The crossing of the border, and the end of the journey, could bring relief, or even a sense of liberation. Yet for many refugees, the journey was only the start of their suffering. Converging on the swelling metropolitan centres – Lahore, Amritsar, Delhi, Karachi – refugees struggled for survival. Many of them ended up in sprawling, squalid camps: the largest of them all, the Kurukshetra Camp, housed over 250,000 refugees. Others were resettled as far away as Madras and even the Andaman Islands. The flow of refugees between East Pakistan and West Bengal has been much less studied, yet eastern India, too, witnessed a refugee movement of vast proportions, transforming completely the landscape of Calcutta.[35]

In all, the Partition of India generated the movement of about 20 million refugees, with 12 million of them moving across the boundaries of the divided Punjab. Not for the first time in this chapter, we are faced

[34] Urvashi Butalia, *The Other Side of Silence: Voices from the Partition of India* (London: Hurst, 2000), 81, 92.

[35] Joya Chatterji, *The Spoils of Partition: Bengal and India, 1947–67* (Cambridge: Cambridge University Press, 2007).

with describing a movement of people on a scale 'without parallel', or as 'one of the largest displacements of people in the twentieth century'.[36] China's war refugees; the exodus of Indians from Burma; the refugee movements of India's Partition – taken together, they do quite probably represent movement on a scale unprecedented in human history.

South Asia was not alone in experiencing the mass migration of people in the years immediately after the war. No sooner had the anti-Japanese War of Resistance ended than China turned in on itself, with a resumption of the conflict between Nationalist and Communist forces. As Mao Zedong's forces put the GMD on the defensive, northern China experienced constant warfare, and was 'filled' with refugees. Among the refugees were students that the GMD had evacuated from Manchuria and elsewhere. By September 1948, Beijing was home to 20,000 or 30,000 'volatile student refugees', Nanjing another 20,000, and Wuhan at least 10,000. As the Communists advanced through China, 'refugees were fed and sent home whenever possible'.[37] The final exodus came in 1949, with the flight of the Nationalist armies and their supporters to Taiwan. The movement began in early 1949, and peaked in the late summer and early autumn, involving up to 3 million people in all. Refugees were resettled in Taiwan, often displacing local people, and moving into the housing and military property vacated by the Japanese departure.

Conclusion

In the period between the 1870s and the 1930s, Asian migration was spurred above all by the transformative force of capitalism, backed by the armed force of empires. In the 1930s and 1940s, states – warfare states, imperial states, and national states alike – compelled migration, even as they tried to control it. The years of Depression and war were a watershed in reorienting Asia's patterns of migration. They put into reverse a circuit of migration that had moved millions since the 1870s. At the same time, the war created new patterns of migration in the journeys of refugees, forced labourers, and displaced people. In the aftermath of the war, imperial and national administrators redrew the map of Asia, trying to stem the new flows of people. The mobility of wartime built on earlier networks of migration, while creating new ones, and leaving a legacy that would confront Asian states for over a generation.

[36] Khan, *The Great Partition*; Zamindar, *The Long Partition*, 6.
[37] Spence, *Search for Modern China*, 507.

4 Migration, Development, and the Asian City, 1950–1970

It was night when the tailors arrived in the city. Groaning and clanking, the train pulled into the station while an announcement blared like gibberish from the loudspeakers. Passengers poured into the sea of waiting friends and families. There were shrieks of recognition, tears of happiness. The platform became a roiling swirl of humanity. Coolies conducted aggressive forays to offer their muscular services.

Ishvar and Omprakash stood frozen on the edge of the commotion. The sense of adventure that had flowered reluctantly during the journey wilted. "Hai Ram," said Ishvar, wishing for a familiar face. "What a huge crowd."

Rohinton Mistry, *A Fine Balance*[1]

In the 1930s, large empires – British, Dutch, French, American, and Japanese – controlled Asia. By 1950, Asia was divided into nation-states. Between 1945 and 1949, India, Pakistan, Burma, Sri Lanka, Indonesia, and the Philippines became independent. The Communist revolution in China created two states – the People's Republic of China and a *de facto* nationalist state in Taiwan – as did the partition of Korea into North and South Korea: both divisions last to this day. The breakup of empires and the drawing of new borders produced countless refugees (Chapter 3). It also produced a patchwork of minority populations within each new set of borders. Each new state faced the historical legacy of the mass immigration of an earlier era (Chapter 1), with the presence of large populations of what imperial administrators had once called 'foreign Asians': primarily people of Indian and Chinese origin.

New forms of citizenship assumed congruence between where people were born, where they lived, and where their loyalties lay. The presence of diasporas, or people of migrant origin, challenged this equation. Distinguishing migrants from locals, identifying and resettling refugees and displaced peoples: these endeavours became central to the new states' assertions of authority, and their definitions of citizenship.

[1] Rohinton Mistry, *A Fine Balance* (New York: Knopf, 1996), 153.

Borders were contested. Their gatekeepers guarded them zealously. Their contours were etched in blood. New technologies were introduced to police the movement of people across frontiers: passports, visas, residence permits, identity papers, and voter registration or ration cards. New states made grand promises to their citizens and sought to control entry and exit into their political communities. The era between the end of the Second World War and the 1970s saw a decline in *international* migration within Asia. However, in an era when virtually all post-colonial states believed in planning and heavy state intervention in the economy and society, millions of people were mobilised to traverse their new countries. They did so in the name of 'development', the overwhelming idea of the age.

In the name of development, states expanded, and attempted to bring more and more aspects of social and economic life within their purview. State-led programmes of development induced or impelled millions of Asians to uproot themselves and their families in the thirty years after 1945. Less regulated were the journeys that tens of millions of Asians made to the cities. In the decades after the Second World War, Asian urbanization accelerated. The populations of cities such as Jakarta, Bangkok, and Kuala Lumpur grew rapidly, as did Delhi, Bombay, Lahore, and Karachi.

All of this took place at a time of unprecedented population growth in Asia. Internal migration policies often took their place alongside other kinds of intervention: birth control and public health campaigns, and attempts to increase food production. Population growth lent dynamism to the migration of populations, but it also limited the ability of even the most ambitious and most coercive planners to realise their visions of 'progress'.

Migrants and Citizenship

The new states that proliferated in Asia after the Second World War had to balance the demands of ethnic nationalism with the fact that their boundaries were inherited from the imperial structures from which they were created. The idea that nations each constituted the homeland of a particular majority ethnic community was a commonsense proposition in the mid-twentieth century. Yet many of Asia's new nations were conspicuously multi-ethnic, multi-religious, and multi-lingual. Given the heterogeneity of Asia's population – partly a consequence of the migrations considered earlier in this book – the new international borders both united and divided people. As Robert Cribb and Li Narangoa have written, new international borders left many ethnic groups 'without a state of their own'; they created 'ethnic enclaves included in larger ... political units', and they left 'pools of people as minorities on one or both sides of the frontier'. The political transition produced many 'orphans of empire'.[2]

In the years after 1945, this had three related consequences with regard to the movement of people. First, as we have seen in the case of India's Partition, the new borders made migrants of people fleeing to get to the other side of the new frontiers. They fled violence, or sought the security of belonging to an ethnic or religious majority. The refugee flight at the time of India's Partition was the greatest in scale, but countless smaller movements of population took place across the new borders. Many of these experiences of displacement were as traumatic as those surrounding Partition. The Rakhain, Arakanese-speaking Buddhists, began an exodus across the borders of East Pakistan into Burma; conversely, the Bengali-speaking Muslims of the Rohingya community found themselves driven out of Burma, often by military force, to seek refuge in East Pakistan. In both cases, new international borders divided the space within which these ethnic groups had long circulated freely. The internal administrative divisions of the British Empire, in this instance, came to constitute the border between two sovereign states: East Pakistan (later Bangladesh) and Burma.

The agonies of India's Partition continued well into the post-colonial period. As East Pakistan, in the 1960s, felt increasingly oppressed by the West Pakistani political and military elite, a movement for cultural and political autonomy arose, spearheaded by the Awami League. Political tension erupted into civil war in 1971, with an invasion of East Pakistan by West Pakistani military forces, followed by brutal pogroms against Bengali intellectuals and supporters of the Awami League. That year, over 9 million refugees from East Pakistan poured into India, nearly rivalling the original Partition in scale. Housed in refugee camps, in some border regions Bengali refugees came to account for 30 per cent of the population. The Indian state spent over $200 million on refugee relief. Eventually, and partly as a result of the pressure of the refugee influx, India and Pakistan went to war in December 1971. The Indian military victory paved the way for the creation of the newest South Asian state: Bangladesh.[3]

---

[2] Robert Cribb and Li Narangoa, 'Orphans of Empire: Divided Peoples, Dilemmas of Identity, and Old Imperial Borders in East and Southeast Asia', *Comparative Studies in Society and History*, 46, 1 (2004): 164–187.

[3] Pia Oberoi, *Exile and Belonging: Refugees and State Policy in South Asia* (New Delhi: Oxford University Press), 104–135.

A second consequence of the new, post-1945 borders worked in the opposite direction. The new borders immobilized people that had once been mobile: sojourning labour migrants, diasporas, and transnational families. Many of Asia's diasporas found that the new nation-states of Asia had no place for them. Their long-distance networks, once contained within the British Empire, were broken up by the formation of territorial states. The Jewish and Armenian diasporas of Asia, which had once stretched from Baghdad to Singapore (via Bombay, Rangoon and Calcutta), began another set of migrations in search of security: to Australia, New Zealand, Canada, the United States, or Israel. To this day, there remain in many of Asia's port cities immaculately preserved Armenian churches, where often there are few Armenians left. In their silence, they speak of absence.

On a larger scale, the circular migrations that had connected Southeast Asia with both India and China became difficult. Indian and Chinese residents of Southeast Asia's new nations were faced with a choice between settlement and return. They rarely determined the terms on which those choices were offered. Writing about the Hadrami Arab diaspora caught between Southeast Asia's new nations, Engseng Ho deploys an effective metaphor: 'the naval blockade of old, which had caught people short on both sides, within and without, was now a permanent, global institution'.[4]

The third consequence of the process of nation-state formation is that both displacement and immobilization, in their different ways, left in place significant minorities within the new borders. Some of these minorities had never moved: their minority status came from borders having moved around them. Other minorities were descended from an earlier generation of migrants, many of whom had moved during Asia's great age of migration (Chapter 1): in this category we count the presence, throughout Southeast Asia, of large populations of Indians and Chinese.

The Biography of a Passport

One of the most pervasive tools for enforcing the new borders of nations was the passport. As a travel document, the passport has a long history in Europe. As earlier chapters have shown, imperial authorities began in the nineteenth century to use passports to control the movement of their subjects across frontiers: regulating the *hajj* provided the occasion for an expansion of passport facilities. In the post-colonial era,

---

[4] Ho, *The Graves of Tarim*, 306.

however, passports gained unprecedented power as a tool of government. Passports were no longer just travel documents, but also documents of citizenship: a tool through which states sifted citizens from aliens. In the unsettled and uncertain conditions of Asia's decolonization in the 1940s, passports came into use on a scale never seen before.

Examining just one passport, which has survived in the National Library of Singapore, suggests that there remained room for ambiguity in the late 1940s and through the 1950s, in the precise relationship between empires and nations, between migrants and settlers, and between citizens and aliens.[5]

Subramania Natarajan, an accountant, was born in 1907 in Palur, South India. On 6 December 1948, the Indian Embassy in Rangoon issued him a passport. The date, of course, indicates that the passport was issued well after the independence of India, and of Burma. The passport was not, however, an Indian passport. The passport identified Natarajan as a 'British subject'. In this period of flux, when the definition of Indian citizenship was still open to question, there seemed no contradiction in the Indian Embassy in Rangoon issuing a British imperial passport. But under 'nationality', the document identified him as 'Indian (by birth)'. It indicated a 'home address' in the town of Cuddalore, in Tamil Nadu. To make things more complicated, this was a special passport, valid only for travel to: 'India, Burma, Pakistan, Ceylon, Siam, Indonesia, Singapore, Malayan Union, United Kingdom'. The passport contained transit visas for Ceylon and Burma, and a list of foreign exchange transactions marked the advent of an era of national economies, with national currencies. Also attached, however, was a 'certificate of identity' entitling Natarajan to stay 'permanently' in Malaya, accompanied by a ration card issued not by the government but by P. Govindasamy Pillai, a prominent Indian general goods store on Singapore's Serangoon Road. For all the fevered concern of new states with policing their boundaries, a great many people proved difficult to identify. Products of the movements of an imperial age, they did not fit easily within the new binary categories of citizens and aliens.

On a much larger scale, Vazira Zamindar has shown the many ways in which the passport system failed to comprehend or control the movement of people between India and Pakistan. However clear they appeared to be as documents of citizenship – of national inclusion or exclusion – passports failed to identify all of their bearers: 'the

---

[5] The passport has been digitized by the National Library of Singapore, and is available at: www.sgebooks.nl.sg/details/170000001.html, last accessed on 24 May 2010.

"undefined" then emerged as this category of moving people that became caught within ... the passport system'. Zamindar details many cases of Indians who went to Pakistan without documentation – to visit ailing relatives, for example – only to find that the only way they could return 'home' was by obtaining a Pakistani passport and an Indian visa. When they 'over-stayed' those visas (in their own homes), many were arrested, and their cases came through the courts, which decided, arbitrarily, whether they were 'citizens' or 'migrants'.[6]

Indian and Chinese Minorities in Southeast Asia

But the real difficulty is the question of citizenship. Now, these Indians abroad – what are they? Are they Indian citizens?.
Indian Prime Minister Jawaharlal Nehru in 1948

With the end of the Chinese Civil War in 1949, overseas migration from China virtually ceased for three decades. The main exception to this trend came in the continuing (and illicit) flow of Chinese to Hong Kong, at the rate of about 40,000 annually through the 1950s; from Hong Kong, significant numbers of Chinese did continue their journeys overseas. International migration from India continued, but on a significantly reduced scale, compared with the colonial era. India's international migration sought new routes: to the West, and later to the Middle East (Chapter 5). The two great streams of migration that had played a central role in shaping Asia's capitalist development and its population geography in the late-nineteenth and early-twentieth centuries had come to an end. But those earlier migrations had left a significant legacy. In every new nation in Southeast Asia there resided significant Chinese and Indian minorities. Their experiences in the post-colonial era were mixed, but for many of them, their 'migrant' origins were a source of disadvantage and discrimination many generations after their forebears had made their journeys across the Bay of Bengal or the South China Sea.

A snapshot of Indian and Chinese minorities across Southeast Asia reveals both how large and how widespread these communities were in the post-colonial era. In 1947, The Federation of Malaya and the Straits Settlements had a population of 2.95 million Chinese and 600,000 Indians; taken together, these 'minorities' were as numerous as the territories' Malay 'majority'. A similar number of Chinese lived in post-colonial Indonesia, though there they made up only 2 per cent

---

[6] Zamindar, *The Long Partition*, 208.

of the overall population. More than 1 million Chinese lived in Thailand, though their number was always difficult to determine, due to the unusual extent of inter-marriage and assimilation with the local Thai population. At the time of Burma's independence, there remained 600,000 to 700,000 Indians in the country, despite the large exodus during the war (Chapter 3). Indochina had a Chinese population of more than a million, with 400,000 Chinese in the Saigon-Cholon region of southern Vietnam alone.[7]

In each of these countries, Indian and Chinese communities had founded themselves on a tradition of sojourning. Many maintained family connections with India and China. In the post-colonial era, circulation became difficult. Every new state in Southeast Asia imposed restrictions on fresh migration from India and China. The governments of new nations in Southeast Asia feared, implicitly or explicitly, that their resident Indian and Chinese minorities would serve to increase Indian or Chinese influence in the region. As one Burmese representative to the 1947 Asian Relations Conference put it: 'It was terrible to be ruled by a Western power, but even more so to be ruled by an Asian power. Burma was naturally frightened by the possibility that British imperialism may be substituted by an Indian or a Chinese imperialism'.[8] The Indian and Chinese governments, too, sought to restrict further emigration from their shores. Indian and Chinese communities in Southeast Asia faced difficult choices of citizenship. In 1950, Indonesia presented the Chinese with a clear choice of citizenship: either they were to register with the Chinese consulate as Chinese citizens, or else they had to opt for Indonesian citizenship.

The pressures came from their home states too. The Indian government after independence insisted that Indians overseas had a clear choice to make about whether they would take Indian citizenship or settle permanently abroad and seek local citizenship: for many, such as the Tamils of Sri Lanka, neither option was open. The Chinese state took a different view, at first. The Communist government in Beijing held to the Chinese law of nationality dating back to 1909, which claimed that anyone born of a Chinese father, anywhere in the world, was a Chinese national. This position weakened through the early 1950s, and ended officially with the Chinese–Indonesian treaty

[7] Virginia Thompson and Richard Adloff, *Minority Problems in Southeast Asia* (Stanford: Stanford University Press, 1955).
[8] *Asian Relations: Report of the Proceedings and Documentation of the First Asian Relations Conference, New Delhi, March-April 1947* (New Delhi: Asian Relations Organization, 1948), 90.

on nationality, hastily hatched together in the coffee shop of Jakarta airport in 1955.[9]

The Chinese in Indonesia faced considerable insecurity and uncertainty over their future. In the midst of the Indonesian Revolution (1945–49), violent attacks on Chinese took place in 1946. Chinese shops were looted. Anti-Chinese sentiment had been present within Indonesian nationalism from the 1910s, and it resurfaced after Indonesia's independence. The position of the Chinese in Indonesia fluctuated in tandem with the international relations between the Indonesian and Chinese governments: Chinese in Indonesia, however long-settled, were always viewed as a potential 'fifth column', representing Beijing's interests. Public criticism of the Chinese escalated from the mid-1950s. In 1956, a prominent businessman assailed Chinese 'citizens of foreign descent'. The local Chinese, in his view, could never truly be Indonesians; they remained migrants in perpetuity. '*Totok* father, *totok* mother', he cried, 'such a man is a foreigner ... Do these people feel themselves Indonesians?' Indonesian President Sukarno passed a series of laws in the late 1950s restricting the ability of Chinese to participate in retail trade outside urban areas. More than 100,000 Chinese Indonesians fled the country amid the fear and anxiety that ensued, many of them on boats sent by the Chinese government.[10] They were resettled in China, though many faced bitter disappointment, and further prejudice, when they arrived there.

Novelist and journalist Pramoedya Ananta Toer intervened in the public debate in the early 1960s. He defended Indonesia's Chinese, highlighting their long history of settlement in the Indies, and describing them as 'strangers who are not foreign'.[11] Pramoedya suffered for his advocacy of the Chinese cause: alongside his other literary and political interventions, it cemented his reputation as a dangerous dissident in the eyes of the authorities. Pramoedya was imprisoned for decades on the notorious penal settlement of Buru Island.

In the orgy of violence that followed the military coup of 1965, which brought General Suharto to power, thousands more Chinese were killed. Thereafter, Indonesia's Chinese faced conflicting pressures of assimilation and exclusion. Many Chinese opted to take, or were forced to adopt, Indonesian-sounding names. The Suharto regime placed restrictions on the performance of Chinese cultural festivals, on Chinese-language

[9] G.H. Jansen, *Afro-Asia and Non-Alignment* (London: Faber, 1966).
[10] Kuhn, *Chinese Among Others*, 287–289.
[11] Pramoedya Ananta Toer, *The Chinese in Indonesia: An English translation of Hoakiau di Indonesia [1960]*, trans. Max Lane (Singapore: Select Books, 2008), 76.

education, and on the Chinese press. Yet the Chinese could never fully assimilate. Their official identity cards were encoded to indicate their Chinese origins. Their migrant origins were thus marked in perpetuity. Nevertheless, the Chinese remained essential to Indonesia's economy: many Indonesian Chinese rose to positions of immense wealth during the Suharto years, using government connections, or working in partnership with indigenous Indonesians to circumvent rules giving preferential treatment to 'sons of the soil'.

Malaysia saw a more carefully negotiated compromise and accommodation between an indigenous majority and Chinese and Indian ethnic minorities. Indians, and especially Chinese, constituted a much larger proportion of Malaysia's population than Indonesia's, and for that reason their claims could not be ignored. Malaysia's path to independence in the 1950s was crafted as a compromise solution, led by a coalition of conservative communal parties, each representing their respective ethnic communities: Malays, Chinese, and Indians. In return for recognition of Malay primacy, preferential access to certain kinds of employment and education, and the overarching sovereignty of the Malay sultans, Indian and Chinese residents of Malaysia were granted full rights of citizenship, and allowed to maintain their respective community organizations. Before this solution could be enacted, the Chinese-dominated Malayan Communist Party had first to be defeated: the Emergency, declared in 1948, sought to defeat the Communist rebels and to detach the rebels from their base of support among the large population of Chinese 'squatters' in the hinterlands of Malaysia. Among the lasting effects of the British counter-insurgency was the establishment of fortified 'New Villages', in which up to 500,000 Chinese were forcibly resettled, but where they were provided with land, housing, and social services.

The choices and the constraints faced by diasporic minorities in new nation-states varied widely. The Tamil population on Sri Lanka's plantations, descended from migrants in the nineteenth and early twentieth centuries, faced almost total exclusion from the new polity. Hundreds of thousands of Tamil labourers were excluded from Sri Lankan citizenship under the terms of the 1948 constitution. After the failure of an attempted agreement in 1954, these people became stateless, since the Indian government refused to accept them as citizens. Negotiations between the two states resumed, and in 1964, an accord was reached allowing for the 'repatriation' of Tamils of Indian origin from Sri Lanka's estates. Over the next two decades, more than 330,000 people were repatriated to India from Ceylon. Many of the repatriated Tamils were born in Sri Lanka, and had few connections with the Indian 'homeland' to which they were returned forcibly. Repatriated Tamil workers from Sri Lanka returned to their 'ancestral villages' to find themselves strangers, with no recognition and few prospects of employment.[12]

One feature of almost all post-colonial states in Southeast Asia was their emphasis on the special place of peoples deemed indigenous, the *pribumi* (Indonesia) or *bumiputera* (Malaysia): the 'sons of the soil'. The *pribumi* had a prior claim to citizenship and, often, preferential access to jobs, education, housing, and social services. These ideas usually had their roots in the structures and pronouncements of the late colonial state, in its search for local collaborators. Dutch and British officials, by the early twentieth century, often blamed 'foreign Asians' for the oppressions of the Malay, Javanese, or Burmese villager, the better to deflect any anti-colonial sentiments that might be brewing. On the view of many Southeast Asian nationalists, the 'indigenous' peoples of the region had to be protected from the waves of migrants from the vast lands of India and China who threatened to engulf them. The politics of nativism made migration across national frontiers ideologically as well as legally anomalous in the post-colonial era.

Migration and Development

In the 1950s, millions of people were on the move in India and China, building the new nations that the political upheavals of the 1940s had produced: one was a democracy, the other a one-party Communist state. Both countries were vast, poor, and hungry for 'development'. Few ideas were as powerful in post-colonial Asia as development. The word was rich with meaning. Development promised a better life for millions of people: better housing, sanitation, access to health care, and employment. In the imagination of many nationalist leaders and professional economists, development also had a much more specific meaning: massive, state-directed industrialization. The influence of a Marxist analysis of imperialism was strong on the generation of Asian leaders that assumed the reins of state power in the 1940s, including those who were not inclined towards Communism. Many believed that Asian nations would not be free until they built themselves into self-sufficient, industrialized economies.

As an idea, however, development reached much farther than the coterie of experts and technocrats who planned and orchestrated it. The promise of development evoked powerful emotions: excitement, hope,

[12] Valli Kanapathipillai, *Citizenship and Statelessness in Sri Lanka: The Case of the Tamil Estate Workers* (London: Anthem, 2009).

expectation, and patriotic commitment to building new nations of the future. Development had a strongly visual aspect to it: large concrete dams were, across Asia, one of the most powerful symbols of the age. Dams epitomised the power of technology, and symbolized the ability of wise statesmen to prevail over nature. Images of development circulated through popular cinema, through propaganda posters featuring well-tended fields and beaming children, and through the speeches of Asia's politicians. Without understanding the power of these images, it is difficult to comprehend the energy and hope with which vast numbers of people moved to the new sites of modernity: the factories, the construction sites, and the dams. They moved not only in search of employment, but also in the service of modernity and progress. At the same time, the project of development legitimized the expansion of state power in many directions, and migrants often felt this power harshly. Many of the journeys people undertook in the name of development were far from voluntary: they were uprooted, displaced, threatened, and 'resettled', by the force of states at the height of their power.

India

The migration of population within the country will have to be regulated and controlled in accordance with the Master Plan.
            The Indian National Congress's Planning Committee in the 1930s

India's planners knew, from the moment they dreamed their dreams of an industrial future, that development would involve the movement of large numbers of people. From as early as the 1920s, Indian nationalists and even some colonial administrators argued that Indians should not go overseas in search of work when their labour was needed for India's own industrialization. Writing in the late 1930s, members of India's national planning committee – a group of Congress politicians, scientists, and industrialists – predicted that 'internal migrations will come inevitably in the wake of [the] planned industrialization of the country'.[13] After independence, the architects of India's Five Year Plans for industrial development recognised that their vision of the future involved considerable internal migration.

During the 1950s, in Sunil Khilnani's apt description, India 'fell in love with the idea of concrete'. At the heart of India's development strategy was a series of massive projects. The largest of them all was

---

[13] National Planning Committee, *Population*, chaired by Radhakamal Mukherjee and edited by K.T. Shah (Bombay: Vora & Co., 1949), 28.

the Bhakra-Nangal dam in Punjab, 'a 200 metre-high concrete wall stretched half a kilometre across a jagged Himalayan gorge'.[14] The Damodar Valley project in Bengal was modelled on the Tennessee Valley Authority of the 1930s, but on an even larger scale. Some of the Tennessee Valley scheme's original architects travelled to India as consultants. State-owned steel plants emerged to feed the needs of the nation's industrialization. Smaller works of irrigation, road-construction, and infrastructural development accompanied the showcase projects.

The history of the state-owned steel plant at Bhilai illustrates the ways in which development projects spurred internal migration in India.[15] Built with Russian assistance between 1955 and 1959, in a small village in the central India, the Bhilai Steel Plant was one of the largest in the world. Bhilai symbolized the industrial future that Nehru envisaged for India: the Prime Minister called it 'a symbol and portent of the India of the future'. In the words of the anthropologist Jonathan Parry, Bhilai was 'as much about forging a new kind of society as about forging steel'. The new plant drew in tens of thousands of workers from the length and breadth of India. By 1961, its workforce already numbered over 18,000. By that time, 60 per cent of Bhilai's male population came from other states, and 78 per cent of the population was between fifteen and thirty-four years old. A 'vast army' of unskilled workers arrived in Bhilai to lay the foundations for the plant's construction: they came from *dalit* communities in Andhra Pradesh and Orissa, and from further south. They came, too, from the surrounding districts and from across neighbouring Bihar.

The migration of more highly skilled workers followed. Many of them had worked in other development projects on the way, as in the case of one of Parry's informants, who arrived in Bhilai in 1958, having worked on the Damodar project in Bengal, and then spending five years in Jamshedpur, centre of the Tata steel empire. Gradually, migrant workers began to bring their families with them: migrants from South India were the first to do so. Bhilai became a microcosm of India, a living manifestation of the 'post-independence ideology of national integration'. But divisions of class, caste, and region continued to shape life in Bhilai. Employees of the steel plant, as public sector workers, formed the 'aristocracy of labour' in Bhilai; they were most likely to settle down

---

[14] Sunil Khilnani, *The Idea of India* (London: Penguin, 1997), 61.
[15] Jonathan P. Parry, 'Nehru's Dream and the Village "Waiting Room": Long-Distance Labour Migrants to a Central Indian Steel Town', in Filippo Osella and Katy Gardner (eds.), *Migration, Modernity and Social Transformation in South Asia* (New Delhi: Sage, 2004), 217–50.

and to bring their families with them. Those who worked in the private and informal sectors, living on the outskirts of the planned company town and servicing the plant, were more likely to be sojourners, circulating between Bhilai and their rural homes across India.

As so often, networks of kin and fellow-villagers made the journeys of Bhilai's migrants possible. Given traditions of both regional and overseas migration from many regions of India (Chapter 1), networks of recruiters and agents were often of long standing. Migrants left for Bhilai having heard of its bountiful opportunities from fellow villagers; when they arrived, they often stayed with others from their native place. If they were lucky, they used local connections to secure jobs for themselves. Yet when Parry interviewed many of these migrants, he found that their narratives tended to be strikingly individualistic. A powerful sense of self-realisation emerges from the migrants' stories: They recall the 'magically enchanted technology' with which they built a vast plant from 'nothing'; most of Parry's interviewees were keen to distance themselves from their 'backward' rural pasts. Parry's findings are important. They suggest that the romance of development was indeed a powerful force motivating tens of thousands of Indians to migrate in the Nehruvian era. Even if these motivations were not there at the outset – or if they existed alongside the more pressing need for income and employment – they were later internalized by many migrants to towns such as Bhilai.

Underpinning long-distance migration to India's new showcases of industrial modernity was a myriad of shorter journeys.[16] Women, moving to their husbands' villages upon marriage, undertook the overwhelming majority of migrant journeys in India. In the language of anthropology, this was a result of a 'tradition of caste endogamy combined with village exogamy': people tended to marry within their caste groups, but outside their immediate village communities. Most people who changed their place of residence in India during the 1950s and 1960s moved within their own districts. In the heyday of India's post-colonial developmental state, marriage networks underwent a process of extension and expansion. Women moved farther from their homes. The networks of suitable and potential matches grew as communities dispersed.

Alongside migration for marriage, India's rural population experienced considerable mobility over short distances in the 1950s and 1960s. Men, and some women, moved from rural areas to other rural areas for seasonal agricultural work; they went to work on the construction of roads and dams, electrical plants and irrigation works. The

---

[16] This section is based on Myron Weiner, *Sons of the Soil: Migration and Ethnic Conflict in India* (Princeton: Princeton University Press, 1978).

larger irrigation works across India attracted hundreds of thousands of labourers from their surrounding regions. A stark sense of India's landscape under transformation emerges towards the end of Bengali director Satyajit Ray's *Apu Sansar* (1959), the third film in his famous 'Apu Trilogy'. Grief-stricken after the death of his wife in childbirth, Apu abandons his son and his responsibilities, and sets out as a wanderer, finding odd jobs along the way. He ends up working in a coal mine 'somewhere in Central India'. In passing, Ray's camera shows India's industrial revolution reshaping the arid rural landscape.

Migrants moved along networks forged by connections of kinship and ethnicity. Low-caste landless labourers from Andhra Pradesh and Rajasthan, for instance, travelled all over the country as manual labourers. They were organized by labour bosses (*sardars*); out of season, they found their way into the cities for casual labour as rickshaw pullers or construction workers. Thousands of families moved into the newly opened Himalayan regions, once notoriously malarial but 'cleared' for settlement by the use of the chemical insecticide DDT in the 1950s. Conversely, millions were displaced by the projects of India's modernism. The construction of large dams, in particular, made unwilling migrants of whole communities. Their livelihoods were ruined, their communities broken, and they received little or no monetary compensation.

Climatic disaster threatened millions of people in India despite the political faith of the time that technology could conquer nature. At moments of crisis, migration – usually over short distances – surged, particularly where government relief works were provided to relieve food shortages and dearth. In what is widely considered a clear success story in the Indian state's approach to famine prevention after 1947, the government responded to a prolonged drought in the western state of Maharashtra in 1970–73 by providing public relief works. At its height, in May 1973, 5 million people each day attended the relief works, receiving a cash wage in return for labour building roads and bridges, and breaking stones. Women were well represented among the villagers who travelled, often quite some distance, to attend the works.[17] On other occasions, less-organized population movements occurred in search of security and relief. Post-independence India never experienced anything on the scale of the famine-related migrations of the late-Victorian era (Chapter 1), yet the vulnerability of a peasantry close to bare subsistence meant that crisis migration could, and did, occur frequently.

India's developing middle class experienced considerable mobility in the Nehru era. India's new colleges, universities, and technical

---

[17] Jean Drèze, 'Famine Prevention in India', in Jean Drèze and Amartya Sen (eds.), *The Political Economy of Hunger*, vol. 2 (1990), 13–122.

institutes were at the forefront of aspirations for a modern future, even as primary and secondary education suffered neglect. The number of college and university students in India increased from 360,000 in 1950 to 2.9 million in 1972. At the pinnacle sat the famed Indian Institutes of Technology and the medical and engineering colleges of the big metropolitan centres; but there were hundreds of smaller institutions that drew in young people and their hopes for advancement. For a class of professionals, the plans for India's development created many opportunities and occasioned many journeys. The Indian Railways, one of the largest employers on earth, moved its administrative and managerial staff around the country. India's expanding ranks of government servants, too, circulated widely. The experience of the author's own family during the 1950s and 1960s is, perhaps, representative: this middle-class Tamil family from south India dispersed widely, while maintaining a base in Tamil Nadu. One family member worked in New Delhi, for the Indian Railways; another circulated widely around Kerala and Tamil Nadu, working for the Auditor-General's office; another worked for the Tatas in Jamshedpur. In the younger generation, both men and women moved away from home (both within and beyond south India) to study in teacher-training institutes and medical, engineering, and commercial colleges throughout the country.

We need to keep the scale of migration in post-independence India in perspective. Migration was not the norm; 95 per cent of Indians in 1971 lived in the states in which they were born, and many had never left their home districts.[18] Yet migration, over both short and long distances, was essential to India's social and economic transformations in the 1950s and 1960s. Migration across India embodied the ideologies of national integration and planned modernization; many of the migrants felt themselves to be agents of modernity and the vanguard of India's efforts to build an industrial future.

China

In 1968, a raging tide of youth, a raging tide of hot blood, a raging tide of innocence surged towards the countryside, the mountains and the vast wildernesses.

Ma Bo

It is a common perception that the Mao era in Chinese history marked an interruption in the country's history of internal and external migration

---

[18] Weiner, *Sons of the Soil*, 19.

that would not resume until the economic liberalization of the 1970s began. In terms of international migration, this perception is more or less true. There was minimal international migration from China between 1949 and the 1980s. Nevertheless, and despite strict controls over internal migration, the two decades after 1949 witnessed substantial migration within China. Much of this migration was decreed and directed by the state, but there remained a significant degree of spontaneous migration, particularly between rural areas. These population movements remain relatively little studied, but Diana Lary's important overview of the period provides many insights into the extent and scale of migration. Many of these migrations appeared, in Lary's description, as 'epic and heroic movements, designed to transform man and nature'; many more were forced movements, or migrations of desperation.[19] Statistics are unreliable, as a significant proportion of internal migration in Mao's China simply went unreported. Official sources suggest that between 25 million and 30 million people changed their registered residence (*hukou*) between 1949 and 1978. Scholars estimate that 32 million people moved *each year* between 1958 and 1960 alone.

In the immediate aftermath of the Communist victory, millions of refugees were resettled or returned to their homes (Chapter 3). Demobilized soldiers were resettled, both Communist cadres and defeated Guomindang troops. In order to construct a new state, and consolidate Communist authority, more than 130,000 loyal northern cadres were transferred to the more volatile southern provinces in the early years after the revolution. In the interregnum between the defeat of the Guomindang and the establishment of Communist authority, millions of peasants made their way to the cities. This was an unorganized, uncontrolled migration, and one that the new authorities found deeply alarming. It was in response to a wave of unplanned urbanization that, by the early 1960s, the *hukou* system of registration emerged in its full form. Thereafter, the *hukou* system put a significant brake on further urbanization until the late 1970s.

With the consolidation of Communist authority, and the inauguration of the first Five Year Plan for economic development in 1953, a new series of migrations began, orchestrated by the state. Migration in service of China's socialist transformation took place over huge distances. The quest to 'strengthen the border' provided the impetus for millions of people to migrate. The core institution governing this movement was

---

[19] The discussion draws on Diana Lary, 'The "Static" Decades: Inter-Provincial Migration in Pre-Reform China', in Frank N. Pieke and Hein Mallee, *Internal and International Migration: Chinese Perspectives* (Richmond: Curzon, 1999), 29–48.

the Production-Construction Military Corps (known as the *Bingtuan*), organized on quasi-military lines. The *Bingtuan* absorbed hundreds of thousands of migrants, prisoners, and political exiles, putting them to work clearing land and on quarries and irrigation works. The political vicissitudes of the 1950s and 1960s produced new waves of exiles and forced migrants. After the Anti-Rightist campaign of 1957, when Mao Zedong turned brutally on his perceived internal opponents after having first encouraged them to speak freely, more than 500,000 people were exiled to isolated labour camps on the frontiers.

Between 1949 and 1961, nearly 6 million people moved to Manchuria. The first wave of migrants was made up of former soldiers, who settled on military farms. Poor peasants from Shandong followed soon afterward. A further 6 million people moved to Xinjiang in the same period, together with smaller movements to Yunnan, Tibet, and Inner Mongolia. In contrast to the settlement of these frontier areas in the late Qing and Republican eras (Chapter 1), these movements were orchestrated by the state, even though they did come to involve more spontaneous movements too. On China's borderlands, and deep in the interior, Han Chinese settlers made new lives for themselves. Those employed on state farms were housed in barracks, their lives carefully regulated. Others formed more autonomous settlements, seeking to re-create – as an earlier generation of Han migrants had done – the social and cultural structures of the Chinese heartland in 'alien' territory. Many Han workers, even after generations of settlement on the frontier, looked back to their *laoxiang* (home place) in Hunan or Shandong.[20] Disillusion characterized the experience of many of the migrants to the frontier, who felt cut off from all they held dear – their homes, the graves of their ancestors, their family connections. The rate of return migration, mostly illicit, was up to 50 per cent in some areas.

There were two overarching motivations for this movement of people towards China's frontiers. The explicit motivation was to ease the 'pressure of population' in the heartland, particularly from the densely populated regions of the east coast, north China, and the Yangzi valley. The second aim, seldom acknowledged openly, was to alter the balance of population in the country, diluting the population of non-Han minorities in the border regions by encouraging Han immigrants, and thus minimizing the chance of oppositional ethnic mobilization. Migration policy was part of a much broader strategy of population management, an attempt to engineer the geographical distribution, the

[20] Mette Halskov Hansen, *Frontier People: Han Settlers in Minority Areas of China* (London: Hurst, 2005).

ethnic composition, and indeed the overall size of the population in the interests of the state and of national development. In their motivation, planned population movements in China had much in common with concurrent movements in Indonesia and the Philippines. Frontier migration had a significant effect on the population composition of China's border regions. Migration to Xinjiang meant that by the early 1960s, more than one-third of the region's population was Han Chinese; the ratio of Han to Mongol in Inner Mongolia doubled in the same period, from 6:1 to 12:1.

'Strengthening the border' was not the only motivation for planned migration in China after 1949. An even greater number of people, perhaps, moved in service of the country's industrial and agrarian transformation. In China, as in India, large dams were the symbol of the age: a symbol of the triumph of the technological state over nature. In the two decades after 1949, about 2,500 large- and medium-sized dams were built in China, alongside tens of thousands of smaller dams. The dams were often ecologically destructive, and many failed to achieve their aims of water control. The Sanmen Dam on the Yellow River, for instance, silted up almost immediately after its construction; it also displaced over 600,000 people. In all, China's large dams displaced over 5 million people during the 1950s and 1960s. 'Local resettlement may not seem like migration', Diana Lary writes, 'but the uprooting could be as severe as a long range move, and almost always had negative connotations'.[21]

The fear of imperialist invasion, in the paranoid atmosphere of the Cold War, also led to the establishment of munitions factories in China's interior that required migrant labour. One of the largest and most celebrated of the new inland factories was the Panzhihua steel mill in Southwestern Sichuan, which attracted over 50,000 migrants each year between 1965 and 1971, in an area where there were, reportedly, only seven Han families in the early 1960s. Situating a huge factory in a small area in a remote mountainous valley produced major problems of water and air pollution, with long-term consequences that persist to this day.[22] Another transported factory – known as Factory 420 – was established in the western city of Chengdu in the 1950s, and provides the subject for a recent film by Chinese director Jia Zhangke, *24 City* (*Ershisi Chang Ji*). Combining documentary footage of former factory workers with fictionalized elements and the use of actors, Jia evokes

[21] Lary, 'The "Static" Decades', 37.
[22] Judith Shapiro, *Mao's War Against Nature: Politics and Environment in Revolutionary China* (Cambridge: Cambridge University Press, 2001), 142.

the heroic era of socialist migration in China, in the past of a factory that is about to be demolished to make way for luxury apartments. The moving testimony by former factory workers speaks of migrant labour motivated by an ethos of sacrifice, and the depth of commitment to the revolution that many workers felt. It is clear from Jia's oral histories, as from other ethnographic work, that the identity of many of China's mobile industrial workers in the 1950s and 1960s was bound up with official ideologies of development, struggle, and social transformation.

The purely destructive elements of China's socialist transformation played an equal role in forcing people to uproot themselves. The disastrous failure of Mao's Great Leap Forward (1958–61) – a state-directed attempt to massively boost China's productivity through collectivization and rural industry – produced a famine that killed anywhere from 30 million to 50 million people. In flight from starvation, millions of Chinese moved in search of relief and survival. These were desperate migrations, and in such conditions that even the Chinese state found them impossible to control or to regulate. Shandong province was among the worst affected by the Great Leap famine. About 1.5 million people left the province in 1960, in search of subsistence. Many drew on family networks established in an earlier era, linking Shandong to Manchuria and the far northeast. The famine migration of the Great Leap era illustrated, starkly, both the costs of China's socialist transformation, and the limits of the state's control over human movement. Illicit migration to Hong Kong burgeoned in these years. Between 1959 and 1962, as many as 142,000 people entered Hong Kong from China; many of them were detained and deported.[23]

The Great Leap made way for the tumultuous 1960s in China, when Mao Zedong attempted to harness the revolutionary enthusiasm of the Chinese masses to undermine the forces of caution within the party and the state, in a campaign known as the Great Proletarian Cultural Revolution. Politically motivated migrations came to the fore. Above all, this period witnessed the mass movement of young people from the cities to the countryside, as agents of Mao's permanent revolution. Between the early 1960s and the mid-1970s, more than 20 million young people moved to the countryside. They went 'up to the mountains and down to the villages' (*shang shan xia xiang*), in a social upheaval that had few precedents, in China or elsewhere.

Many of these 'educated youth' were absorbed within the Production-Construction Army Corps in frontier areas. They were set to work in

[23] Agnes S. Ku, 'Immigration Policies, Discourses, and the Politics of Local Belonging in Hong Kong (1950–1980)', *Modern China*, 30 (2004), 336.

an assault on nature that has few, if any, precedents. Environmental historian Judith Shapiro has written of the 'intimate link between the suffering of people and the abuse of land, because of forcible, state-sponsored relocations'. The frontier migrations did untold damage to the rainforests of Yunnan (home to a significant portion of China's bio-diversity), the forests and deserts of Xinjiang, the grasslands of Inner Mongolia, and the mountains of Guizhou and Sichuan.[24]

Diana Lary rightly notes that these movements were so 'improba-ble' that only novels and fictionalized memoirs have come close to cap-turing the experience and its devastating consequences for all those involved. One such account, direct and moving, comes from the pen of Ma Bo, who was sent to join the Mongolian Army Corps. It was 'not an eastward crusade', he writes, 'yet history was about to be written; not a mass migration, yet tens of thousands of households would taste the bitter fruit of parting'. For eight years, he laments, 'we had laboured for this. And it was worse, for we had wreaked unprecedented havoc on the grasslands'; Ma Bo and his contemporaries had worked like 'beasts of burden, only to commit unpardonable crimes against the land'.[25]

The Philippines, Indonesia, Vietnam

India and China were not alone in witnessing internal migrations in support of national development. The Philippines and Indonesia, too, pursued projects of state-sponsored, or state-directed migration. Both programmes had an eye on the 'population problem', and used planned migration as a way of redistributing people from the densely-populated centres to more distant frontiers of both archipelagos: Sumatra and the outer islands of Indonesia, and the southern islands of the Philippines. In both cases, too, the migration programmes also stemmed from a desire to change the ethnic or religious balance of the population, as a way of reducing the possibility of regional separatism or minority unrest.

From the time of the Philippine's independence in 1946, the new state encouraged the large-scale migration of Christian Filipinos from poor areas of the north and central regions of the country to the sparsely populated, predominantly Muslim, southern region of Mindanao. In the late 1940s and early 1950s, more than 100,000 Christian Filipino settlers moved to the southern Philippines. By the late 1960s, Muslims

[24] Shapiro, *Mao's War Against Nature*, 142–143.
[25] Ma Bo, *Blood Red Sunset: A Memoir of the Chinese Cultural Revolution*, trans. Howard Goldblatt (New York: Viking, 1995), 1; 352–353.

constituted a poor minority of the population of Mindanao, having been a majority in every part of the region in 1950. The tensions caused by this mass migration from the north produced the conditions for the development of a Muslim separatist political movement that has lasted to this day. Demographic change was not the only source of tension. Christian Filipino settlers were offered land on favourable terms, had preferential access to public facilities, loans, and support from the state. Their settlements were well connected with the commercial towns by a network of roads, which largely bypassed Muslim areas. The language of 'colonization' was used explicitly: the Philippine state used a programme of officially sponsored migration to colonize, finally, the part of the archipelago that had resisted Spanish conquest.

The Indonesian resettlement programme, known as *transmigrasi*, or transmigration, was on an altogether larger scale, and with origins in the colonial period. From the early twentieth century, the Dutch colonial state had encouraged the movement of Javanese labourers to Sumatra, gradually to replace the Chinese migrant workforce. Javanese workers on the Sumatran plantations were given small plots of land, encouraging settlement rather than circular migration. At the same time, the Dutch state devised a distinctive project of colonization, envisaging the establishment of enclaves or villages of Javanese settlers in Lampung residency, in Sumatra. By 1940, about 144,000 Javanese had been settled in Lampung, with another 50,000 in other parts of Sumatra, as well as in Kalimantan and Sulawesi. The Japanese conquest of Indonesia put an end to migration between Java and the outer islands. Many settler families suffered during the Japanese occupation; their villages were easy targets for Japanese labour recruiters.

Soon after the end of the Indonesian Revolution, plans for the resumption of transmigration emerged, now imbued with the ideology of national development, and an urgency born of revolution. The 'overpopulation' of Java haunted the imagination of Indonesia's new technocrats and planners, as much as it had preoccupied the Dutch before them. Initial plans for transmigration were on an enormous scale: on one plan, 31 million people would move within thirty years. The actual numbers were much smaller. Between 1950 and 1958, over 185,000 people had moved from Java to Sumatra and, in smaller numbers, to other islands. If we include spontaneous migrants, not officially supported, and the local-born children of settlers, nearly 300,000 people lived within designated 'transmigration areas' by the end of 1958.[26] As the Sukarno

[26] J.M. Hardjono, *Transmigration in Indonesia* (Kuala Lumpur: Oxford University Press, 1977).

government moved in a more radical direction, community organizations and political parties became involved in transmigration, moving their own supporters and adherents, not least as a way of establishing a political foothold in the outer islands. The year of Indonesia's political nightmare, 1965, was also the greatest single year of transmigration in the period between 1950 and the 1970s: that year, more than 53,000 people moved, many of them under the auspices of political parties and other non-governmental organizations.

Like so many other state-sponsored programmes of development, transmigration encountered unforeseen obstacles. Many of the migrants had little idea what they were moving to. 'I put everything I own into a plastic sack and came here in a big boat with my husband', recalled one migrant many years later.[27] Often the land chosen for settlement was unsuitable for cultivation, or it had not been cleared in time. The soil was inappropriate, in many cases, for wet rice cultivation. Settlers arrived to find that there were competing claims to the land they lived on, often from shifting cultivators with customary rights to the land. Later, logging companies that had been granted concessions by other branches of the Indonesian state also staked their claims. Landless migrants from Java or Bali were promised land, but their title was insecure, and often their holdings were too small to be profitable. Provincial governments resented the high-handedness of the transmigration authority, which settled migrants with little reference to local needs or concerns. Javanese migrants often remained in enclaves, poorly integrated with local populations. Transmigration projects often had a deleterious effect on the customary rights and the standards of living of local people. They were imbued with a paternalistic ideology that sought to 'civilize' communities that practiced shifting cultivation by providing them with the Javanese example of sedentary agriculture.

Transmigration flourished despite these obstacles. Spontaneous migrations over both long and short distances rose to match, or even exceed, the number of state-sponsored settlers. The Indonesian transmigration project was distinctive in its longevity. Long after China's modernist migration projects had fallen into decline, Indonesian transmigration continued to flourish. Between 1968 and 1990, more than 1.3 million people moved from Java to the outer islands – increasingly, now, to places such as Irian Jaya, rather than to Sumatra. By 1988, non-Sumatrans made up over 80 per cent of Lampung's population. From the 1970s, the Indonesian authorities used technology to identify suitable sites for settlement: satellite photographs and sophisticated mapping technology. There was a corresponding rise in the ecological

[27] 'Java's Mixed Result Migration', *International Herald Tribune*, 9 October 1992.

destructiveness of the programme. By the 1980s, between 8,000 and 12,000 square kilometres of forest were felled each year to make way for settlement. Technology did not always prevent disastrous miscalculation. The Indonesian state shipped large bulldozers, at great cost, to Irian Jaya in the 1980s, to find that the trees were less than half the size anticipated; the massive machines ripped out all of the topsoil in the area.[28]

Throughout this time, the Indonesian state also used forced migration as a form of political punishment. During the religiously-inspired separatist revolt led by the Darul Islam movement in the 1950s, local villagers who had supported the rebels were resettled thousands of miles across the archipelago. From the 1960s, Buru Island – one of the Maluku islands in eastern Indonesia – became Indonesia's most notorious political prison. Among its residents, from 1965 to 1979, was Pramoedya Ananta Toer. It was on Buru Island that Pramoedya, denied paper, recited orally to other prisoners his epic 'Buru Quartet' of novels on Indonesia's modern history; fortunately, his listeners managed to transcribe them and smuggle them out. In this extract from his memoirs, Pramoedya evokes an ironic sense of continuity with the past when describing his voyage to Buru. In suggesting that his journey belonged within the sweep of Indonesia's maritime history, while also invoking the history of slavery and indentured labour, Pramoedya draws our attention to both the continuities and discontinuities between the 'developmental' migrations of the 1960s and earlier patterns of both free and forced mobility.

Don't listen, shut your ears to the laboured breath of this rusted and asthmatic vessel. Like our distant ancestors in the age of migration we are on a voyage of discovery, a journey toward a new land and life. Only our education gives us the knowledge that we are passing through the waters of our own country, a maritime nation of more than thirteen thousand islands.

But the lesson that now seems more real, more easy to comprehend, is the one that was drilled into us by the chief warrant officer of Salemba Prison: "The only right you have is to breathe!"... We no longer have the right to look at the sky, or so it seems, much less dream of claiming it, even a small part of it, as our own. We are coolies on Captain Bontekoe's ship, the kidnapped Chinese in Michener's ship bound for Hawaii; we are the four million Africans loaded onto British and American ships for transport across the Atlantic.[29]

In Vietnam, too, over a million people moved. They formed part of a state-organized migration of people from the Red River delta to the

---

[28] 'Centrifugal Force', *Time*, 11 November 1991.
[29] Pramoedya Ananta Toer, *The Mute's Soliloquy: A Memoir*, trans. Willem Samuels (New York: Penguin, 1999), 8–9.

hills of the north, and later to the central highlands. After 1954, the Vietnamese state saw the settling of the highlands by Viet migrants as strategically essential to securing the country's frontiers. The state embarked on what Andrew Hardy calls 'rule by mobilization', using quasi-military techniques of mass mobilization to persuade or pressure hundreds of thousands to move. The majority of Hardy's interviewees, old people who had migrated in service of socialist transformation, saw themselves as 'volunteers'. The level of enthusiasm and ideological commitment to building a new country was very real, and powerfully remembered. So too were the bitter disappointments and the sense of broken promises that often followed. In seeking to balance desire with ambivalence, Hardy chooses to call these migrations 'semi-voluntary'; his description might apply just as well to the other post-colonial migrations we have considered thus far.[30]

Migration and High Modernism

The states that planned for the migration and resettlement of workers – to fortify frontier regions and to staff new factories, to build dams and clear forests – saw their populations as a resource to be managed. Most, if not all, post-colonial states in Asia adhered in the 1950s and 1960s to some version of what James C. Scott called 'high modernism', by which he meant a 'strong ... even muscle-bound, version of the self-confidence about scientific and technical progress'. Inherent in this way of seeing the world was confidence in 'the mastery of nature (including human nature)' and a belief that states could bring about 'the rational design of social order'. The movement and resettlement of population was essential to this process.

In creating new areas of migrant settlement – China's military farms, India's factory towns, the transmigration districts of Sumatra – post-colonial states sought to create what Scott would call 'state spaces' – spaces where populations were open to order, planning, surveillance, and control. We have seen throughout this chapter the high human cost that schemes of this nature could extract. The planned migration and resettlement of population, as Scott reminds us, 'almost always disrupted or destroyed prior communities ... [with] their own unique histories, social ties, mythology, and capacity for joint action'.[31]

[30] Andrew Hardy, *Red Hills: Migrants and the States in the Highlands of Vietnam* (Copenhagen: NIAS, 2003), 150–262; 283–290.
[31] James C. Scott, *Seeing Like a State: Why Certain Schemes to Improve the Human Condition Have Failed* (New Haven: Yale University Press, 1998), 4, 191.

Undoubtedly, for countless thousands of those who moved in service of post-colonial development, Scott's narrative of cultural loss and subjection to authoritarian control would hold true. The most brutal instance of migration impelled by a state's fantasies constituted high modernism in reverse: the de-population of the Cambodian capital Phnom Penh in 1975 by Pol Pot's Khmer Rouge forces, in their quest to re-create a rural Cambodia of fantasy, cleansed of the corruption of the city. The cost in lives lost, and in lasting damage to the fabric of Cambodian society, was incalculable.

To see the mass migrations of the post-colonial era purely in terms of authoritarian state planning would be a partial view. Even the most planned societies witnessed countless unregulated, informal, or spontaneous migrations. Despite the best efforts of the Chinese state to control migration, there remained much scope for individual and family initiative. This was even more the case in India where, despite the pretensions of the planners, most migration followed familiar networks of kin and fellow villagers. Aggregate statistics of migration represent the outcome of countless individual decisions.

Furthermore, to attribute too much power to state officials may lead us to ignore the very real enthusiasm with which millions traversed land and sea in the age of development. The ideology of 'high modernism' may have emanated from the corridors of state, but it also had many popular manifestations. Belief, motivation, and even faith drove people to uproot their lives and their families in genuine enthusiasm for the project of making their countries (and themselves) modern.

Finally, we must remember that even the most concerted and coercive official attempts to control migration were met with evasions, large and small. This becomes clear if we look to Burma. After the military coup of 1962, Burma became one of the most authoritarian and paranoid of all Asian states; Burma's rulers aimed to seal hermetically the country's external borders, and to control movement within them. Yet Burma remained a much more mobile society than the state imagined. In his marvellously vivid 'tales of everyday people', collected through the 1970s and 1980s, the Burmese writer Mya Than Tint (1929–1998) depicted a country in constant motion. Sketch maps showing the journeys that people made, as chance, fate, desperation, or ingenuity kept them on the move, accompany some of the life histories that Mya Than Tint collected. One of the stories suggests that Burma's external borders remained porous in the 1970s and 1980s. In search of survival, in a country driven to economic ruin by mismanagement, illicit mobility provided attractive, and dangerous, opportunities. As one fisherman-turned-smuggler told Mya Than Tint:

It's dangerous work, making the trips to Penang. There's so much stress what with worrying about the Navy patrol boats and the storms and the *Pashu* Malay pirates. They don't just steal your boat. They chop your head off and throw your body into the sea. ... I gave up and went off to Tamu and from there to Morre and Prinaga, doing some smuggling. I had no money of my own, so I was hiring myself out. I was a carrier. For example, we used to smuggle bikes in from Bangladesh. We'd ride them down the side-roads in the jungle so as to avoid the customs posts on the way to Tamu. ... Otherwise we'd bring in Indian *longyis* or make-up, or betel ingredients or bits of machinery.[32]

Borders restricted mobility, but they also stimulated it. As Mya Than Tint's story illustrates, borders were dangerous places, where quick profits could be made at great personal risk. Closed economies and currency restrictions turned border regions into the sites of thriving black markets – including black markets in human labour.

Despite the determination of state planners to plan and orchestrate migration in interests of national development, migrant networks continued to exercise an agency of their own. This was particularly true in Asia's growing cities, which drew in an increasing proportion of Asia's mobile people in the post-colonial era. The final section of this chapter therefore picks up the story of Asian urbanization: the journey to the city.

Asia's Urbanization, 1945–1970

In the 1950s, the world's urban population more than doubled, from 313 million to 655 million. Asia's cities accounted for a significant portion of this increase. The population of Metropolitan Manila grew from 1.3 million in 1948 to 2.1 million by 1960. The population of Greater Bombay grew from 2.8 million in 1951 to 4.1 million just a decade later. Urbanization was even more rapid during the 1960s. In that decade, the Indian urban population grew by nearly 30 million. In sum, the proportion of urban residents in Asia grew from 17.4 per cent in 1950, to 24.7 per cent in 1975, by which time the total urban population in Asia was close to 600 million.

Western and Asian policymakers regarded the urban growth with alarm. Many viewed it as a symptom of the 'population explosion' that threatened the Third World. If resettlement projects represented an attempt by states to solve the 'population problem', unplanned

---

[32] Mya Than Tint, *On the Road to Mandalay: Tales of Ordinary People*, trans. Ohnmar Khin and Sein Kyaw Hlaing (Bangkok: White Orchid Press, 1996), 111–112.

urbanization very often signified the breakdown of those plans and controls. Even the most thoughtful outside observers of Asia's rural cultures experienced a visceral reaction to its growing cities. Writing of an encounter with Calcutta, the anthropologist Claude Lévi-Strauss described his sordid impressions: '...filth, promiscuity, disorder, physical contact; ruins, shacks, excrement, mud; body moistures, animal droppings, urine, purulence, secretions, suppuration'.[33]

Many migrants to Asia's post-colonial cities were refugees from the conflicts that arose from national revolutions, civil wars, and colonial counter-insurgency. As we have seen (Chapter 3), India's Partition produced well over 10 million refugees across the borders in both directions. Many of these refugees ended up in Delhi and Lahore, Calcutta and Bombay. Half a million Punjabi refugees arrived in Delhi after Partition, many of them settling in squatter settlements on the outskirts of the city; Bengali refugees in Calcutta, similarly, congregated in vast squatter settlements that contained hundreds of thousands of people. The cultural composition of the cities changed dramatically. With the arrival of refugees and the departure of many Muslims, Delhi was by the 1950s an overwhelmingly Punjabi city. The influx of 500,000 Sindhi and Gujarati refugees into Bombay transformed its character. Bombay's housing shortage, already acute before 1947, meant that up to a million people slept on the streets in the late 1940s.

Other parts of Asia, too, saw urbanization driven by conflict. The armed nationalist struggle in Indonesia, together with a myriad of local rebellions, drove people to the cities. The population of Medan, Sumatra's largest city, grew even faster than Jakarta's: it grew by 50 per cent between 1930 (the time of the last pre-war census) and 1960. The anti-Communist war in the jungles of Malaya uprooted many people, as did the colonial policy of resettling Chinese forcibly in 'new villages', where they could be kept under surveillance. As the conflict in Vietnam grew increasingly bitter, Saigon grew considerably in size: as American bombs targeted Vietnam's jungle, the proportion of South Vietnam's population in urban areas grew from 15 per cent to 65 per cent. As Mike Davis has written, 'counterinsurgency and civil war were the most ruthlessly efficient levers of informal urbanization in the 1950s and 1960s'.[34]

Another 'lever' of urbanization was deepening rural poverty at a time of rapid population growth. The 1950s and 1960s were a time of rapid population growth throughout Asia. Asia's total population (including India and China) grew from 1,399 million in 1950 to 2,397 million

[33] Claude Lévi-Strauss, 'Crowds', *New Left Review*, 15 (1962), 3–6.
[34] Mike Davis, *Planet of Slums* (London: Verso, 2006), 55.

in 1975. Despite rapid urbanization, the majority of that increase took place in rural areas. As we have seen in this chapter, almost all post-colonial states in Asia opted for large-scale projects as a means to bring about rural development: the concentration of agricultural production in larger and ostensibly more efficient units of production. In the absence of widespread land reform, this meant that the problem of landlessness worsened over time. Those families with land found their holdings so small as to be unviable. Asia's smallholders found government policy stacked against them, in favour of large farms and plantation agriculture. The emergence of technological solutions to agricultural development in the form of high-yielding and drought-resistant seeds – a process known as the 'green revolution' – meant that food production per capita kept pace with population growth, and food prices in urban areas remained relatively low. This came at the expense of agrarian employment. Agrarian poverty was a major stimulus, sending young people to the cities. Just as in the nineteenth century, families spread risk: some children sought cash incomes in town, while others stayed behind to work the land. However, writing of Bombay, Rajnarayan Chandavarkar described a growing trend in the 1950s and 1960s of new migrants coming from conditions so distressed that there were no rural homes left to maintain connections with.[35]

Housing was the first, and greatest, problem that new migrants to the city faced. It was the fundamental problem of urban life in post-colonial Asia (as it was throughout the Third World). Most migrants to the city arrived with people they already knew, and at least initially they stayed with others from their home villages or regions. New migrants to the cities gravitated towards squatter settlements or to inner-city slums. Squatter settlements were particularly common in the cities of South and Southeast Asia. The outskirts of Rangoon swelled with slums and village-like settlements inhabited by people in flight from conflict or poverty. By the early 1960s, estimates held that there were 750,000 squatters in Jakarta, 100,000 in Kuala Lumpur, and up to 250,000 in Singapore: in each case, squatters accounted for about 25 per cent of the urban population. The figures for Indian cities were higher; many squatters there did not even have built structures to inhabit, and 'squatted' on the streets.[36]

Lacking legal title to their land, squatters were vulnerable to the attentions of the authorities, often in collusion with property developers who

[35] Rajnarayan Chandavarkar, 'From Neighbourhood to Nation', in Neera Adarkar and Meena Menon, *One Hundred Years, One Hundred Voices: The Millworkers of Girangaon: An Oral History* (New Delhi: Seagull, 2004), 7–80.
[36] T.G. McGee, *The Southeast Asian City: A Social Geography of the Primate Cities of Southeast Asia* (London: G. Bell & Sons, 1967), 159.

coveted the land that the squatters inhabited. Basic sanitation was lacking in many of the squatter settlements. Medical and educational facilities were inaccessible to most. Squatters lived, as Terence McGee put it, in 'fear of eviction; fear of fire; fear of crime – fear is the governing force of the squatter area'. On occasion, however, squatters acted together to assert their rights to the city. Their presence in the heart of Asia's capital cities made them difficult to ignore indefinitely. In India, squatters exercised the vote; at election time, at least, politicians had to pay some attention to them. In Delhi in the 1950s, there was a brief period during which squatters' needs and concerns were given serious consideration by the authorities. Alongside the squatter settlements, most of Asia's metropolitan centres had densely populated tenement slums. In Southeast Asia, these slums were largely the preserve of Chinese communities, a survival of the 'Chinatowns' of the colonial era. Upper Nanking Street in Singapore was in the 1950s one of the most notorious slums in all of Asia; today it is an air-conditioned shopping mall.

Insiders and Outsiders in the Post-Colonial City

With few exceptions, post-colonial cities in Asia were built upon colonial cities. New migrants to the city found their place among migrants of an earlier generation. As we have seen (Chapter 2), multiple diasporas shaped the topography of Asia's colonial cities, particularly the port cities. The urban landscape of colonial Asia was marked by segmentation and segregation. From the time of the early modern port cities such as Melaka, different ethnic groups inhabited separate quarters of the towns. Yet the late-colonial period also saw the life of the city dissolving these divisions, in the worlds of popular culture and entertainment, and through the expansion of capitalist cultures of consumption. Urban migration after 1945 added to, as it also disrupted, this pre-existing juxtaposition of cultures, neighbourhoods, and diasporas. Traditions of urban cultural pluralism helped to absorb newcomers in the 1950s and 1960s. But the influx of newcomers put those cultures of accommodation under strain. Over time, the large cities of Asia were taken over by migrants from their immediate hinterlands.

Describing Southeast Asia's 'primate cities' in the 1960s, McGee wrote that each was 'a mosaic of cultural and racial worlds, each invoking the memory of other lands and people'.[37] Existing patterns of residential concentration in Kuala Lumpur (commonly known as KL), for instance, began to break down as Malay migrants to the city began to

---

[37] McGee, *The Southeast Asian City*, 24–25.

form squatter settlements both within and on the outskirts of the city. Older communities were broken up by urban redevelopment; the middle classes dispersed towards new 'dormitory suburbs' such as Petaling Jaya. Overwhelmingly a Chinese and an Indian city in the colonial period, KL became more consciously Malay in the 1950s and 1960s, as it emerged as the capital city of independent Malaysia. In KL, as in Jakarta, Manila, and Bombay, most new migrants to the city gravitated towards the informal sector. They became petty traders, street hawkers, food vendors, messengers, and drivers of taxis and rickshaws.

In Bombay, too, an older cosmopolitan culture came into conflict with an insistent provincialism and a claim upon the city by 'sons of the soil'. With the coming of Indian independence and the arrival in Bombay of hundreds of thousands of refugees, many small communities that had played a key role in Bombay's history went into decline. Jews, Parsis, and Armenians had all contributed to the development of Bombay's public culture. After 1947, many Jews and Armenians began to leave, making new homes in Israel or Australia. Decades later, though, one eighty-nine-year-old Jewish millworker responded sharply when asked why he had not chosen to emigrate to Israel: 'I am Indian', he declared, 'why should I go to Israel?'[38]

The composite culture of Bombay emerged from the meeting of regional migrants and long-distance diasporas from across the Indian subcontinent and beyond. Bombay, Rajnarayan Chandavarkar wrote, 'teemed with people of every faith. Its wadis and gullies echoed with the sound of every language spoken by residents who had migrated from all over the subcontinent'.[39] The popular culture of the city was a composite, and yet individual neighbourhoods retained dense connections with other parts of the subcontinent. Bombay, one might say, contained numerous internal diasporas. Matunga, for instance developed as a Tamil neighbourhood. In microcosm, its residents re-created something of the social landscape of South India and a culture that was constantly reinforced by new arrivals from Madras. Many of these migrant groups occupied particular niches within the urban economy. Myron Weiner observed that 'the city's milk is delivered by migrants from Uttar Pradesh, the port labourers are from Andhra, the clerical personnel are from Tamil Nadu, and construction workers are from Rajasthan'.[40] Many of these niches of migration and economic specialization had roots in the colonial era. The economic and social transformations of

[38] Adarkar and Menon, *One Hundred Years*, 111.
[39] Chandavarkar, 'From Neighbourhood to Nation', 47–48.
[40] Weiner, *Sons of the Soil*, 46.

the 1950s and 1960s created new networks, but also allowed some of these older connections to flourish.

Throughout India, the 1960s saw the rise of 'sons of the soil' movements, whose claims were similar in tone and nature to those of indigenous nationalist groups in Southeast Asia. These groups argued that natives of each region ought to receive preferential treatment in the distribution of jobs, housing, and benefits. On numerous occasions, the movements turned violent and targeted migrant groups – or the descendents of migrants. The rise of the Shiv Sena in Bombay, formed in 1966, pitted the claims of the Marathi 'sons of the soil' against those of migrants in the city. On many views, at the time and subsequently, it was a struggle between a cosmopolitan and a provincial vision of Bombay's future.

Migration in the Imagination

The quintessential journey of the post-colonial era was the journey to the city. In most parts of Asia, the 1950s and 1960s was a period of rapid and massive urbanization. But the journey to the city was also a journey of the imagination. Few narratives were more common in popular cinema, in novels or short stories, than the journey to the city. It was a story that afforded much repetition: the innocent young man from the countryside arrives in the city, astounded by the allure of its glittering lights. Urban tricksters dupe him, he struggles amid the city's anomie and isolation, and yet he finds the exhilarating possibility of freedom, often in the form of romantic love. The journey to the city came to signify something more than simply movement. The city represented a different and more modern way of life.

Representations of the Asian city came in many hues, encompassing resignation and optimism, satire and celebration. Japanese director Yasujiro Ozu's exquisite *Tokyo Monogatari* ('Tokyo Story', 1953) tells the story of two elderly parents making the journey to Tokyo to visit their children. Amid the frenetic pace of life in what remained the largest city in Asia after the war, where families lived cramped in small suburban apartments, the children have little time for their visiting parents. The parents accept this neglect stoically and with good grace. The loss of community – the rupture between the country and the city – emerges as a defining feature of the journey to the city.

The cinematic celebration of India's great metropolis, Bombay, was more exuberant. The 1950s witnessed the flourishing of Bombay's film industry ('Bollywood'), and the city itself was a character in many of the films of this era, alongside a flurry of historical epics. Bombay cinema drew liberally on the 'theatre of the street', the rich and plural popular culture that had developed in working-class districts such as Girangaon, a product of multiple migrations from every corner of the subcontinent. The films of Raj Kapoor, such as *CID* and *Shree 420*, epitomised the lure of the metropolis. They reflected the broader values of Nehru's India: a commitment to modernity and mobility, together with a concern for social justice. In *Shree 420* – named, ironically, for the section of the Indian penal code dealing with vagrancy – the innocent Raj Kapoor finds his way into the bewildering bustle of Bombay. He is homeless. He sleeps on the street, only to find that even the streets are governed by rising land values. In time, he finds a sense of community there. He ekes out a living, and he falls in love. The city allows him, in the end, to transform himself into a successful and wealthy man. He uses his power magnanimously, and justice prevails. The cinematography evokes Bombay at 'street level': the crush of people, the bright lights, the motorized transport, and a world full of strangers and migrants.

Other depictions of the Asian metropolis used satire to overcome despair. In the short stories of Pramoedya Ananta Toer, the thousands of new migrants who arrived in Jakarta each day found themselves in the city's dark underbelly. It was a world of slums and squatter settlements, mired 'in the shit of the *kampung* residents'. Housing was scarce, and jobs were hard to come by. Heat, crowds, and dust made everyday life a struggle.

It was hot in those days. And vehicles, tens of thousands of them, sprayed dust on sweating bodies. And the dust was composed of a number of things: dry snot, horse dung, bits of motor tires, bits of tires from bicycles and *betjak* and perhaps also bits of tires of my own bicycle which the other day slipped along the roads which I was now passing. And this dust of many kinds stuck, with the sweat, like glue to the body.

... Between the darkness and the last crimson rays in the west my bicycle skipped along the small road in front of the palace. The palace – bathed in electric light. God knows how many thousand watts.

In another of Pramoedya's short stories, 'News from Kebajoran', a prostitute who had moved to Jakarta to make a living thinks wistfully of her family and her village home. The 'territory' where she waits for clients is just a few yards from the palace, where Indonesia's new authorities exercise their power. Ironically, the installation of new lamps to illuminate the palace mean the prostitutes have to move along the road to ply their trade in darkness. But 'to protest to the authorities' about her plight 'would be futile', since, like thousands of other migrants, 'she is not registered as an inhabitant in the city and, officially, she is not yet even born – nor has she ever set foot in Djakarta'.[41]

Conclusion

In this chapter, I have shown that in the post-colonial era, international migration in Asia declined whereas internal migration within new nation-states flourished. The formation of new nations and new borders put up barriers to migration, and differentiated between citizens and aliens. Diasporas and migrant communities came under pressure; some faced eviction, and even statelessness. Asia's new states were ambitious. They sought the industrial and social transformations encapsulated by the promise of development. In the service of development, tens of millions of Asians moved. They moved to factories and cities, to agricultural settlements, and to the construction sites of large dams. Many others were displaced from their homes to make way for 'progress'.

Whether we are discussing long-distance migration for labour on plantations, or the process of urbanization, certain conditions emerge as crucial: the importance of family or village networks; the maintenance of connections across space and time; the development of ethnic neighbourhoods within plural societies. Internal and international movements alike involved a sense of excitement and possibility, and often, too, of alienation. All of these features connect overseas and domestic migration, in the colonial and the post-colonial periods. Particularly in the vast, continental nations such as India or Indonesia, migration to the metropolitan centres would have been no less strange or disorienting than migration overseas.

This chapter has emphasized the greater importance of the modern state in orienting patterns of migration in the 1950s and 1960s. Here, too, we can discern a continuum: there were many precedents in colonial labour recruitment policies for the modernist strategies of mobilizing labour pursued after 1945. When the Vietnamese state recruited workers for its projects of socialist modernization, many recruits already had experiences, within their families, of migration. 'Officials recruiting labour for distant projects had long been familiar figures in Vietnam', Andrew Hardy reminds us. 'Only the contract and the destination were

---

[41] Pramoedya Ananta Toer, *It's Not an All Night Fair* [Bukan Pasar Malam, 1951], trans. C.W. Watson (Singapore: Equinox, 2001), 4–5; Pramoedya Ananta Toer, 'News from Kebajoran', in *Tales From Djakarta* [*Tjerita Dari Djakarta*, 1963], trans. Nusantara Translation Group (Singapore: Equinox, 2000), 23–42.

new'. Shandong peasants recruited by the Maoist state for labour in northern China might have felt similarly.

Hardy suggests we can identify 'cultures of migration' that transcend the divide between internal and international migration, as well as the colonial and post-colonial eras. Of Vietnamese migrants, he writes:

> After abstraction of the differences and details of their life stories, we are left with what they shared: their courage, their response to a situation at home, their insertion into networks combining ancient and modern elements and their intention – after a few weeks or a few years – to return to the place they had left. This common ground is what I call their culture of migration.[42]

The idea of a 'culture of migration' draws our attention to the more tangible ways in which internal and international migration are connected. Communities or families with histories of overseas mobility were more likely to migrate internally, and vice versa. If we return to the Bhilai steelworkers interviewed by Jonathan Parry, we find that as new frontiers of Asian migration opened up in the 1970s (Chapter 5), many workers moved between periods of work within India, in Bhilai, periods spent in the Middle East, and periods spent back 'home' in Kerala. The upper-caste Tamil and Bengali families that developed a culture of circular migration within India were the first to move as skilled professionals to the United States from the 1960s and 1970s.

Finally, we find throughout the post-colonial era that the opponents of migration used similar political language. The 'sons of the soil' movement in Bombay, and the anti-immigrant rhetoric of Malay or Indonesian nationalism, drew on similar ideological tendencies and employed similar patterns of political language. These included the rise, from the early twentieth century, of 'nativism': a belief that being indigenous to a particular territory accorded special political and economic rights, and a broader sense that migration was a problem.

Many of Asia's great metropolitan centres were products of earlier eras of migration. They were shaped by diasporas and their interactions with one another and with the colonial state. During the 1950s and 1960s, the hinterlands came to assert their dominance over the port cites of Asia, at the expense of their external or oceanic connections. The era of globalization, which began in the 1970s, saw another shift in that balance.

---

[42] Andrew Hardy, 'Culture of Migration and Impact of History in Wartime Indochina: A Game of Chance?' in Beatriz P. Lorente et al. (eds.), *Asian Migrations: Sojourning, Displacement, Homecoming and Other Travels* (Singapore: Singapore University Press, 2005), 50–68: 57–59.

5   Asian Migrants in the Age of Globalization, 1970–2010

I'm thankful for my life as a migrant worker. It has given me the opportunity to make myself strong and it has taught me how to get on with others, and that if you try you can do anything. The long journey of the migrant worker presents even more opportunities than it does challenges. I wish all those who are working away from home more success and happiness and less unhappiness and worries. I wish that through their diligent work they will realize their dreams!

Wang Ziangfen, 'Looking Back I am Proud'[1]

The 1970s marked another turning point in the history of migration in Asia. The balance of economic power within Asia began to shift, with the economic rise of East and Southeast Asia, and the growing power of the oil-producing nations of the Middle East. These economic transformations opened new frontiers of migration. As the post-colonial projects of national development began to falter, the international dimension of migration grew once again, facilitated by cheaper air travel and communications.

Asian migration in a global age continues to follow regional patterns, taking people from South Asia, Indonesia, and the Philippines to the growth economies of Southeast Asia (particularly Malaysia and Singapore), and to the Persian Gulf. Construction workers from the south-western Indian region of Kerala, from Pakistan and Bangladesh, have made possible the transformation of Dubai from desert settlement to metropolis. Filipina and Indonesian domestic workers have become essential to the reproduction of middle-class households in Singapore and Hong Kong. The last three decades have also seen an increase in the movement of skilled professionals and many students across national frontiers in Asia. Inter-Asian migration forms part of a continuum that includes movement to the United States, Australasia, and Europe. Indeed, a majority of the world's 215 million 'international

---

[1] Arianne M. Gaetano and Tamara Jacka (eds.), *On the Move: Women in Rural-to-Urban Migration in Contemporary China* (New York: Columbia University Press, 2004), 297; translation by the editors.

151

migrants' – people who live outside the country of their birth – now live in the developed world.

But the real dynamism in the growth of Asian migration since the 1970s comes from the intersection of internal and international migration. Alongside an expansion in international migration, accelerated internal migration has led to the growth of 'mega-cities' in Asia (cities of over 10 million people), which attract hundreds or thousands of new migrants every week. This mass movement is particularly evident in China, where earlier strict controls over migration and settlement in urban centres have fragmented. This has produced the largest and most rapid urbanization in recorded history. Mumbai, Jakarta, Manila, and Dhaka are not far behind Chinese cities such as Guangzhou or Shenzhen in their capacity to attract migrants and to serve as a focus for migrants' dreams of a better future.

Building on the argument of Chapter 4, this chapter shows that internal and international migrations are still linked. In the era of globalization, internal and international migrations are consequences of the same underlying forces: sharpening inequalities between regions, and between city and country; the move towards more flexible, transnational production; ecological degradation and natural disaster. Both rural–urban migration and overseas migration are driven by the globalization of new cultures of consumption and new aspirations through the expanding reach of satellite television and electronic communications. Migrants in Asia are the agents of globalization, and often its most vulnerable victims. The final section of the chapter will highlight the new forms of immobility – and even incarceration – that accompany the expansion of mobility in Asia's age of globalization.

Globalization

Countless books and articles have appeared since the 1990s on the subject of 'globalization'. There is broad agreement that globalization describes the increasing economic, political, and cultural inter-connectedness of the world, reflected in an expansion of trade, production, communications – and human migration. It also refers to the growing consciousness of these changes: a heightened awareness of living in 'one world'. The geographer David Harvey describes globalization as 'time-space compression'.[2] Historians have argued that there is nothing particularly new about these processes. They originate – on different views – in

---

[2] David Harvey, *The Condition of Postmodernity: An Enquiry into the Origins of Cultural Change* (Oxford: Blackwell, 1990), 240.

the transformation of Eurasia's empires in the early modern period; in the expansion of European maritime imperialism from the fifteenth century; in the industrial revolution and the great migrations of the nineteenth century.[3] As we have seen, Asia in the second half of the nineteenth century underwent such a process of 'time-space compression' (Chapter 1).

Contemporary globalization represents an intensification and acceleration of a longer-term historical process. Economic and technological changes dating from the 1970s lend contemporary globalization its velocity and its particular characteristics. The abandonment of the Bretton Woods system of fixed exchange rates – inaugurated as part of the post-Second World War international order – led to an unprecedented increase in financial flows across national borders. The enthusiasm for deregulation and privatization spread throughout the world, often via the influence of international financial institutions. This boosted levels of foreign direct investment. Industrial production became more flexible, and truly transnational. Rather than manufacturing products in large factories close to their retail markets, large corporations took advantage of cheaper shipping to extend their supply chains. Globally dispersed factories specialised in manufacturing small component parts rather than finished goods; trade within transnational corporations expanded, as did the process of sub-contracting.

Technological transformations made possible these economic shifts. The 1970s saw the advent of cheap air travel on a mass scale, epitomised by the arrival of the Boeing 747. The revolution in electronic communications, culminating in the World Wide Web, marked the most significant expansion of global information since the invention of the printing press, the telegraph, and the telephone. But these older technologies, too, gained in importance. The advent of fibre optic cables from the 1980s made international telephone communication much cheaper than it had ever been. Containerized shipping revolutionized global trade, creating huge industrialized container ports offshore, utterly dissimilar from the port cities of the age of empire. Approximately 90 per cent of the world's international trade is still transported by sea. Seafaring Asians – from the Philippines, India, Indonesia, South Korea, Thailand, Singapore, Malaysia, and China – constitute a majority of these ships' crews.

Asia has been central to the process of globalization, not least because Asia is home to the majority of the world's labour force. Globalization,

[3] A.G. Hopkins (ed.), *Globalisation in World History* (London: Pimlico, 2001).

in turn, has transformed the economic map of Asia. The period since the early 1970s has seen the rise to prominence of the small, oil-producing states of the Persian Gulf: the United Arab Emirates, Bahrain, Qatar, and Kuwait. After the Organization of Petroleum Exporting Countries (OPEC) precipitated a significant increase in the price of oil in 1973, the Gulf states underwent an abrupt transformation from isolated desert states into aggressively modern metropolitan centres. They quite literally 'fuelled' globalization, and – as we shall see – became the largest importers of Asian migrant labour.

In East Asia, the rapidity of Japanese industrialization after the Second World War served as a boon to the economic development of the region as a whole, beginning with South Korea and Taiwan. In the 1960s, Japanese companies began to set up plants to manufacture electronic components, computer chips, televisions, and radios in Singapore and Malaysia, where labour costs were cheaper. This, together with heavy American investment and access to American markets, stimulated a second wave of industrialization and growth in Singapore, Malaysia, and Thailand. All three countries were staunchly conservative, capitalist, and pro-Western in the Cold War. They took advantage of the opportunity to specialise in export-led development. It was in these countries that Export-Processing Zones – tax-free areas located near the ports, designed to attract transnational capital – made their first appearance in Asia. Throughout the 1980s, and until the Asian financial crisis of 1997–98, Singapore, Malaysia, and Thailand all boasted average annual growth rates in Gross Domestic Product of over 8 per cent; the Philippine economy, by contrast, grew by an average of 1.8 per cent annually in the 1980s.

From the 1980s, the market-led transformation of China has strengthened the weight of East Asia in the global economy. With unprecedented rapidity, China became the manufacturing powerhouse of the world. Other socialist states, notably Vietnam, followed this path. As Singapore and Malaysia specialized in higher value-added goods and services, mass production – of garments and footwear in particular – moved to China, Vietnam, and Indonesia.

Widening regional inequalities have resulted from the impact of globalization on Asia. A stark gap divides those regions that have benefited from the expansion in global trade and commerce and those that have not. The contours of inequality are both inter-national and intra-national. The imbalance in economic growth and job opportunities between different regions acts as a crucial motor of both international and internal migration.

The Mobility Revolution, Revisited

Since the 1970s, Asia has undergone – for a second time: the first was in the 1870s (Chapter 1) – a mobility revolution. One major force propelling this revolution is agrarian decline. Across rural Asia, population growth and the spread of agrarian markets increased pressure on land and produced growing inequalities in access to land. This combined in many places with decreasing productivity resulting from soil erosion and environmental degradation. Natural disaster, too, remains an engine of migration, though usually of a temporary nature, and usually over short distances. Annual flooding displaces up to 500,000 people each year in Bangladesh, leading to temporary migration to Dhaka and other urban centres; scientists have shown that climatic unpredictability has increased in the last two decades, because of climate change. In the Mekong Delta of Vietnam, too, more severe flooding has stimulated a greater level of migration to urban areas in the 1990s and 2000s.[4]

In the nineteenth century, too, environmental degradation and episodes of catastrophe drove tens of thousands off the land, in search of security; many of them travelled from India and China to the lands of Southeast Asia (Chapter 1). In contrast with events in the nineteenth century, the Asian frontier has now closed. There are few, if any, sparsely populated cultivable lands left. The new environmental migration is almost entirely destined for urban areas, both internally and internationally. The history of international migration control in the twentieth century, which we have traced in this book, has placed higher barriers to entry in the way of international migrants, compounding the compulsion to head, first, to the mega-cities in their own countries. Given the magnitude of overall population growth, and their already strained infrastructures, the capacity of the cities to incorporate an even larger flow of migrants is open to question. Many Asian mega-cities are themselves vulnerable to rising sea levels and more intense cyclones.

But those urban centres also provide contemporary Asia with its economic dynamism. The growth of export-oriented manufacturing industry has led to the increasing availability (and financial attractiveness) of non-farm work for those fortunate enough to be able to obtain such jobs. The burgeoning informal sector of Asia's growing cities has absorbed millions who lack the skills, the networks, or the luck to secure formal industrial jobs. Jobs in the informal sector are precarious. They

---

[4] *In Search of Shelter: Mapping the Effects of Climate Change on Human Migration and Displacement* (New York: CARE, 2009), 13–15.

might vanish as quickly as they appear. Faster and cheaper transportation, often a legacy of the development projects of the 1960s and 1970s (Chapter 4), increased mobility. Tarred roads, more frequent ferry services, and cheaper air travel – all brought migration within closer reach of an ever-greater number of people. The transport industry itself employs millions of people across Asia.

As the rest of this chapter will show, the mobility revolution has spurred both internal and international migration in Asia. Scholars treat the two processes separately, but they are both the product of the social and economic conditions outlined earlier; their effects on migrants and their families are often comparable. Internal and international migrations are often in fact directly connected. In some cases, internal migration acts as a stepping stone to more lucrative opportunities for overseas migration: young people move first to their local provincial capitals, before embarking on longer journeys to national capital cities, or beyond national borders. Internal and international migration may be connected, too, at the level of the family. Throughout Asia, families adopt migration strategies that spread risk through diversification: one son or daughter goes to the Middle East, another to an urban centre closer to home, while the rest of the family remains on the land. In his work on migrant workers in the Indian steel town of Bhilai (discussed in the previous chapter), Jonathan Parry found that many of these migrant workers had themselves worked for a period overseas, or currently had family members in the Gulf or in Southeast Asia.[5] In other circumstances, internal and international migrations are locked together in a hierarchy of paths open to families. Only those with some land or capital to begin with can finance international migration, with its promise of greater returns. The poorest are more likely to migrate over shorter distances.

Routes of migration are segmented. They reflect the inequalities of economic globalization and the very different life chances that market-driven economic growth, or its absence, create for different sections of the population.

Asian Urbanization, 1970–2010

The most spectacular result of the growth in mobility in Asia since the 1970s has been the scale and pace of urbanization. Thousands of young men and women each day arrive in Shanghai, Mumbai, Jakarta, Manila, and Bangkok in search of livelihoods, survival, and advancement. Collectively they are bringing about the most rapid urbanization

---

[5] Parry, 'Nehru's Dream'.

Table 5.1 *Population of Asia's 'Mega-Cities'*

City	Population (in millions)		
	1975	2000	2015 (est.)
Tokyo	19.8	26.4	27.2
Mumbai	7.3	16.1	22.6
Kolkata	7.9	13.1	16.7
Dhaka	2.2	12.5	22.8
Delhi	4.4	12.4	20.9
Shanghai	11.4	12.9	13.6
Jakarta	4.8	11.0	17.3
Osaka	9.8	11.0	11.0
Beijing	8.5	10.8	11.7
Karachi	4.0	10.0	16.2
Metro Manila	5.0	10.0	12.6

Source: United Nations, *World Urbanization Prospects: The 2001 Revision Data Tables and Highlights* (New York: United Nations, 2002), 9.

in human history. In 1950, 231 million Asians lived in urban areas, approximately 17 per cent of Asia's total population. In 2000, that figure was 1.22 billion urban residents, 35 per cent of all Asians. Within the next two decades, more than half of Asia's population will live in cities, significantly more than half in East and Southeast Asia. One conspicuous area of urban growth is in the so-called 'mega cities', with populations in excess of 10 million people (Table 5.1). No fewer than eleven of the world's seventeen mega-cities are in Asia. Smaller cities are growing rapidly, too. In 2000, there were 166 Chinese cities with populations over 1 million (compared with just 9 in the United States).[6] India's urbanization, by contrast, is more focused on the growth of a smaller number of extremely large cities, with some growth of medium-sized cities, and the relative stagnation (economic and demographic) of small cities.

The greatest of all the rural–urban migrations in Asia (or anywhere) has been underway in China since the late 1970s. As we have seen, until the 1970s, strict controls on urban residence under the 'residence permit' (*hukou*) system kept Chinese urbanization in check. When these controls began to break down with the advent of Deng Xiaoping's (1904–1997) market-driven reforms, China's urban centres received a 'peasant flood'.[7]

[6] Mike Davis, *Planet of Slums* (London: Verso, 2006), 11–12.
[7] Dorothy J. Solinger, *Contesting Citizenship in Urban China: Peasant Migrants, The State, and the Logic of the Market* (Berkeley: University of California Press, 1999); Kuhn, *Chinese Among Others*, 321–382.

According to estimates, more than 200 million Chinese have moved from the countryside to the cities since the 1970s, constituting a vast 'floating population' without precedent. In 2004, there were an estimated 1.6 million migrants in Beijing, 3.3 million in Shanghai, and 12 million in the cities of Guangdong, at the heart of the Pearl River Delta's industrial revolution: the new city of Shenzhen alone was home to over 6 million migrant workers.

These millions of migrants provide the labour for China's ascent to its position as the manufacturing centre of the world. A significant proportion of them are women. Apart from the sheer scale of this labour force, structural factors make it cheap and easily exploitable. Though the *hukou* system no longer works effectively, the majority of urban migrants are nevertheless in the cities unofficially. Not recognised as formal urban residents, they lack access to social security, medical care, and educational facilities for their children. Given that the *hukou* was in effect an internal passport, many undocumented workers in China's cities face a situation akin to that of undocumented migrants who have crossed international borders. One migrant interviewed by sociologist Lee Ching Kwan put it simply: 'we are second-class citizens', he said, 'and not even that sometimes, just beasts in the eyes of the police'. Exploited by both the state and the market, 'migrant workers have no rights at all, because we are not locals'.[8] Access to urban *hukou* accentuates inequalities between different groups of migrants. The last two decades have seen a steady commoditisation of urban *hukou*; only the wealthiest migrants are in a position to purchase a more recognised status in the city. Others spend several thousand yuan to buy 'provisional' urban residence permits for the Special Economic Zones, which do not give them any rights to social services or social protection.

Migrants in China's cities have since the 1980s been vulnerable to harassment, detention, and sudden deportation to the countryside. Such was the experience of one of Beijing's largest migrant quarters, Zhejiangcun ('Zhejiang Village'). A settlement of more than 100,000 people – mostly migrants from the Zhejiang region specializing in small-scale, family-based garment production – Zhejiangcun was raided in 1995: nearly 10,000 homes were destroyed and more than 18,000 residents were sent back to their villages. Such was the tenacity of this group of migrants, however, that before long, the settlement had reformed and returned to business as usual. In Guangdong, Lee Ching Kwan has highlighted an increasing tendency for migrant workers to

[8] Lee Ching Kwan, *Against the Law: Labour Protests in China's Rustbelt and Sunbelt* (Berkeley: University of California Press, 2007), 198.

turn to labour arbitration and China's labour law to seek redress when their wages are unpaid, when they are injured in the workplace, or when they are subject to violence and indignity by their employers. If they are often unsuccessful in their claims, this nevertheless indicates a shift in migrant workers' consciousness of the avenues open to them, and their increasing ability to use the central state's promises of fairness against bosses and corrupt local officials.[9]

In common with so many of the currents of migration this book has examined, migration to Asia's cities in the age of globalization depends on informal networks of information, capital, housing, and emotional support. Labour contractors, or 'jobbers', play a pivotal role in facilitating both rural–urban and intra-rural migration in India. Similarly, migrants to China's cities depend on informal connections: on kinsmen and fellow villagers. Now, as in the past, these networks are fragile. They can unravel as quickly as they form.

Even for those with access to regular employment, the struggle for survival in the city can be relentless. Asia's urban migrants swell what Mike Davis has called a 'planet of slums'; Davis reminds us that 'the five great metropolises of South Asia (Karachi, Mumbai, Delhi, Kolkata, and Dhaka) alone contain about 15,000 distinct slum communities whose total population exceeds 20 million'.[10] Migrants to the cities dwell in makeshift structures made up of recycled materials: sometimes no more than cardboard. Many sleep on the streets. Slums are under constant threat of demolition by the state and by private developers. The threat of fire looms large, along with the perennial problems of unsanitary conditions and a visceral lack of privacy.

The Chinese phrase – the 'floating population' – describes well the transient and insecure condition of many of Asia's migrant workers. In China, as in other parts of Asia, urban migrants maintain close connections with their rural homes. Most Chinese migrant workers retain land rights in rural areas, contracted from the state for tenures of up to thirty years. Rural land rights constitute both a buffer and a source of pressure. Landholdings are usually insufficient for subsistence, and require an additional income in order to be viable; yet they do offer some security in times of unemployment. With the onset of the global economic crisis in the second half of 2008, reports began to emerge of a mass return movement of labourers to the Chinese countryside, involving over 20 million people, or about 15 per cent of China's total migrant workforce. The intention of eventual return to their rural

---

[9] Kuhn, *Chinese Among Others*; Lee, *Against the Law*.
[10] Davis, *Planet of Slums*, 26.

homes is widespread among China's migrant workers in the cities. Most continue to identify themselves as 'peasants' rather than as 'workers'. The aspiration to return to their rural homes and open a small shop is widespread; so, too, is a powerful collective memory of rural suffering, and a sense that urban migration represents the possibility of progress, however often it remains unrealised.[11]

The idea that rural homes represent a buffer against the vicissitudes of the urban labour markets needs qualification. In China, the degree of rural decline in inland provinces means that for an increasing number of migrant workers, the possibility of return is precarious. In South and Southeast Asia, where urban migrants are less likely to have land-holdings, the security offered by rural homes is more fragile still.[12]

International Migration, 1970–2010

Alongside Asia's urban revolution, increasing prosperity and increasing inequality stimulated a resurgence in international migration in Asia. Some of the routes of migration were entirely new; others were built on long historical connections, including many described earlier in this book. Two main circuits of Asian migration established themselves from the 1970s: the first, from the 1970s, involved the migration of millions of short-term contract workers, both skilled and unskilled, from South Asia, the Philippines, Indonesia, and Thailand to the oil-producing states of the Middle East. The majority were men working in construction, though an increasing proportion of women made the journey from the 1980s to work in domestic service and in the leisure industry.

The second circuit of Asian migration, which took off during the 1980s, drew migrants from South Asia, Indonesia, the Philippines, Burma, and Vietnam to the growing economies of Southeast Asia: Singapore, Malaysia, and Thailand. The migration of young women for domestic work constitutes a significant proportion of this movement, as does the movement of male construction and manual workers. Both streams of migration have grown in scale over the past decade, and both involve large numbers of undocumented ('illegal') migrants.

Exporting Labour

Because of new inter-regional economic inequalities, and new opportunities for migration, some countries in South and Southeast Asia have

[11] Lee, *Against the Law*, 205–226; Tania Branigan, 'Downturn in China Leaves 26 Million Out of Work', *The Guardian*, 2 February 2009.
[12] Jan Breman, 'Myth of the Global Safety Net', *New Left Review*, 59 (2009), 29–36.

specialized in the export of labour. From the 1980s, the Philippines emerged as the foremost exporter of labour in Asia. By the 1990s, the Philippines was second only to Mexico as a source of migrants in the world. From the time of the oil crisis of 1973, the Philippine state opted to promote migration as a strategy for bolstering the country's foreign-exchange reserves. Since the Philippines' economic crisis coincided with the boom in the Gulf (as will be explained later), there was a ready market in the Middle East for Filipino construction workers. In the next two decades, migration from the Philippines grew rapidly, and involved an increasing number of Filipina women. In 2001, an estimated 7.4 million Filipinos were working abroad. Of these, 3.1 million were temporary contract workers, the rest more permanent emigrants (2.7 million) and illegal or undocumented migrants (1.6 million). Since the early 1990s, over 600,000 people each year have departed from the Philippines for employment overseas.[13]

The Philippine state promoted migration actively, initially as a temporary measure, but with increasing awareness that it was a permanent feature of the Philippines' economic strategy. Under the direction of the Overseas Employment Development Bureau, and then the Philippines Overseas Employment Agency (POEA), the government promoted Filipino labour abroad, oversaw recruitment, and sought – often half-heartedly – to champion the rights of Filipino workers abroad. The dependence of the Philippine economy on migrant remittances is striking. In 2003, remittances through formal channels reached $7.6 billion, amounting to 10 per cent of Gross Domestic Product. Formal channels accounted for only around one-third of overall remittances, the majority of which were sent through personal contacts, or small agencies. From the 1970s, total remittances have outstripped total foreign direct investment in the Philippines by between 10 per cent and 60 per cent.

The Philippines is distinctive in Asia in the extent to which migration is a formal state strategy. More recently, other countries have sought to follow this example. In the 1990s, the Indonesian state sought to foster more actively the export of labour. However, in the other major labour exporting region of Asia – South Asia, including India, Pakistan, Bangladesh, Nepal, and Sri Lanka – the state has less involvement in the process of migration. One significant difference, of course, is the significance of migration as a proportion of the population. Even if comparable numbers of Filipinos and Indians travel abroad for contract

[13] Rochelle Ball, 'Trading Labour: Socio-Economic and Political Impacts and Dynamics of Labour Export from the Philippines, 1973–2004', in Amarjit Kaur and Ian Metcalfe (eds.), *Mobility, Labour Migration and Border Controls in Asia* (Basingstoke: Palgrave, 2006), 115–138.

work each year, Indian migrants, unlike their Filipino counterparts, constitute a tiny fraction of the country's overall working population. Perhaps a better comparison would be with particular regions of South Asia, rather than with India as a whole. Parts of the Indian state of Kerala, for instance, depend on migrant remittances for up to 50 per cent of local income.

Most unskilled, international migration in Asia takes place under the control of recruiters, sub-recruiters, moneylenders, and a range of other intermediaries. Asia's 'migration industry' is a lucrative business worth billions of dollars. A true estimate of its size is impossible to calculate because so much of it operates underground, or at least at the margins of legality. The main variable lies in the degree to which the industry is regulated: it is under closer scrutiny in the Philippines, and operates with almost complete impunity across most of South Asia. The potential for abuse is enormous, and often realised.

Migration scholars Stephen Castles and Mark Miller see the 'migration industry' as a distinctive feature of Asian migration in global perspective.[14] These networks of recruitment have deep historical roots. As we have seen, colonial states lacked the reach and the local knowledge to undertake the recruitment of labour for plantations and other forms of agricultural or industrial production. They relied on local intermediaries, whose networks reached deep enough into the Indian village to overcome obstacles to mobility. In the case of China, the state played almost no role in organizing migration in the nineteenth century. The persistence and revival of these networks in the twentieth and twenty-first century were made easier by the deep ambivalence that many Asian states feel about migration. Asian nationalists held that the migration of their people overseas was a sign of national failure and humiliation. They felt that international migration would no longer be necessary in the post-colonial era. Yet as promises of development faltered, international migration increased again. Unwilling to acknowledge this phenomenon and its implications, most Asian states prefer to turn a blind eye to migration, allowing the private migration industry free rein.

The Lure of the Gulf

In the first decade of the twenty-first century, a significant proportion of all of the cranes in the world were found in Dubai. It is, alongside Shanghai, the 'world's largest construction site', filled with projects of

[14] Stephen Castles and Mark J. Miller, *Age of Migration*, 4th ed. (Basingstoke: Palgrave, 2009).

Plate 5.1 **Construction site in Dubai (2008). In the early twenty-first century, Dubai was in the midst of a massive construction boom; South Asian migrant workers – just visible in the photograph, dwarfed by the scale of the structure they are building – constitute the majority of Dubai's construction labour force.** *Photograph by Sunil Amrith.*

the kind depicted in Plate 5.1. Urban theorist and historian Mike Davis has described twenty-first century Dubai as 'an emerging dreamworld of conspicuous consumption'.[15] Dubai's construction frenzy has seen the construction of the world's tallest building and its largest airport; the biggest amusement park on earth; an underwater hotel; and a development of artificial islands, each shaped like one of the world's continents, each available to the highest bidder. This was before the global financial crisis of late 2008, which brought Dubai to the verge of default a year later. At the time of writing (March 2010), many of those buildings now lie empty and unfinished. Nevertheless, the speed and scale of Dubai's metamorphosis from a small trading port to a global metropolis symbolizes the transformation of the Persian Gulf since the 1970s.

Asian migrant labour is at the heart of this transformation. Since the 1970s, millions of short-term contract workers from South Asia, Southeast Asia, and other parts of the Middle East have travelled to the states of the Gulf, providing between 70 per cent and 95 per cent of their labour force, and nearly all of their manual labour.

Bahrain was the first of the Gulf states to import labour, after the discovery of oil there in 1932. Fears about the potentially subversive influence of Persian migrants led the authorities to turn to British India. After the Second World War, the pattern spread to other parts of the Middle East. Saudi Arabia's ARAMCO employed more than 2,400 Indians and Pakistanis by 1952, and the Kuwait Oil Corporation, nearly 3,000. The number of migrants grew steadily through the 1950s and 1960s. Arabs were in the majority, Palestinians in particular, but a continuing stream of migrants came from South Asia. As well as manual workers, many skilled workers made the journey: technicians, engineers, electricians, architects. The oil shock of 1973–74 precipitated mass migration. Beginning with workers from neighbouring Arab countries, the inflow of migrant workers soon included men from South Asia, Turkey, Iran, Afghanistan, South Korea, the Philippines, Thailand, Malaysia, and Indonesia. In 1970, there was a total of 660,000 foreign workers in the Gulf States, most of them Arabs; by 1980, there were more than 6 million. By 1980, Kuwait employed people from sixty-eight countries. Foreign workers, by this stage, made up 70 per cent to 80 per cent of the workforce in most Gulf countries.[16] They built and ran the schools and hospitals, airports and hotels, airlines and ports that resulted from the region's oil wealth.

[15] Mike Davis, 'Fear and Money in Dubai', *New Left Review*, 41 (2006), 47–68.
[16] Roger Owen, *Migrant Workers in the Gulf* (London: Minority Rights Group, 1985); Myron Weiner, 'International Migration and Development: Indians in the Persian Gulf', *Population and Development Review*, 8, 1 (1982), 1–36.

From the outset, a fundamental feature of migration to the Gulf was its short-term and oscillating nature. Settlement was out of the question for the migrant workers to the Gulf. From the 1950s, each of the Gulf states defined restrictively their laws of citizenship, making naturalization difficult, if not impossible. This gap between citizens and short-term migrants came to define the societies that emerged from the 1970s: a small number of local citizens enjoyed benefits on a scale unimaginable almost anywhere else in the world; their lifestyles were made possible by the labour of foreign workers, who enjoyed few benefits and fewer rights.

The migrants' absence of legal protection has been compounded by their dependence on the 'migration industry'. Already by the early 1980s, workers had to pay up to US$1,000 to recruiters to secure a job in the Gulf. To raise those sums of money, equivalent to several years' earnings for poor South Asian families, many prospective migrants contracted loans from local moneylenders at very high rates of interest; others sold or mortgaged family land. Their willingness to do so emphasizes the substantial wage differential between their home regions and the Gulf. Most Asian labour migrants, in the 1980s as in the 1880s, begin their journeys deeply in debt. Fraud and coercion are pervasive, ranging from the provision of fake documentation and falsified contracts, to large-scale human trafficking.

With rapid development and economic diversification, the composition of the migrant workforce began to shift. As states such as Dubai aimed to make themselves less dependent on oil, the service sector absorbed a larger proportion of migrants. By the late 1980s and early 1990s, more of the migrants to the Gulf were women – from the Philippines, South Asia, and Indonesia – employed as domestic workers, waitresses, hostesses, and in the sex industry.

The social world of migrant labour that had emerged in the Gulf states by the late 1990s was unprecedented in its scale and its concentration. In 2005, the United Arab Emirates alone had 2.7 million migrant workers, about 20 per cent of them working in construction. A clear majority of the 500,000 or so construction workers are from South Asia: India, Pakistan, Bangladesh, Nepal, and Sri Lanka. Migrant workers live far from the centre of the growing metropolis of Dubai, housed in labour camps, safely out of sight of tourists, wealthy expatriates, and Emiratis. The largest of these camps, Sonapur ('City of Gold', in Hindi and Urdu) houses over 100,000 people. With the exception of a few 'model labour camps', conditions are overcrowded, with up to ten people sharing dormitory rooms that are just 10 square feet in size. In many cases, the camps lack sanitary facilities and even running water. Despite the substandard conditions, many employers deduct a portion of workers' salaries as 'rent'.[17] The camps are guarded closely. Even in such conditions, however, the camps have developed their own cultural and social life: the universal language of Hindi cinema and film music; ceremonial meals to greet newcomers or to see off men heading home; a game of cricket from time to time.

Construction workers earned an average of US$175 each month in 2006.[18] Their shifts can stretch for up to 14 hours, in heat that in summer can exceed 40 degrees Celsius. Workplace accidents are common (and usually unreported). Some employers provide medical facilities for injured workers, but few workers have access to any sort of compensation. Many workers are simply deported if they are injured in the workplace. Undocumented workers find themselves in a particularly vulnerable position if anything goes wrong. Nobody keeps count of mortality rates among migrant workers. The arrival home of migrant workers' bodies in coffins is an experience all too common among families in South Asia.

The most common complaint among workers is the withholding of wages by employers. Nearly universal is the practice of withholding two or more months' salary – along with the workers' passports – as security. When boom turns to bust, as it did in 2008–09, many workers found that their employers had simply vanished, and they were left with months of unpaid wages and without their travel documents. Recruiting agents routinely pass on to workers the costs of their work visas and air travel, although this is illegal. Many workers are subject to 'contract switching', arriving in the Gulf to find their wages much lower than promised.[19]

In the absence of trade unions, recourse to arbitration through official channels rarely, if ever, results in fines for offending employers.[20] In 2005 and 2006, however, migrant workers in the UAE (United Arab Emirates) staged unprecedented public protests. In September 2005, up to 1,000 migrant construction workers blocked Sheikh Zayed Road, the multi-lane highway that is Dubai's main thoroughfare.[21] In March 2006, thousands of workers went on strike when their employer, a Belgian construction company, refused a wage increase.[22] The ostensible

17 'Blood, Sweat, and Tears', Al-Jazeera English [AJE], broadcast on 18 August 2007; Human Rights Watch, Building Towers, Cheating Workers: Exploitation of Migrant Construction Workers in the United Arab Emirates (New York, 2006).
18 Human Rights Watch, Building Towers, 7.
19 Ibid., 36–37.
20 Ibid., 12.
21 Davis, 'Fear and Money', 67.
22 Hassan M. Fattah, 'In Dubai, An Outcry from Asians for Workplace Rights', New York Times, 26 March 2006; Human Rights Watch, Building Towers, 25.

leaders of the protest were arrested, along with many others. A number of workers were deported. The longer-term effects of the protests on labour conditions remain to be seen.

The migrant networks that bring hundreds of thousands of South Asian, Southeast Asian, and Arab workers to the Gulf states are a product of the 1970s. Yet the Gulf states also remain central to much older networks of circulation and exchange, which intersect with the new global flows at many levels. Dubai is home to up to 450,000 Iranian exiles, many of them Sunni Muslims from the Bastak region of southern Iran. Flows of migration, and trade by *dhow* – in televisions, computers, refrigerators, scrap metals, and clothing – between the two coasts of the Arabian Gulf remain vital. Iranian exiles are estimated to control around 30 per cent of Dubai's real-estate market.[23] In the Bastakiya district of Dubai, 'rows of tall wind-towers and rectangular, coral-stone houses with beautifully carved wooden doors and windows are testimony to a strong connection with Iran'.[24] Similarly, the Indian Ocean connections that have for centuries linked the Middle East to South Asia continue to thrive. Small communities of Hindu merchants still play an important role in the region's trade, as they have for centuries. Now these Indian Ocean connections have intersected with other forces of globalization, making Dubai a central node in the networks of Indian organized crime. In Dubai, South Asia's drug trade, Bombay cinema, human trafficking, and religious politics collide. Through the 1990s, Dubai was home to India's most notorious gangster, Dawood Ibrahim, thought to be behind the 1993 bombings in Bombay that killed hundreds. Here, as elsewhere, the changes of contemporary globalization have not displaced, but rather built upon and diverted, older flows of people, goods, capital, and ideas.[25]

Southeast Asian Miracles

By the 1980s, a second pole of attraction for Asian migration emerged: the rapidly growing economies of Southeast Asia. By the end of the twentieth century, Southeast Asia attracted an even greater number of Asian migrants than the Middle East. The labour shortage that necessitated the import of hundreds of thousands of migrant workers was in part a result of annual economic growth rates exceeding 7 per cent; it was also a result of demographic change. Between

[23] Davis, 'Fear and Money', 56.
[24] 'Dubai Iranians Hurt By International Sanctions', *Kuwait Times*, 29 December 2007.
[25] Appadurai, *Modernity at Large*.

Table 5.2 *Estimated Stocks of Migrant Workers in Asia*

Countries of origin	Number of migrants	Main destinations
Southeast Asia		
Burma	1,100,000	Thailand
Thailand	340,000	Saudi Arabia, Taiwan, Burma, Singapore, Brunei, Malaysia
Laos	173,000	Thailand
Cambodia	200,000	Malaysia, Thailand
Vietnam	340,000	Korea, Japan, Malaysia, Taiwan
Philippines	4,750,000	Middle East, Malaysia, Thailand, Korea, Hong Kong, Taiwan, Singapore
Malaysia	250,000	Japan, Taiwan, Singapore
Singapore	150,000	Worldwide
Indonesia	2,000,000	Malaysia, Saudi Arabia, Taiwan, Singapore, South Korea, United Arab Emirates
TOTAL	8,313,300	
South Asia		
India	3,100,000	Middle East
Pakistan	3,180,973	Middle East, Malaysia
Bangladesh	3,000,000	Middle East, Malaysia
Sri Lanka	1,500,000	Middle East, Malaysia
Nepal	4,000,000	Middle East, India, Malaysia
TOTAL	14,780,973	
North East Asia		
China	530,000	Middle East, Asia and the Pacific, Africa
North Korea	300,000	China
South Korea	632,000	Japan
Japan	61,000	Hong Kong
TOTAL	1,523,000	

Source: Graeme Hugo, 'Migration in the Asia-Pacific Region', Global Commission on International Migration (2005), 9.

1970 and 2003, Asia's overall population (including India and China) almost doubled, but the population growth rate fell by almost half. The average number of children borne by each woman in Asia fell from 5.4 in 1970 to just 2.4 in 2003. In that time, the proportion of Asia's population resident in urban areas grew from 24 per cent to 40 per cent.

But these demographic trends were unevenly distributed. Malaysia, Thailand, and Singapore underwent the fertility transition first, and attracted migrants from Indonesia, the Philippines, and South Asia, where fertility rates fell later. The migrants were drawn from the burgeoning ranks of young people.[26]

As Table 5.2 indicates, Southeast Asia's migrant networks converge on Malaysia and Thailand, which are countries of both immigration and of emigration. Like Singapore in the nineteenth century, Malaysia and Thailand are transit points for the onward migration of Asian labourers farther east, as well as destinations in their own right.

The significant majority of migration in Southeast Asia consists of unskilled and semi-skilled contract workers. Many cross borders undocumented and undetected. Thailand, for instance, attracts overland migrants predominantly from neighbouring countries: Burma, Laos, and Cambodia – though recent years have seen an increasing number of migrants from South Asia (Bangladesh, in particular). They work in construction, on fishing boats, and in the agricultural sector. Since many, or most, of them are in Thailand 'illegally', migrant workers face considerable insecurity and are vulnerable to abuse from the police and the Thai authorities, not to mention labour recruiters and a myriad of intermediaries. The International Labour Organization (ILO) estimated that in 2002 there were 1.1 million Burmese, 111,000 Laotians, and 88,000 Cambodians legally in Thailand. In addition, there are between 700,000 and 2 million undocumented Burmese workers in Thailand.[27] Thailand also sits at the centre of Southeast Asia's malign webs of human trafficking.

The economic boom that Malaysia witnessed in the 1980s, and the increasing difficulty of getting local people to undertake poorly paid manual labour, led to a significant influx of migrant labour. Peninsular Malaysia saw the arrival of hundreds of thousands of construction workers from Indonesia, Bangladesh, Nepal, India, and Pakistan, and from across the Thai border. Many, and possibly a majority, of these workers were undocumented, as seen in the numbers that came forward to have their status regularized during brief periods of amnesty, in 1991–92 and again in 2005.

The conditions experienced by the migrant workers, the insecurity of their status, and their indebtedness to migrant recruiters of different

[26] Graeme Hugo, *Migration in the Asia-Pacific Region*, report for Global Commission on International Migration (2005).

[27] Graeme Hugo, 'Women, Work and International Migration in Southeast Asia: Trends, Patterns, Policy', in Kaur and Metcalfe (eds.), *Mobility, Labour Migration and Border Controls*, 73–114.

kinds are similar to those faced by migrants to the Middle East, as outlined earlier. Neighbouring Singapore, wealthier still, also imports unskilled labour on a large scale. In the case of Singapore – a small island with tightly policed borders – most, though not all, of the migrants are documented. In Singapore and Malaysia alike, legal migrant workers arrive on short-term visas, with no possibility of settlement. Work visas tie migrant labourers to a single employer. As in the Middle East, labour rights are scarce.

The vulnerability of migrant workers in the growth economies of Southeast Asia became clear when economic growth went abruptly into reverse, as it did during the financial crisis of 1997–98, and again at the time of writing this book in 2008–09. Thousands of workers were left unemployed, owed several months' salary. For most of them, legal avenues of redress were either unavailable or prohibitively expensive. In recent years, voluntary organizations in Singapore and Malaysia have championed the rights of migrant workers, with success in a number of individual cases.

Many workers have been deported, returning home in shame to face their creditors and their disappointed families. In a powerful collection of photographs, Malaysian artist Simryn Gill presented anonymous portraits of unfinished buildings from across Southeast Asia, in the wake of the economic crisis of 1997. In their eerie emptiness, and in the absence of the workers who built them, the buildings in Gill's photographs attest to the fragility of an economy built on speculation; a fragility felt most acutely by migrant workers. A similar sense of alienation pervades Tsai Ming-Liang's 2006 film, *I Don't Want to Sleep Alone*, set in Kuala Lumpur in the aftermath of the last Asian economic crisis. The film features an unfinished, empty building as a recurring motif, amid the lives of characters that include South Asian migrant workers out of work.[28]

Backdoor to Sabah

Eastern Malaysia provides a third nodal point for migration in Southeast Asia. Much of this migration takes the form of cross-border migration within the archipelagic, maritime world linking eastern Malaysia, the southern Philippines, and Indonesia. As Maruja Asis has shown, migrants from western Mindanao – the 'southern back door' to the Philippines – follow a 'centuries-old path to Sabah', that now happens

[28] Simryn Gill, *Standing Still* (Cologne: Verlag der Buchhandlung Walther König, 2004); Tsai Ming-Liang, *I Don't Want to Sleep Alone* (2006), DVD: Axiom Films, 2008.

to cross an international border. Circulation continues through the region that historian James Warren called the 'Sulu Zone' – in the nineteenth century, a region that was closely integrated politically and economically, and a major centre of slave raiding – but under a new regime of national borders and border controls. The 1970s saw a significant increase in migration from the southern Philippine island of Mindanao to the Malaysian state of Sabah (on the island of Borneo), coinciding with a rise in civil strife in the southern Philippines and the advent of Sabah's oil boom. The majority of Filipino and Indonesian residents of Sabah are undocumented. On one estimate, they make up more than 55 per cent of Sabah's workforce, and are found in the construction and plantation sectors, as well as in the service sector in the towns. Like undocumented migrants everywhere, they are vulnerable to the attentions of the police, subjected to sudden raids, deportation, and extortion. Sabah is home to up to 40 per cent of Malaysia's total migrant work force of about 1.7 million people.[29]

The Feminization of Migration in Asia

Finally, I thought to myself, how come all the bosses I met were of the same nature?.

Chinese migrant woman in Harbin

One of the most striking features of Asian migration – both internal and international – is the rising proportion of female migrants. This is part of a broader tendency towards the feminization of work under the conditions of flexible mass production brought about by globalization. The rise of export-oriented production, particularly in the garment and shoe manufacturing industries, has created openings for a feminization of the workforce. Employers view female workers as having more manual dexterity than do men, while being more docile and significantly cheaper. A number of the tasks undertaken by smaller units of production – etching circuit boards, sewing – are similar to tasks that women have been 'socialised' into 'in the household production unit'. In factories across Asia, women almost invariably occupy the lowest rung of hierarchical workplaces segmented by gender, class, race, immigration status, or nationality.[30]

---

[29] Maruja M.B. Asis, 'The Filipinos in Sabah: Unauthorized, Unwanted and Unprotected', in Santosh Jatrana, Mika Toyota, Brenda S.A. Yeoh (eds.), *Migration and Health in Asia* (London: Routledge, 2005), 116–140.

[30] Amarjit Kaur, *Wage Labour in Southeast Asia Since 1840: Globalization, the International Division of Labour and Labour Transformations* (Basingstoke: Palgrave, 2004), 188–189.

Mobility has given millions of Asian women greater autonomy. Women constitute between one-third and one-half of China's 'floating population', and many of them express a desire to gain 'more experience in life' as a primary motivation for migration. Though they confront many prejudices in urban areas, as rural outsiders, China's migrant women often experience a significant sense of transformation in the process of moving to the cities.[31] Anthropologist Yan Hairong has pointed to a significant cultural shift in attitudes towards migration in her study of female migration for domestic service from rural villages in Wuwei County, Anhui Province, to China's cities. Women from Wuwei county had a long tradition of migration for domestic work, though for decades they felt the stigma of this 'feudal' form of employment at a time when public discourse elevated the farmer and cultivator as the heroes of the Chinese revolution. From the 1980s, however, female migrants from Wuwei increasingly regarded the countryside as a backward, distasteful place, in contrast with the gleaming modernity of the cities.[32] For many Chinese women, migration is a means to self-transformation, yet always undertaken in the context of family networks and obligations. The quotation that opens this chapter gives the view of a Chinese migrant woman whose experience of migration 'has given me the opportunity to make myself strong and it has taught me how to get on with others'. She wrote of her 'rich and colourful' spare time, and her relentless quest for self-improvement – reading newspapers, attending lectures, and learning English.

For many others, the experience of migration was one of humiliation, which they recall with 'bitter tears'. One migrant to Harbin, in China's far northeast, reflects on the indignities she faced as a young woman:

The year I turned twenty, I started life as a real migrant worker. I went to a restaurant in Harbin to work as a waitress. Every day I got up at four o'clock in the morning and worked continuously till eleven or twelve at night when the restaurant closed. I served food, washed the dishes, looked after the guests, and cleaned the tables and chairs. I was so busy my feet hardly touched the ground, but still I was often scolded by the boss. Overwork, poor wages, and not enough sleep made all the wages exhausted ... I could put up with low pay, but what I couldn't put up with was insults from the boss. I can do without anything except my dignity.[33]

[31] Gaetano and Jacka (eds.), *On the Move.*
[32] Yan Hairong, *New Masters, New Servants: Migration, Development and Women Workers in China* (Durham, NC: Duke University Press, 2009).
[33] Li Jianying, 'Working for Myself', in Gaetano and Jacka (eds.) *On the Move,* 304–308.

Even this woman, however, was later successful in opening her own beauty salon, before ultimately returning to her rural home to get married.

Everywhere, migrant women balance their newfound freedoms with a sense of obligation. Mary Beth Mills, in her work on Thai women from rural areas who migrate to Bangkok, found that they balanced their desire to be 'modern' – often manifested in particular kinds of consumption: the purchase of lipsticks and fashionable clothing – with their obligation to be 'good daughters'.[34] Consumption offers a powerful means of self-fashioning for young migrant women in Asia, who often gather to go window shopping on pay day; but the shopping malls of Asia's cities also remind them painfully that their wages are never quite enough. Many migrant workers are motivated by the distant dream of being able to afford a life of material comfort.

Women play an increasingly prominent role in Asia's international migration, too. By the early twenty-first century, 72 per cent of overseas migrants from the Philippines, 73 per cent of migrants from Indonesia, and 65 per cent of Sri Lankan migrants were women (by contrast, 99.9 per cent of Bangladeshi overseas migrants were men).[35] The majority of these female migrants find employment as domestic workers. With increasing wealth and the rising participation of middle-class women in the labour force in countries such as Singapore and Hong Kong, the demand for domestic workers grew substantially in the 1980s. In the early years of the twenty-first century, there were about 2 million migrant domestic workers in Asia. Prosperous Singapore and Hong Kong were the largest employers of migrant domestic workers, most of them from the Philippines, Indonesia, and Sri Lanka.

As in other fields of unskilled migration in Asia, recruitment for domestic work was overwhelmingly undertaken by private agencies. Nicole Constable found among Filipina domestic workers in Hong Kong in the 1990s that three-quarters of them had left the Philippines in debt to recruiters, and many had to take out further loans in Hong Kong. In the 1990s, as Indonesia tried to replicate the Philippines' success in using overseas migration as a means of earning foreign exchange, training camps were established in Java for prospective migrants. Many of the camps are run by private companies, and charge significant sums for admission. By the year 2000, over 150,000 Indonesian women each year travelled abroad for domestic work. One young Indonesian woman described to anthropologist Catharina Williams the path that took her

[34] Mary Beth Mills, *Thai Women in the Global Labour Force: Consuming Desires, Contested Selves* (New Brunswick, NJ: Rutgers University Press, 1999).
[35] Hugo, *Migration in the Asia-Pacific Region*, 18.

to Hong Kong as a domestic worker: 'My experience was that it was hard to find a job after finishing high school... financially, we could not afford my further studies, as my parents were farmers. Then almost every night we heard on the radio that they needed domestic workers. I wanted to have the experience of working abroad. Well I was not so sure, but it must have been a divine provision'. In the Philippines and Indonesia alike, recruitment agencies subject domestic workers to a training regime designed to make them obedient, unassertive and unthreatening in the eyes of employers.[36]

Working in private households, domestic workers are perhaps even more open to abuse than their male counterparts in the construction sector. In most countries in Southeast Asia, even the most rudimentary labour laws do not cover domestic workers. Their workload often begins at 4 or 5 AM, and continues until late in the evening. Many domestic workers get a day off once a month, if that. Their isolation in the workplace makes solidarity, let alone organization, difficult, to say nothing of the restrictive laws that prevent them from forming unions. Rarely are the domestic workers' home governments willing or able to defend their rights in the international arena, given the dependence of the sending countries on the continued flow of migrants overseas. The public outrage occasioned in the Philippines by Singapore's execution in 1995 of a Filipina domestic worker convicted of murdering another domestic worker and the Singaporean child in her care marked a notable exception to the general inaction on the part of migrants' own governments.

By no means are female domestic workers simply victims. Many enjoy rich social lives in their cities of work, and the process of migration is often a means of personal transformation. This transformation can be seen in their attire, in their acquisition of new skills, and in their sense of achievement through personal sacrifice. Many aspire to return home and embark on small businesses, often by the establishment of small general goods stores. Convivial gatherings of Filipina domestic workers on Sundays assert their claim to public space in Hong Kong and Singapore. Since the 1980s, particular shopping centres in Singapore have been filled with Filipino restaurants, bars, shops, beauty salons, remittance agencies, and, more recently, internet cafes, where migrants can communicate with their families at home. Activities organized by churches, hometown associations, and other social networks play a significant role in the lives of many migrant domestic workers. A significant

---

[36] Nicole Constable, *Maid to Order in Hong Kong: Stories of Migrant Workers* (2nd ed., Ithaca: Cornell University Press, 2007); Catharina Purwani Williams, *Maiden Voyages: Eastern Indonesian Women on the Move* (Singapore: ISEAS, 2007), 139.

element of this social world takes place on-line, in blogs, and in chat-rooms and social networking sites. Since the 1990s, the level of activism on the part of Filipina migrant domestic workers has increased, in Hong Kong in particular. The United Filipinos in Hong Kong and the Asian Domestic Workers Union organized to protest against new regulations imposed on migrant workers by the Hong Kong government, and against the Philippine government's attempts to control remittances. In the twenty-first century, these migrant workers' associations have become notably multi-ethnic in composition.[37]

After domestic work, the next largest industry involving female migrant workers in Asia is the 'entertainment' industry, which involves a spectrum of work, from dance and musical performance to prostitution. Japan is the destination for most female entertainers – predominantly from the Philippines and Thailand. For decades, entertainment visas provided the only legal means of temporary migration to Japan. These regulations left women open to abuse. Thousands ended up in Japan illicitly, often by entering the country on tourist visas, and staying on. On one recent estimate, there are over 400,000 female migrant entertainers and 150,000 migrant sex workers in Japan. Organized crime plays a significant role in the Japanese and Korean entertainment industries. There are many reports of migrant women being forced into prostitution, having arrived in Japan to work as singers or bar waitresses.

The line between migration for work in the entertainment industry and human trafficking is blurred. Thailand has long been at the centre of Asia's trafficking networks. Thailand is the destination of women and children trafficked for sex work from Burma, Cambodia, Laos, and Yunnan (in southern China). On one estimate, 20,000 Burmese girls work in Thailand's brothels. Many of these women and girls, together with a significant number of Thais, then travel to Japan and to Europe. Trafficked women and children are subject to particularly appalling levels of abuse, from their 'clients', from the mafias that control their movement, and from corrupt police and government officials. South Asia has its own networks of trafficking, of which Mumbai is the epicentre. Young children from across South Asia end up in Mumbai's brothels, after being abducted by or sold to traffickers. Many of the trafficked girls in Mumbai's brothels come from impoverished highland regions of Nepal. The story of just one Nepali girl, interviewed by the Panos Institute, might stand for many. Deceived into thinking she was working as a courier for a diamond merchant, she was drugged and abducted, ending up in a Mumbai brothel. She spoke of the 'many girls

---

[37] Constable, *Maid to Order*, 160.

that are taken away with the promise of marriage', only to be sold into sexual slavery. 'Most of the girls sold there are from the hills [of Nepal]', she said, 'just like me, they were coaxed, misled and taken there'.[38]

A third, and growing, reason for the migration of women across Asia is marriage. Transnational marriages in Asia have been on the increase since the 1990s. Many of these marriages are arranged by international agencies. These agencies take Filipina, Thai, and Vietnamese women to Japan and Taiwan; ethnic Korean (Chosonjok) women in China to South Korea, leaving Chosonjok men in China to look to North Korea for brides; and women from China to Hong Kong, Taiwan, South Korea, and Singapore. In 2003, 32 per cent of all marriages in Taiwan were between Taiwanese men and foreign women. In meeting a 'bride short-age' in rural Taiwan or Korea, migrant wives often create one in their home regions. Recent work by anthropologists cautions us against the stereotypes of the 'mail order bride', and shows that marriage migrants need not necessarily be cast in the role of victims. Personal ambition, fantasies, dreams of better lifestyles, and different ideas about gender roles and family life underlie the decision of many women to find part-ners overseas. Often the reality does not match the fantasy.[39]

Skilled Migration in Asia

Although most Asian migrants – both male and female – are unskilled contract workers, there has been a corresponding rise in the migration of highly skilled professionals and of students across Asia.

The elite among this group of migrants constitute the new managerial class of the global economy – bankers, software designers, management consultants, entrepreneurs, and property developers. This movement of skilled people within Asia continues to include more traditional pro-fessional migrants, too: doctors, engineers, and architects. Increasingly prominent within this conspicuously mobile group are Asia's new media elites: designers, artists, winners of television singing contests, film stars, sports broadcasters, and music television presenters. Many among this group enjoy what anthropologist Aihwa Ong has called 'flexible citizenship': they carry multiple passports and move seamlessly across national borders in search of profit, opportunity, or adventure. Their circulations bridge Asia with other centres of global finance

---

[38] Panos London, *Voices from the Mountain: Oral Testimonies from Nepal* (London, 2003).

[39] Nicole Constable (ed.), *Cross-Border Marriages: Gender and Mobility in Transnational Asia* (Philadelphia: University of Pennsylvania Press, 2005).

and technology: New York, London, Los Angeles, and Silicon Valley. Within Asia, the most significant corridor within which elite migrants circulate is that linking Singapore and Hong Kong: geographer Howard Dick calls this 'main-street Southeast Asia', and argues that, for this new elite, urban centres are more integrated with one another than with their respective hinterlands.[40]

Alongside this Asian migrant elite is a much larger movement of skilled workers. Since the 1980s, thousands of migrant nurses – predominantly Filipina, but also Burmese, Chinese, and Malayali – have migrated across Asia to fill shortages: first to the Middle East, and later to places like Singapore and Hong Kong. Skilled technicians, too, have moved in large numbers, including marine engineers – Filipino, Bangladeshi, or Chinese – working in Southeast Asia's burgeoning shipping industry. As Megha Amrith's work on Filipina migrant nurses in Singapore has shown, these skilled migrants often occupy an ambiguous class position, lacking the easy mobility of the migrant elite, but seeking to differentiate themselves from the masses of their unskilled migrant countrymen and women. Gains in professional status, or in the right to settlement and citizenship in the countries to which they move, are often hard-won.[41] Many, however, undergo a process of 'de-skilling' as a result of migration, employed in jobs well below their levels of qualification, yet earning higher wages than they would in more senior positions at home. The impact of skilled migration on sending countries – what has been called the 'brain drain' – has occasioned concern and comment since the 1980s. In the Philippines, for instance, an estimated 30 per cent of IT professionals and 60 per cent of physicians have emigrated permanently.

One of the most significant movements of skilled people is the movement of students – particularly (though not exclusively) university students. Between 1998 and 2003, there were an estimated 2.6 million Asian students studying outside their own countries; Chinese, Indian, and South Korean overseas students each numbered more than 400,000. A significant proportion of these students study outside Asia: primarily in Australia, the United States, Canada, and the

[40] Howard Dick, 'Southeast Asia as an Open System: Geo-Politics and Economic Geography', in Paul H. Kratoska, Remco Raben, and Henk Schulte Nordholt (eds.), *Locating Southeast Asia: Geographies of Knowledge and Politics of Space* (Singapore: Singapore University Press, 2006), 250–274; Aihwa Ong, *Flexible Citizenship: The Cultural Logics of Transnationality* (Durham, NC: Duke University Press, 1999).

[41] Megha Amrith, '"They Think We Are Just Caregivers": The Ambivalence of Care in the Lives of Filipino Medical Workers in Singapore', *The Asia Pacific Journal of Anthropology*, 11, 3–4 (2010), 410–427.

United Kingdom. However, the number of students migrating within Asia increases each year. As China's own university system expands, there has been an increase in the number of Asian students travelling *to* China for their higher education, Thai students in particular. Japan, for its part, seeks to expand the number of Asian students in its university system, from 118,000 in 2008 to 300,000 by 2012.[42] In 2005, Singapore hosted 66,000 students, most of them from Southeast Asia, China, and India; by 2012, this number is likely to exceed 150,000.[43] In many cases, student migration serves as a prelude to more permanent settlement abroad.

While countries like Singapore aim to attract highly skilled Asian professionals, their home countries seek to draw them back. Following the example of Taiwan, China and India have both made efforts in the twenty-first century to encourage their diasporas to invest in their homelands, and to encourage migrant professionals to return. A significant number have begun to do so, as rapid economic growth creates opportunities and boosts salaries. In 2004, the Indian government instituted a partial concession to the ban – in place since 1955 – on dual citizenship. Tellingly, the Indian government's efforts were directed largely towards Indians in the West, with a more ambivalent view towards working-class Indians settled elsewhere in Asia.

Migrant Connections

The thousands of migrants whose journeys this chapter has considered rarely, if ever, act as lone individuals. While individual suffering and self-realisation form an important part of the story of global migration, it is essential to remember that most migrants' journeys are undertaken in the context of their relationships and obligations to their families and local communities. The suffering that migrants endure in Jakarta's slums, Dubai's labour camps, or as domestic workers in Singapore households takes on an entirely different meaning if we view the migrants not in isolation but in relation to the communities they have left behind. The expansion in Asian migration has created dense webs of connection between distant places. Through these connections, familial affections and family obligations orient migrants' actions and expectations, even over long distances. In the idiom used

---

[42] Castles and Miller, *Age of Migration*, 125–147.
[43] Brenda S.A. Yeoh, 'Singapore: Hungry for Foreign Workers at All Skill Levels', Migration Information Source (January 2007), http://www.migrationinformation. org/profiles/display.cfm?ID=570, last accessed on 2 September 2009.

by families in northern Pakistan, migrant sons in the Gulf 'save there, eat here'. A powerful ideology links the struggle and suffering of male migrants who travel and 'save' so that their kinsmen at home can 'eat' their savings.[44]

Challenging the 'tragic' view of migration in the age of globalization, Jean-François Bayart argues that, more than anything else, migrants are motivated by the 'quest for personal reputation by means of gifts that are skilfully made public knowledge'. It is chiefly in the eyes of their families and local communities that migrants aim to 'achieve respectability'. It is in recounting stories of migration to those back home that migrants' journeys take on an 'epic' quality.[45]

Through the 1980s, one of the most common ways in which migrants' narratives were communicated with their families was through recorded audiocassettes. Fortnightly or monthly, migrant construction workers would record messages to send home to their families. Many workers' families, and workers themselves, were (and are) illiterate, and the cassettes had the added immediacy of emotional connection provided by the migrant sons' and daughters' voices. The power of Yasmine Kabir's tragic documentary *My Migrant Soul* – the story of a Bangladeshi migrant, Shahjahan, who dies in a Malaysian detention centre – comes from the film's narration in the voice of Shahjahan himself, taken from audio letters that his grieving family gave to the filmmaker.

Since the 1990s, the rapid expansion of cheap international phone calls has emerged as the most important way in which migrant workers maintain communication with their homes (Plate 5.2). Anthropologist Steven Vertovec calls cheap phone calls the 'social glue connecting small-scale social formations across the globe'.[46] The global volume of long-distance calls increased from 12.7 billion call-minutes in 1982 to 154 billion in 2001. Although the United States remains the centre of the global network of international phone communication – 25 per cent of all international calls are made from the United States – the volume of calls within Asia is increasing.

The ease of instant communication with families left behind is something that distinguishes contemporary migrations from earlier ones. The ability to speak regularly, even daily, with distant family members allows migrants to participate in family decisions, and to maintain

---

[44] Francis Watkins, '"Save There, Eat Here": Migrants, Households and Community Identity Among Pakhtuns in Northern Pakistan', in Osella and Gardner (eds.) *Migration, Modernity and Social Transformation*, 59–82.

[45] Bayart, *Global Subjects*, xi, 188.

[46] Steven Vertovec, 'Cheap Calls: The Social Glue of Migrant Transnationalism', *Global Networks*, 4, 2 (2004): 219–224.

Plate 5.2 **Vendor of calling cards in Singapore (2010).**
This stall is located in a district of Singapore frequented
by migrant workers: the profusion of long-distance call-
ing cards compete for consumers' attention, each offer-
ing attractively cheap ways of staying in touch with home.
Photograph by Sunil Amrith.

relationships. Phone calls may ease, but also sharpen, the pain of family separation and loneliness. For many Filipina domestic workers, leaving children behind in the Philippines in order to care for the children of middle-class families in Singapore or Hong Kong, phone calls become central to the practice of long-distance parenting. Though family separation is a very common experience in the Philippines, traditional gender and parenting roles remain powerful, and absent migrant parents – particularly mothers – often continue to exercise a primary parental role over the telephone.[47]

Remittances, of course, are at the core of almost every migrant journey. Remittances have meaning beyond their financial value. Remittances create or cement relationships between migrants and their families, and are associated with powerful emotions: debt and gratitude; expectation and obligation; pride, shame, and aspiration. We might recall what Chen Da wrote in 1938 about the impact of remittances from the Nanyang on south China's villages: 'Money and ideas about the spending of money flow together through the same channel. In a number of ways the material contributions and the intellectual contributions are intertwined'.[48]

In every Asian city that hosts large numbers of migrants, lines outside the offices of remittance agencies are a common sight. Plate 5.3 shows the office of a Bank of India remittance centre in Singapore.

Others – including up to 40 per cent of Bangladeshi migrants in Southeast Asia and the Middle East – rely on the centuries-old *hawala* system to transfer money. There is a sense of achievement in sending money home, and a nagging feeling that it is never quite enough. For example, Mohammad Ismail, a thirty-year-old Bangladeshi worker in the marine industry in Singapore, went directly to the remittance office when he managed to recover several months' unpaid wages. 'I am happy that after three months I can finally send money home', he stated plainly, 'it's not much money. But it's useful for my wife and child'.[49] The fact that many migrants' families owe large amounts, often as a result of the migrants' hefty recruitment fees, adds a darker edge to the sense of familial debt. Such ambivalence is perhaps a universal aspect of the working-class migrant experience.

Remittances circulate within a broader exchange of gifts and objects of special value. Anthropologist Pnina Werbner has shown how the

---

[47] Rhacel Salazar Parreñas, *Children of Global Migration: Transnational Families and Gendered Woes* (Stanford: Stanford University Press, 2005).
[48] Ta Chen, *Emigrant Communities*, 84.
[49] 'Migrant Dreams', *AJE*, broadcast on 18 August 2009.

Plate 5.3 **Remittance centre, Singapore (2010). This branch of the Indian Overseas Bank in Singapore, which was established during the first phase of large-scale Indian emigration overseas, specializes in sending remittances to India, and is used primarily by migrant workers.** *Photograph by Sunil Amrith.*

circulation and ceremonial movement of 'food, clothing, cosmetics, jewellery' and other objects imbued with particular value provide a significant means of connection within migrant worlds. Particular goods come to embody specific places or moral qualities. This flow of gifts and goods often involves objects of spiritual significance: pictures of saints, relics, prayer mats, beads, or scented oils. Thai construction workers in Singapore participate in Buddhist rituals of 'merit-making', wherein they make collective donations in support of particular projects – temple improvements, the construction of schools or clinics – in their home villages. The envelopes containing the donations are rich with symbolism, and cement the connectedness between migrant workers and their rural homes.[50]

---

[50] Pnina Werbner, 'Global Pathways. Working Class Cosmopolitans and the Creation of Transnational Ethnic Worlds', *Social Anthropology*, 7, 1 (1999), 17–35; Pattana Kitiarsa, 'Village Transnationalism: Transborder Identities among Thai-Isan Migrant

Plate 5.4 **Migrant family's house in Rural Kerala (2008). Houses built by 'Gulf money' in Kerala are easy to identify. They are built in conspicuously modern style – reflected in their bright colours, and forms of architecture – and they stand out from those of their non-migrant neighbours.** *Photograph by Sunil Amrith.*

Nowhere is the impact of remittances more clearly marked on the landscapes of migrants' home regions than in the form of housing. For many migrants and their families, the priority in using remittances – after paying off debts – is the construction of a new family home (Plate 5.4).

Among the formerly 'untouchable' Izahava community of Kerala, 'Gulf money' has allowed some families to challenge local caste hierarchies, building villas much grander than those of upper-caste villagers.[51] The furnishing of new dwellings with the latest consumer goods provides another way of marking one's distinction as a result

Workers in Singapore', Asia Research Institute Working Paper 71 (National University of Singapore, August 2006).
[51] Filippo Osella and Caroline Osella, 'Migration, Money and Masculinity in Kerala', *Journal of the Royal Anthropological Institute*, 6, 1 (2000), 117–133.

of migration: sewing machines, refrigerators, colour televisions, and now mobile phones and computers. Remittances also play a crucial role in diversifying families' livelihood strategies. They may be invested in education, or in farming; the need to keep up these investments often spurs further outward migration.

To build a 'comfortable home' in their rural localities remains the ultimate aspiration of most urban migrants in China. Rachel Murphy's work in Jiangxi province has shown that the ability to construct a house with earnings from the city is crucial 'in enabling villagers to achieve the goal of self-respect'. The contrast between the homesteads of migrants' families, and those who have not been able to send sons and daughters to the city, is sometimes stark. The houses, in Jiangxi as much as in Kerala, are furnished with the most expensive consumer durables the family can afford. These desired consumer goods form part of a broader flow of material things from the city to the countryside: branded goods and markers of fashionable urban culture, including magazines, popular music, and films. In the words of one of Murphy's informants, a former farmer whose family had benefited from migration to the city:

The first year that someone has migrated, the family eats their fill, after the second year the family wears new clothes, after the third the family builds a new house, and after the fourth year, a bride is taken. Since time immemorial, the Chinese farmer has had three life goals: to eat so that the stomach is full, to build a house, and to marry. You ask how do they spend their remittance, well that's how.[52]

The final stage in the cycle of connection between migrants and their homes is the moment of return. Often migrants return, only to depart again for another spell of work far from home. Yet the moment of return remains deeply significant. Filippo and Caroline Osella discuss the ways in which the returned migrant appears in popular cinema in Kerala: in a taxi from the airport, weighed down by his gold chains, and boxes upon boxes of gifts and consumer goods. The cinematic migrant is possessed of a new confidence and a new moral code, as he produces a bottle of Johnny Walker Red Label whisky to share with his friends.[53] The reality of return is usually more ambivalent. Migrants return to find their family relationships under strain, after years of separation; they often contrast the poverty of their homes unfavourably with the

---

[52] Rachel Murphy, *How Migrant Labour is Changing Rural China* (Cambridge: Cambridge University Press, 2002), quote on p. 103.
[53] Osella and Osella, 'Migration, Money, and Masculinity', 123.

modernity of their places of work, no matter how difficult their working conditions.

For many young migrants – both male and female – the ultimate goal upon their return is marriage. Urban employment has led to a significant inflation of the bride price in China and of dowries in South Asia. Migrants who have done well in the city, or working abroad, might find that their value on the marriage 'market' is significantly increased. Tales abound of once-despised young men who find after their return that their prospective in-laws now treat them with respect.

Yet the vast social mobility that migration can offer – epitomised by the returned migrant 'made good' – serves only to highlight the importance of chance, luck, or fate in determining who will 'make it' among the greater number of migrants who return home disappointed and broken. Too many families experience the most difficult return of all: the return of the bodies of their beloved sons or daughters who have died away from home.

As in an earlier age of Asian migration (Chapter 2), the networks that connect migrants with their homes serve as a powerful conduit for new ideas, new cultural practices, and new world views. Migration facilitates the transmission of new religious ideas, as it has for centuries. It is often in terms of familiar religious idioms and rituals that migrants and their families seek to legitimise their newfound wealth in the community, and to transform wealth into status. Muslim women from eastern Sri Lanka, who work as domestic servants in the Gulf, often bring back with them more orthodox, 'Arab' views of Islamic practice. They take to wearing the *burqa*. In the new houses they construct, they institute firm distinctions between male and female, public and private space. Far from signifying a lack of modernity, it is precisely because returned migrants associate piety with wealth and modernity that they seek to replicate this at home. In reinforcing pious behaviour, returned migrants increase their own status as wives and mothers in the household.[54]

Mobility and Immobility

A fundamental characteristic of contemporary globalization is that while capital and goods can cross borders with ease, human beings cannot. The upsurge in human mobility that this chapter has charted

---

[54] C.Y. Thangarajah, 'Veiled Constructions: Conflict, Migration and Modernity in Eastern Sri Lanka', in Osella and Gardner (eds.), *Migration, Modernity and Social Transformation*, 141–162.

is neither unfettered nor smooth. Internal and international migrants negotiate complex regulations over their movement. Individuals' prospects of mobility are shaped by the documents they carry – passports, residence permits – or their ability to pay for forged ones. A significant proportion of human mobility under the conditions of globalization is undocumented, working through the gaps in official regulation and surveillance; it is facilitated by agents, recruiters, forgers, traffickers, and corrupt police or border officials. Those who evade regulations are most vulnerable to abuse and exploitation at the hands of recruiters, employers, and governments alike.

In the process, 'waiting', Jean-François Bayart reminds us, has become an essential feature of globalization. 'Waiting in uncertainty, dirt and stench', he writes, 'are an everyday experience in globalization'. They are 'the equivalent, in advanced capitalism, to the confinement of the slaves'.[55] In this chapter, we have seen many examples of the everyday institutions that keep migrants, or prospective migrants, waiting: the training camps for Indonesian women who wish to work abroad as domestic servants, for instance.[56] The airports, ports, and border checkpoints that thousands of migrants pass through each day function as 'gatekeepers', in part through their ability to make people wait, often in fear and uncertainty.

The 'mobility revolution' in Asia has produced many new kinds of immobility, and even incarceration, of which the camp – the refugee camp or the immigration detention camp – is the most conspicuous symbol.

Asian Refugee Migration

Of late our citizenship has been cancelled and we are no more recognised as citizens of Burma ... One and a half million of our people have been forced to diaspora.

Rohingya Solidarity Movement

The period since the 1970s has seen a continuing flow of refugees across Asia's borders, and an equal or greater number of people displaced within their own countries. In 2006, the United Nations High Commission for Refugees (UNHCR) estimated that Asia hosted more refugees and displaced persons than any other world region: a total of 3.47 million refugees, 1.14 million 'returned refugees', and more than 1.32 million

---

[55] Bayart, *Global Subjects*, 274.
[56] Williams, *Maiden Voyages*, 148–149.

internally displaced persons 'of concern to UNHCR' (indicating that this was but a fraction of the total number of internally displaced persons).[57]

At the turn of the twenty-first century, Pakistan hosted the largest number of refugees – close to 1 million – almost all of them from Afghanistan; an additional 950,000 Afghan refugees were in Iran. The number of Afghan refugees in Pakistan in particular had been significantly larger, but the period since 2001 has seen the return of about 3.4 million refugees to Afghanistan. Until the early twenty-first century, however, many camps for Afghan refugees were in effect permanent settlements, distributed throughout Pakistan, and under the care of the UNHCR. Amid the armed conflict and upheaval that has afflicted Afghanistan since the Soviet invasion of 1979, the UNHCR estimates that more than 6 million Afghans have sought refuge abroad, the vast majority in either Iran or Pakistan.[58] Anthropologist Magnus Marsden has made clear that the life of Afghan refugees in north-western Pakistan is not confined to camps. Many circulate along older networks, affirming and reactivating family, linguistic, and cultural connections that span a mountainous, trans-regional world of Central Asia. Afghan refugees in places such as Chitral, where Marsden works, claim kinship and commonality with local families. The refugee movements sparked by international conflict intersect with ancient diasporic worlds.[59]

The Afghan crisis came in the aftermath of the exodus of refugees from the intertwined conflicts in Indochina in the 1970s. More than 3 million Vietnamese refugees fled the country between 1975 and the early 1990s. The vast majority of them were settled in the West – the United States in particular – yet some of the most traumatic experiences of Vietnam's refugees awaited those who fled initially to other parts of Southeast Asia. Tens of thousands of 'boat people', as they became known, ended up in Malaysia, Thailand, Singapore, and Hong Kong. Many of them embarked on their treacherous journeys across the South China Sea in overcrowded craft, many suffered pirate attacks, during which refugees were murdered, raped, or abducted. Perhaps one in ten 'boat people' did not reach their destinations alive.[60]

Upon arrival in Southeast Asian ports, Vietnamese refugees often received a hostile reception. Malaysia, Thailand, and Singapore all attempted to prevent the docking of Vietnamese boats in their ports,

[57] UNHCR, *State of the World's Refugees, 2006* (Geneva, 2006).
[58] Ibid.
[59] Magnus Marsden, 'Muslim Cosmopolitans? Transnational Life in Northern Pakistan', *Journal of Asian Studies*, 67, 1 (2008), 213–247.
[60] UNHCR, *State of the World's Refugees, 2000* (Geneva, 2000), chapter 4.

using military force to push them back out to sea. Refugees on boats that did manage to lay anchor were held in detention camps as they anxiously awaited resettlement in the West.[61] The most notorious of these detention camps was established in Hong Kong in the late 1980s, and at its height held over 18,000 people, including large numbers of women and children.[62]

Vietnam's neighbours, Cambodia and Laos, were not spared the political upheaval of the 1970s. In Cambodia, the radical Khmer Rouge regime created millions of both internal and external refugees, forcibly resettling the country's urban population in the countryside in the midst of genocide. Thailand bore the brunt of the refugee influx from Vietnam and Cambodia, and later – after the military crackdown on the pro-democracy movement in 1988 – from Burma, too.[63] Thousands of refugees were housed in camps along the Thai–Cambodian border, dependent on relief from the UNHCR. The largest of these camps, Khao-I-Dang, became infamous for the harsh conditions in which its Cambodian residents lived. The Thai government refused officially to recognise these refugees, and alternated between toleration and persecution – often deportation.

Joining the ranks of Asia's long-term refugees are those trans-border communities that remain victims of the national borders drawn in the 1940s and 1950s. The flight of Rohingya refugees from Burma into Bangladesh is a case in point.[64] Persecuted by the Burmese state from the time of independence (Chapter 4), a large Rohingya community sought refuge across the border in Bangladesh. By the early 1990s, more than 250,000 of them lived in border camps run by the Red Crescent Society, the UNHCR, and other international charities. Into the twenty-first century, more than 20,000 refugees continued to live in the Teknaf camp in Bangladesh. The case of the Rohingyas also suggests that even refugee movements are connected with broader circuits of labour migration. From Bangladesh, large numbers of Rohingya men have travelled to Malaysia and the Middle East in search of work; by the 1990s, more than 200,000 Rohingyas were thought to live in the Middle East. And like other kinds of migrants, Rohingya refugees

---

[61] 'Vietnam's Boat People: Victims of war and peace', *International Herald Tribune*, 26 June 1989

[62] Robert Mauthner, 'Humanitarian Help Alone Cannot Solve Refugee Problem', *Financial Times*, 26 June 1989; Frederik Balfour, 'Home Again: Repatriation Money Turns Returnees into Nouveau Riche', *Far Eastern Economic Review*, 4 March 1993.

[63] UNHCR, *State of the World's Refugees, 2000*, Chapter 4.

[64] Willem van Schendel, 'Guns and Gas in Southeast Asia: Transnational Flows in the Burma-Bangladesh Borderland', *Kyoto Review of Southeast Asia* (August 2006).

are increasingly connected to one another, virtually, and through the Rohingya solidarity movement.[65]

Sri Lanka provides a further example of the connection between earlier migrant flows and contemporary forms of displacement. The civil war, which erupted after the anti-Tamil pogroms of 1983, has clear roots in the consequences of the large-scale migration in the nineteenth century for plantation labour in Ceylon. As we have seen (Chapter 4), a significant number of these 'plantation Tamils' found themselves excluded from Sri Lankan citizenship at independence. Since the outbreak of the civil war, the United Nations estimates that more than half a million Tamils have been displaced from their homes and held in detention camps, alongside a significant movement of Tamil refugees abroad: primarily to France, Scandinavia, Australia, and the U.K. After the military defeat of the Liberation Tigers of Tamil Eelam (LTTE) in June 2009, the UNHCR estimated that more than 280,000 displaced Tamils still remained in detention camps in September 2009.[66]

Migration and Detention

Detention is, for millions of migrants, an everyday experience. Refugee camps stand alongside a much wider array of camps, prisons, and detention centres designed to constrain mobility – and to punish those who transgress. In countless ways, states categorize and distinguish between those who can move and those who cannot. If we envision contemporary Asia as a series of maps of migration, we must also pay attention to what Asia would look like if it were mapped by its detention centres. In these places of detention, the distinctions between refugees, asylum seekers, and 'illegal immigrants' begin to blur.

To take just one example, there were seventeen immigration detention centres in Malaysia (known as 'depots') at the end of 2007.[67] An estimated 10,136 people were detained in these camps, some of them for indefinite periods of time. Hundreds of women and children were among the detainees. Their offences were varied: some awaited deportation; others had been rounded up by raids undertaken by RELA, Malaysia's (state-sanctioned) vigilante militia of nearly 400,000 citizen

[65] http://www.arakanyoma.org/featured/salient.php, last accessed on 12 February 2010.

[66] http://www.unhcr.org/refworld/country/LKA.html, last accessed on 16 February 2010.

[67] Global Detention Project, 'Malaysia: Country Profile', http://www.globaldetention. org/countries/asia-pacific/malaysia/introduction.html, last accessed on 1 September 2009; UNHCR, *World Refugee Survey 2009: Malaysia* (Geneva, 2009).

volunteers. For a period, the camps were run by RELA: an indication of the extent to which even immigration control has been privatized, and an ironic counterpart to the privatized nature of the migration industry itself. Members of RELA have the right to bear arms and to detain anyone on the 'reasonable belief that any person is a terrorist, undesirable person, illegal immigrant or an occupier'. Observers noted that between 300 and 400 people shared a single cell in the Lenggeng detention centre; food provision often failed to meet minimal nutritional standards. Between 2002 and 2008, about 1,300 detainees died in detention camps. They died of illness, malnutrition, and – on many reports – torture. A leading Malaysian human rights organization, SUARAM, wrote to the government in April 2009 that 'we have highlighted repeatedly the poor conditions … in immigration detention centres, which include overcrowding, poor sanitation, insufficient provision of food and water, and inadequate access to necessary medical and health services'.[68]

Malaysia is not alone in detaining migrants. To the numbers of detainees in Malaysia's 'depots' we must add the unknown number of refugees and 'illegal immigrants' detained in Thai camps and the unreported numbers of Bangladeshi 'illegals' – some of whom are in fact poor Muslims from West Bengal and Bihar – detained in regular police raids in major Indian cities. We may also include the thousands of rural Chinese migrants detained for being in the cities without permission. Japan, South Korea, and Hong Kong all resort regularly to detaining undocumented migrants and those awaiting deportation. Singapore detains, and regularly subjects to corporal punishment, those who overstay their visas. Undocumented migrants, refugees, and asylum seekers (many of them of Asian origin) are detained in large numbers, too, in Australia, the United Kingdom, the United States, and throughout the European Union.

Conclusion

Although professional historians have intervened rarely in the debate, historical analogies are common in recent discussions of migration in Asia (and indeed elsewhere). Journalists, labour activists, even workers

---

[68] Seth Mydans, 'Foreign Workers Face Campaign of Brutality in Malaysia', *International Herald Tribune*, 9 December 2007; '1300 Foreign Detainees Died Due to Neglect', *The Star* (Malaysia), 18 December 2008; 'Bangladesh Tortured to Death in Malaysia', *The Daily Star* (Bangladesh), 19 April 2009; SUARAM, 'Deaths and Conditions of Migrants and Refugees', 28 April 2009, http://www.suaram.net/node/76, last accessed on 1 September 2009.

themselves invoke the language of 'slavery' in describing the experiences of migrant labour in the Middle East and Southeast Asia; many highlight the parallels between recent migrations and the system of indentured labour in the nineteenth century.[69]

In the lack of autonomy that so many migrant workers in the Gulf and Southeast Asia experience, there are undoubtedly parallels with earlier forms of unfree labour; so, too, are there similarities in the harsh conditions under which they work. Comparisons and even direct continuities are evident in the methods of labour recruitment: in particular, in the powerful sway of labour recruiters and intermediaries who use debt as a tool of power. The contraction of distance, on the other hand, is a significant departure: where the voyages of indentured migrants took weeks or days, today's migrants fly across seas in a matter of hours. This can be empowering – allowing for easier exit when conditions are intolerable – but migrants' lack of access to the means of travel (not least, to their own passports) can counteract this greater proximity between their homes and their places of work.

The political context, however, has changed. Indentured migrants moved within large empires; despite the presence of some dissenting voices, an explicit racism governed these systems of migration: the sense that certain peoples were fit only for unfree labour. Labour migrants today move within a world of nation-states, a world of sovereign equality between nations, underpinned by great inequalities of power and influence. The borders and identity documents that shape contemporary migrants' life chances are recent inventions: a product of attempts to govern earlier migrations (Chapter 4). Some of the arguments used to justify the regime of migrant labour, and the treatment of migrant labourers, have persisted since the eighteenth century: above all, the argument that workers sign contracts of their own will, and that in doing so, they acknowledge that their harsh conditions abroad are still better than conditions at home. By contrast, openly racist arguments about the capacities of different peoples, their suitability for different kinds of work, have now taken the guise of arguments on the basis of 'culture'.

Finally, there is a sense in which earlier struggles for the dignity and rights of migrant workers – including the struggles that led to the end of indentured migration in the early twentieth century – can provide moral and political resources for critics of injustice in the present. The force of international law, and organizations like the ILO, are often weak in the

---

[69] Gaith Abdul-Ahad, 'We Need Slaves to Build Monuments', *The Guardian*, 8 October 2008.

face of the exploitation and abuses that many migrant workers face, but they are not without effect. The greater protections afforded to human and labour rights within the international system, compared with the imperial systems of the past, may make little concrete difference to the lives of those who move under constraint; but many activists, inter-governmental and non-governmental organizations, work tirelessly to give them greater effect.

Conclusion

I have argued in this book that migration has shaped modern Asia. At the dawn of Asia's first age of mass migration, which began in the second half of the nineteenth century, large parts of Asia – Manchuria, the Malay Peninsula, Sumatra – were still sparsely populated. Within half a century, these regions were home to millions. New cities, new forms of intensive agriculture, and new societies emerged. The losers from the new order were, usually, small and mobile communities. The winners were invariably states, and – in different and unequal measures – diasporas, settled peasantries, and urban residents, who benefited from new economic opportunities.

People on the move have taken with them ideas, cultural practices, political movements, social institutions, and religious faith. These ideas and practices have changed in the process of circulation, and they have changed the societies in which they implanted themselves. In studying the history of attempts to control migration, I have also touched on core aspects of state-formation in modern Asia: the drawing of imperial and national borders; the development of new ideas about citizenship; states' increasing concern with knowing, and acting upon, their populations.

Migration in Asian History

We began with the proposition that migration deserves a larger place than it has hitherto been given in large-scale accounts of historical change in modern Asia. The question remains: does putting migrants at the centre of our story make any difference to the 'big picture', the large narratives, of modern Asian history?

Three big narratives have dominated the accounts of historians of modern Asia. The first narrative is the transition from empires to nation-states: from colonial to post-colonial Asia. For the first generation after Asia's independence, and for obvious reasons, the rise of Asian nationalisms – a search for the roots of Asia's modern nations – dominated the attentions of historians. The second narrative is the story of economic transformation: the story of capitalist development, and the rise of some parts of Asia from rural poverty to global economic supremacy, while other regions lagged behind; the transformation of Asian peasants into workers; and massive and unprecedented urbanization. The third narrative is the rise of the modern state. The rise of increasingly ambitious, intrusive states, and their systems of information and knowledge, provide an element of continuity between the colonial and post-independence eras, as these states brought more and more Asians under their control.

A focus on the history of migration does not fundamentally change any of those stories, which remain important ways of understanding the changes – social, political, and economic – that Asian societies experienced over the past century and a half. This book is a complement and not an alternative to the standard accounts of modern Asian history. It does, however, modify our sense of chronology; it points to the incomplete and messy way in which many of those transitions occurred; it suggests that our sense of geography need not always correspond to the borders of modern states (nor those of national academies). Above all, following people's journeys gives us a way to emphasize the centrality of human agency – people's choices, their compromises, their struggles, their suffering – in shaping and negotiating the forces of globalization.

Putting migrants at the centre of the story can help to highlight the interconnected nature of historical change. Take, for example, the history of Asian nationalism: Chapter 2 showed that human mobility played a significant role in allowing ideas of nationhood and nationality to spread across Asia. Modern nationalism in Asia did not emerge purely as a result of 'colonial modernity' or – conversely – from a deep, uncolonized indigenous 'tradition'. It emerged, too, from the interaction of Asian intellectuals of diverse origins, and it spread in part through their journeys home and in the pamphlets and books they took with them. A similar case can be made for the significance of migration in explaining the spread and the longevity of transnational modes of identification. The experience of travel gave a tangible reality to religious universalism. As individual and collective journeys tied together distant places, many people's view of the world began to look rather unlike the maps of bounded territory that modern cartography produced.

Migrant networks across Asia have shown great resilience over two centuries. These networks have in the past, and continue in the present, to cross political boundaries faster than they can be brought under official control. In this light, the idea that modern nation-states exercise complete sovereignty over a defined territory seems fragile: that fragility is an enduring cause of unease among state-builders and rulers across Asia.

Those Who Stayed Behind

A history that emphasizes migration risks over-emphasizing mobility. I have argued throughout that the magnitude of migration in modern Asia has long been under-estimated, but there is the danger of the inter-pretive pendulum swinging too far. Over the long period covered by this book, most Asians were *not* migrants – certainly not long-distance migrants. Histories of migration must not lose sight of those who did not move, and those who stayed behind.

In this book, I have shown that non-migrants, too, were affected by processes of migration. In particular regions of Asia, local economies and societies depended heavily on migration to the extent that many non-migrant families (and, even more, non-migrant family members with migrant relatives) depended on remittances from migration – over shorter or longer distances – for their livelihoods and survival. If we look to periods when migration went into reverse – as it did in the 1930s (Chapter 3), or in 2008–09 (Chapter 5) – it becomes clear that the effects of migration spread much farther than the lives of migrants and their immediate families. Access – or lack of access – to the opportunity for migration continues to serve as a major driver of regional differen-tiation and inequality.

The impact of migration on cultural change, too, reached beyond the immediate families of migrants. Migrant connections brought new ideas, new technologies, new images of desirable lifestyles, and new resources: the circulation of these innovations was never restricted to those who lived mobile lives. Migration – and the broader process of globalization of which it is part – gave to many people who did not travel a sense of connection with a wider world. By the early twentieth century, many urban Asians had an increasingly cosmopolitan sense of living in a connected world, an awareness and openness to cultural and material practices from elsewhere; access to this cosmopolitan world often began with, but was never limited to, those who travelled. Many Asians imbibed new ideas and participated in long-distance connec-tions without leaving the places of their birth.

On a larger scale, I have argued that mobility and immobility are linked inextricably. As some Asians became more mobile in the sec-ond half of the nineteenth century, many more became less mobile. As Chapter 1 showed, the upsurge in Asian migration after 1870 coin-cided with the emergence (and immobilization) of a more settled Asian peasantry. Coercion came into play as often to stop people from moving as it did in forcing them to migrate. Forced immobility could be as damaging to people's lives, livelihoods, and hopes as could forced migration. As Chapter 5 showed, new forms of immobility arise to accompany the increase in migration in the present day.

To study the relationship between those who moved, and those who did not – between migrant and non-migrant members of families; between migrant and non-migrant families; between migrant and non-migrant villages, or even regions – is an area that would reward further attention.

Asian Migration and Global Migration

I have focused deliberately on the history of migration within Asia, in part as a corrective to the existing scholarship. Most recent work on Asian migration focuses on the experiences of Asians who moved to the West, and thus ignores the experiences of the vast majority of Asian migrants. But while the distinction between inter-Asian migration and migration beyond Asia can be useful, it is also arbitrary and artificial. As we have seen, particularly in Chapters 1 and 5, migration within Asia was always linked to global circuits of movement. In the nineteenth century, the same forces – sometimes even the same recruiters – took Indian labourers to Southeast Asia as to the Caribbean. Asian and European migrants alike were moved by, even as they shaped, the forces of globalization.[1] In the present day, migration within Asia often takes place within family networks that reach from North America to Australia.

As an aspect of human experience, migration displays striking similarities in its patterns across quite different societies and under different conditions: this is one reason why as a subject it lends itself to comparative study. I have highlighted general features of Asian migration that are equally true of migration in, for instance, nineteenth-century France: migration depends on informal family networks as much as (or perhaps more than) formal processes of recruitment; women move more often, but less far, than men do; an initial wave of migration can establish a recurring pattern of 'chain' migration; those who move farthest usually have the most to begin with, except where they are specifically recruited under constraint (as was the case with indentured labourers).[2]

---

[1] McKeown, 'Global Migration'.
[2] Paul-André Rosental, 'Between Macro and Micro: Theorizing Agency in Nineteenth-Century French Migrations', *French Historical Studies*, 29, 3 (2006), 457–481.

In global perspective, inter-Asian migration does have some distinctive elements. Even more than other streams of global migration in the late nineteenth century, Asian migration was founded on a tradition of circulation, or sojourning. Simply put, Indian and Chinese migrants were more likely to return home than were their English or German counterparts – though the latter did also undertake circular journeys, as did Italians and eastern Europeans. Though flows of movement across the Atlantic were roughly comparable with flows from India and China to Southeast Asia, many more Europeans settled permanently in North America than did Indians or Chinese in Southeast Asia, or Chinese in Manchuria. The sheer velocity of circulation between different Asian regions is one reason why traditional models of diaspora formation – to the extent that they assume a more-or-less permanent movement of people away from their homelands – work less well in an Asian context, at least until the twentieth century, when mobility in Asia was more constrained.

In part because the settlement of Europeans overseas coincided with the historical moment of Europe's military supremacy in the world, European settlers were more likely to establish their own political institutions wherever they went; they governed themselves under their own rules, while subordinating others.[3] By contrast, most Asian migrants adapted to the political institutions of others – very often, in the modern era, the institutions of Europeans. Still, as we have seen in Chapter 2, Asian migrants did shape, and even transform, the nature of those institutions by virtue of their presence and their engagement with new structures of authority. Furthermore, Chinese migrants in particular retained a good measure of autonomy in their social and political institutions, even under European rule. Many of the cultural and linguistic adaptations made by Asian migrants in the process of migration were eased by the prior and longstanding historical and cultural connections between Asian societies.

Sojourning and circulation were the modal forms of Asian migration in the period from 1850 to 1930. Such circular movements became more difficult in the middle decades of the twentieth century (Chapter 4), but are once again prominent in patterns of labour migration from South Asia to the Middle East or to Southeast Asia (Chapter 5). In part, the persistence of circular migration can be explained by the fact that Middle Eastern and Southeast Asian states discourage the permanent settlement of new migrants; even the descendents of migrants

---

[3] Engseng Ho, 'Empire through Diasporic Eyes: A View from the Other Boat', *Comparative Studies in Society and History*, 46, 2 (2004): 210–246.

sometimes struggle to achieve citizenship and political recognition. As we have seen in Chapter 3, the borders of Asia's new states were hard fought, and often arbitrary. The continued flow of legal and illicit migration across borders, combined with the legacy of earlier migrations, make the idea of an ethnically and culturally homogenous nation-state absurd in Asia – and this makes states anxious. Yet, however reluctant they are to sign up to international conventions, Asian states such as India and Pakistan host more refugees than Western states that proclaim more loudly their humanitarian credentials. And where ethnic, religious, and linguistic differences between migrants and local communities are slight – as in the case of Indonesian migrants to Malaysia, or Bangladeshi migrants in parts of India – the process of settlement and political assimilation takes place relatively unhindered, unofficially, if not officially.

Migration, History, and Memory

A curious visitor, or a reader of this book, would struggle to find a museum of migration anywhere in Asia. The new Singapore History Museum is an exception, along with a small museum in Penang: both give migration a prominent place in the narratives they construct. Rarely, though, do the artefacts of migration (as opposed to caricatured representations of minority cultures) find their place in panoramas of national histories. As Benedict Anderson reminds us, museums have played an important role in defining national identity and providing the symbols and narratives of nationalism. Where citizenship and national identity continue to be tied to a notion of being indigenous, many in Asia prefer to forget their families' or communities' migrant pasts, at least in public.[4] Few school history curricula give much room to the history of migration, preferring to focus on the making of national heroes, and projecting back in time the histories of contemporary nation-states.

Yet memories of migration are everywhere imprinted on the social fabric of most Asian societies. Usually these traces are a taken-for-granted aspect of everyday life and cultural practice. It is hardly possible to walk the streets of an Asian city without stumbling upon some trace of migrant journeys past, some invocation of distant places, some evidence of continuing flows of people, ideas, and material culture. From food stalls (Plate C.1) and sacred architecture to the imprint of cash-crop monoculture on the soil, urban streets and rural landscapes

[4] Benedict Anderson, *Imagined Communities: Reflections on the Origin and Spread of Nationalism*, revised ed. (London: Verso, 1991).

Plate C.1 **Food stall in Singapore (c. 2010). This establishment in contemporary Singapore shows the ways in which different culinary cultures from across Asia have implanted themselves in this city of migrants. The restaurant has individual stalls selling regional specialities from across China, and 'Muslim food', which is itself a hybrid of Malay and Indian styles of cooking and spicing.** *Photograph by Sunil Amrith.*

are a living testament to the importance of migration – and different kinds of mobility – in shaping modern Asia.

The history of Asian migration has relevance beyond the field of Asian Studies. Asia's 'plural societies' presaged the hyper-diverse urban centres of many parts of the world today. As I have shown in this book, Asian migrants managed multiple and overlapping loyalties, shaped their sense of collective identity from many sources, and learned to live among the practices and the languages of strangers. It is impossible to understand global economic transformations without acknowledging the central role of Asian migrant labour in the world's labour force. There are, in histories of Asian migration, political and intellectual resources of enduring relevance to the world we live in; these histories make the idea that Western societies provide the only examples of cosmopolitan tolerance difficult to sustain. By the same token, I have also shown that the West has no monopoly on the persecution of outsiders: the exclusion of migrants, strangers, and refugees.

The forces that have caused the expansion of Asian migration over the past 150 years – unequal economic development; war and political conflict; improvements in transportation and communications; environmental degradation, and now the crisis of climate change – remain powerful, and the magnitude of both internal and international migration within Asia continues to rise.

What is likely, however, is that the key themes of this book will continue to shape the experience of Asia's migrants. They will rely on the networks and connections that kinship and local community provide – to find jobs and security and to carve out new paths of migration. Migration will continue to provoke admirable feats of adaptation and ingenuity, new ideas and new ways of living. It seems likely, too, that migrants will continue to bear the brunt of policies of exclusion, persecution, and even expulsion. Migration will be an ever more central aspect of the Asian experience – with the attendant suffering, the possibility of liberation, and the difficult moral choices that it has always involved.

Guide to Further Reading

This brief guide to further reading is confined to English-language works, or works available in English translation. The books and articles cited here and in the footnotes contain references to a wealth of material in Asian languages.

Chapter 1

The global context for this history of Asian migration is best provided by C.A. Bayly's magisterial *The Birth of the Modern World, 1780–1914* (Oxford, 2004). The best overview of global migration flows is Adam McKeown, 'Global Migration, 1846–1940', *Journal of World History*, 15, 2 (2004), 155–189.

Christopher Baker's seminal article inspired many of the arguments in the present book: 'Economic Reorganisation and the Slump in South and Southeast Asia', *Comparative Studies in Society and History*, 18 (1981), 325–349. For an introduction to labour migration under colonial rule, see Jan Breman's *Labour Migration and Rural Transformation in Colonial Asia* (Amsterdam, 1990). Readers interested in the broader debate about indentured labour might start with the contrasting perspectives in Hugh Tinker, *A New System of Slavery: The Export of Indian Labour Overseas* (London, 1974), and David Northrup's *Indentured Labour in the Age of Imperialism, 1834–1922* (Cambridge, 1995).

The best work on south Indian migration to Southeast Asia remains K.S. Sandhu's classic, *Indians in Malaya: Some Aspects of their Immigration and Settlement* (Cambridge, 1969). My own work on Tamil migration to Southeast Asia can be found in the journal articles cited in the notes, and will eventually appear in a book entitled *Crossing the Bay of Bengal* (Harvard University Press, forthcoming). Philip Kuhn's recent survey of Chinese emigration, *Chinese Among Others: Emigration in Modern Times* (Singapore, 2008), is invaluable, and includes work on the early modern era. On migration to Manchuria, the work of Diana Lary and Thomas Gottschang has been my main source of information and interpretation: *Swallows and Settlers: The Great Migration from North China to Manchuria* (Ann Arbor, 2000).

Readers interested in some of the migrations less fully covered in this chapter can consult a wealth of good work. On Java, see Jan Breman, *Taming the Coolie Beast: Plantation Society and the Colonial Order in Southeast Asia* (New Delhi, 1989). On Burma, Michael Adas's *The Burma Delta: Economic Development and Social Change on an Asian Rice Frontier, 1852–1941* (Madison, 1974) remains essential. For a brilliant account of the illicit movement of people, goods, and ideas across Asian frontiers, see Eric Tagliacozzo, *Secret Trades, Porous Borders: Smuggling and States along a Southeast Asian Frontier, 1865–1915* (New Haven, 2005).

Chapter 2

Useful general works on diasporas include Robin Cohen, *Global Diasporas* (London, 1997), and Stephane Dufoix, *Diasporas* (Berkeley, 2008). A groundbreaking statement on the history of diasporas in Southeast Asia, from which much work has followed, is T.N. Harper, 'Globalism and the Pursuit of Authenticity: The Making of a Diasporic Public Sphere in Singapore', *Sojourn*, 12 (1997). On Chinese diasporic networks, see Adam McKeown, 'Conceptualizing Chinese Diasporas, 1842–1949', *Journal of Asian Studies*, 58, 2 (1999), which adopts a global perspective. Christopher Goscha's work on transnational Vietnamese political networks is exemplary: *Thailand and the Southeast Asian Networks of the Vietnamese Revolution* (Richmond, 1999). On migration and urban popular culture, Meng Yue's *Shanghai and the Edges of Empires* (Minneapolis, 2006) is consistently engaging.

The chapter's discussion of migration and pilgrimage within the world of Islam uses Snouck Hurgronje's account extensively, despite its problems of reliability: *Mekka in the Latter Part of the Nineteenth Century: Daily Life, Customs and Learning: The Moslims of the East Indian Archipelago*, trans. J.H. Monahan (Leyden, 1931). William Roff's classic history of *The Origins of Malay Nationalism* (New Haven, 1967) contains useful material on Singapore's position as a centre of Malay intellectual life. Three recent works have advanced our knowledge considerably: Michael Laffan's *Islamic Nationhood and Colonial Indonesia: The* Umma *Below the Winds* (London, 2003); Joel S. Kahn's *Other Malays: Cosmopolitanism and Nationalism in the Modern Malay World* (Singapore, 2006); and the essays edited by Eric Tagliacozzo in *Southeast Asia and the Middle East: Islam, Movement and the Longue Durée* (Singapore, 2009).

On the Chinese diaspora and its social institutions, Philip Kuhn's survey is a good starting point. The ethnographic research of Ta Chen provides illustrative material in this chapter, and remains compelling: Ta Chen, *Emigrant Communities in South China*, ed. Bruno Lasker (Institute of Pacific Relations, 1940). The institutions of the Indian diaspora in Southeast Asia are much less studied. For an introduction (which says little about Southeast Asia), see Judith Brown, *Global South Asians: An Introduction to the Modern Diaspora* (Cambridge, 2006); also see Claude Markovits's study of the Sindhi merchant diaspora: *The Global World of Indian Merchants, 1750–1947: Traders of Sind from Bukhara to Panama* (Cambridge, 2000).

Chapter 3

Much of this chapter's material on war and refugees in China comes from general histories of the Sino-Japanese war; for an introduction, see James Hsiung and Stephen Levine (eds.), *China's Bitter Victory: The War with Japan, 1937–1945* (Armonk, N.Y., 1992). The work of Stephen MacKinnon on refugees is particularly valuable, vividly recounted in his *Wuhan, 1938: War, Refugees and the Making of Modern China* (Berkeley, 2008).

On the Second World War in Southeast Asia, the two volumes by Christopher Bayly and Tim Harper are definitive: *Forgotten Armies: The Fall of British Asia, 1941–45* (London, 2004), and *Forgotten Wars: The End of Britain's Asian Empire* (London, 2007). Sugata Bose's *A Hundred Horizons: The Indian Ocean in an Age of Global Empire* (Cambridge, MA, 2006) contains a vivid account of the Indian National Army experience.

On the refugee movements during the Partition of India, the best recent history is Yasmin Khan's *The Great Partition* (New Haven, 2007). On Partition's protracted aftermath, see Vazira Fazila-Yacoobali Zamindar's *The Long Partition and the Making of Modern South Asia: Refugees, Boundaries, Histories* (New York, 2007). Urvashi Butalia's compilation of oral histories, *The Other Side of Silence: Voices from the Partition of India* (London, 2000) is essential.

The traumatic displacements of the 1930s and 1940s are perhaps best portrayed in fiction. Amitav Ghosh's *The Glass Palace* (London, 2000), based on extensive research, dramatizes the painful choices and conflicts that war brought to Southeast Asia's diasporas. Pramoedya Ananta Toer brings to life the wartime and post-war experiences of Indonesia in his first novel, *The Fugitive*, trans. Willem Samuels (New York, 1990), and in his short stories.

Chapter 4

A contemporaneous source that contains a wealth of material on Indian and Chinese minorities in Southeast Asia is Virginia Thompson and Richard Adloff, *Minority Problems in Southeast Asia* (Stanford, 1955). Again, Philip Kuhn's *Chinese Among Others* contains a useful synthesis of the contrasting histories of overseas Chinese communities in different Southeast Asian countries after independence. Pramoedya Ananta Toer's essays on the Indonesian Chinese are important: *The Chinese in Indonesia*, trans. Max Lane (Singapore, 2008).

On migration flows within India after independence, Myron Weiner's book remains the essential starting point: *Sons of the Soil: Migration and Ethnic Conflict in India* (Princeton, 1978). Important local case studies have appeared in *Economic and Political Weekly* over several decades. There are illuminating essays by Jonathan Parry and others in the volume edited by Filippo Osella and Katy Gardner, *Migration, Modernity and Social Transformation in South Asia* (New Delhi, 2004).

The history of migration in Maoist China is beginning to receive consideration. An outstanding survey that challenges received wisdom is Diana Lary's 'The Static Decades: Inter-Provincial Migration in Pre-Reform China', in Frank N. Pieke and Hein Mallee (eds.), *Internal and International Migration: Chinese Perspectives* (Richmond, UK, 1999). On migration to China's frontiers, see Mette Halskov Hansen, *Frontier People: Han Settlers in Minority Areas of China* (London, 2005). James A. Millward's outstanding history of Xinjiang – *Eurasian Crossroads: A History of Xinjiang* (New York, 2007) – contains much useful material on migration under the PRC, as does Judith Shapiro's equally fine *Mao's War Against Nature: Politics and Environment in Revolutionary China* (Cambridge, 2001).

Indonesia's human drama of transmigration has yet to find its historian. A policy-oriented study with useful basic information is J.M. Hardjono's *Transmigration in Indonesia* (Kuala Lumpur, 1977). On the Philippines, see Thomas McKenna, *Muslim Rulers and Rebels: Everyday Politics and Armed Separatism in the Southern Philippines* (Berkeley, 1998). On migration in Vietnam, see the superb work of Andrew Hardy: *Red Hills: Migrants and the State in the Highlands of Vietnam* (Copenhagen, 2003).

There is a wealth of literature on Asian urbanization, much of it from the 1970s and 1980s. Terence McGee's pioneering work on Southeast Asia remains important: *The Southeast Asian City: A Social Geography of the Primate Cities of Southeast Asia* (London, 1967). More recently, and with a global perspective, Mike Davis's brilliant *Planet of Slums* (London, 2006) makes for sobering reading. The history of Bombay has produced some particularly fine work, including that of the late Rajnarayan Chandavarkar – see his *History, Culture and the Indian Cities: Essays* (Cambridge, 2009).

Chapter 5

One challenge of writing about migration in contemporary Asia is the sheer volume of material available. Important works on the cultural and political dimensions of globalization include Arjun Appadurai, *Modernity at Large: Cultural Dimensions of Globalization* (Minneapolis, 1996), and Jean-François Bayart, *Global Subjects: A Political Critique of Globalization*, trans. Andrew Brown (Cambridge, 2007).

Much of the case-study material that this chapter draws on comes from specialized journal articles and edited volumes, more fully cited in the notes. Good overviews include Jonathan Rigg's *Everyday Geographies of the Global South* (London, 2007) and the essays in Amarjit Kaur and Ian Metcalfe (eds.), *Mobility, Labour Migration, and Border Controls in Asia* (Basingstoke, 2006).

The cultural impact of contemporary migration has been well studied by anthropologists. A particular focus of recent work has been on the feminization of migration, and the impact of migration on gender roles and family structure. See, among others: Mary Beth Mills, *Thai Women in the Global Labour Force: Consuming Desires, Contested Selves* (Rutgers, 1999); Nicole Constable's *Maid to Order in Hong Kong: Stories of Migrant Workers* (Ithaca, 2007); and *New Master, New Servants: Migration, Development and Women Workers in China* (Durham, NC, 2009), by Yan Hairong. Arianne M. Gaetano and Tamara Jacka's *On the Move: Women in Rural-to-Urban Migration in Contemporary China* (New York, 2004) contains helpful analysis and invaluable extracts from essays written by Chinese migrant women. On the Chinese diaspora in the age of globalization, see Aihwa Ong and Donald Nonini (eds.), *Ungrounded Empires: The Cultural Politics of Modern Chinese Transnationalism* (New York: Routledge, 1997).

On the political struggles of migrant workers in China's cities, see Dorothy J. Solinger, *Contesting Citizenship in Urban China: Peasant Migrants, the State, and the Logic of the Market* (Berkeley, 1999), and the groundbreaking study by Lee Ching Kwan, *Against the Law: Labour Protests in China's Rustbelt and Sunbelt* (Berkeley, 2007). On migrant workers in India, see Jan Breman's *The Labouring Poor in India: Patterns of Exploitation, Subordination and Exclusion* (New Delhi, 2003). On urbanization throughout Asia (and beyond), Davis's *Planet of Slums* is compelling and thoroughly documented.

News sources on migration issues are plentiful. Most major Asian newspapers contain frequent stories on labour migration, as do *Al Jazeera*'s English service, London's *Financial Times*, and the BBC. Bulletins issued by the Scalabrini Migration Centre in Manila (www. smc.org.ph) provide digests of news stories. There is an increasing number of videos on www.youtube.com on questions of Asian migration, including documentaries, news stories, and videos produced by migrants. On the movement of refugees in Asia, the UNHCR's website is an essential starting point for information: www.unhcr.org.

The photographs of Sebastião Salgado capture the frenetic pace of urbanization in contemporary Asia in his *Migrations: Humanity in Transition* (New York, 2000). Migration looms increasingly large in contemporary Asian cinema. Recent highlights include the work of Jia Zhangke on China's transformation, and Thai director Apichatpong Weerasethakul's *Blissfully Yours* (2002). Among recent documentaries, Bangladeshi director Yasmine Kabir's *My Migrant Soul* (2000) is exceptionally direct and affecting.

Index

Abduh, Muhammad, 71
Aceh
  war of resistance, against Dutch,
    27, 69
Afghanistan
  labour migration from, 164
  refugees from, 5, 187
agriculture. *See also* economic
    development; plantations;
    poverty.
  and credit, 31, 93
  and economic inequality, 5, 144,
    155
  and population growth, 144
  and shifting cultivation, 24, 138
  development of, 24
  global crisis in,1930s, 91
  green revolution in, 144
  in early modern Asia, 20
  land rights and, 53, 92, 144, 155,
    160
  Overseas Chinese initiatives in, 44
  relative decline of, 8, 144, 160
  subsistence, 28, 37
air travel
  importance to migration, since
    1960s, 7, 8, 151, 153, 156
Amrith, Megha, 177
Anderson, Benedict, 198
archives
  and study of migration, 13–16
Armenians
  in post-colonial Asia, 120, 146
Asia
  and global connections, 17, 196

  and pan-Asianism, 72, 103
  arbitrary boundaries of, 16
  as space of interaction, 1, 17
  boundaries of, 16–17
  connections across, 2, 17, 18,
    89, 91
  regional boundaries of, 2
Asian Studies, 16, 199
Asis, Maruja, 170
Assam
  migration to, 33, 35
  refugees in, 105
  tea plantations in, 29, 33
Atlantic, migration, compared with
    Asian, 9, 197

Bahrain
  discovery of oil in, 1932, 164
  labour migration to, 164
Bangladesh
  environmentally-induced
    migration in, 155
  independence of, 1971, 119
  migrant remittances to, 181
  migration from, 151, 169, 179,
    188
  migration to India from, 198
  refugees in, 188
Barakatullah, Maulana, 61
Bayart, Jean-François, 179, 186
Bayly, Christopher, 18
Beijing
  Japanese attack on, 97
  migrants in, 158
  refugees in, 116

Bharati, C. Subramania, 73
Bhilai
    development of steel plant in, 128
    labour migration to, 128–29, 150,
        156
Bombay (Mumbai)
    anti-immigrant politics in, 147
    cinematic representations of, 148
    cosmopolitanism of, 146, 147
    ethnic networks in, 146
    film industry of, 147
    growth of, 1950s, 142
    migration to, 144, 146
    Partition refugees in, 143
borders. *See also* decolonization;
        migration, controls over.
    and capital flows, 176
    and international migration, 3
    and mobility, 1, 120, 186
    and refugee movements, 6, 90,
        117, 119, 186
    and trans-border movements, 71,
        119, 170, 188
    arbitrariness of, 194, 198
    control over, 12, 118, 120
    creation of new, after 1945, 6, 90,
        116
    illicit movement across, 142, 169
    internal and international, 158
    war and making of, 90
Bose, Rash Behari, 104
Bose, Subhas Chandra, 105
Bose, Sugata, 17, 105
Breman, Jan, 9
British Empire.
    See also decolonization;
        indentured labour; individual
        country entries.
    abolition of slavery in, 1837, 28, 32
    and destinations of Indian
        emigration, 32
    boundaries within, 119
    control of mobility within, 14, 48,
        92
    end of, in India, 113
    expansion in Southeast Asia, 23

indentured labour in, 37
    shipping routes across, 25, 37
Burma
    British conquest of, 27
    expansion of rice cultivation in, 29
    Indian labour in, 34
    Indian refugees from, 1942,
        105–07
    Indians in post-colonial, 123
    labour migration from, 169
    military coup of 1962 in, 141
    mobility within, 141
    quantity of Indian migration to, 32
    refugees from post-colonial, 119,
        188
    role of Chettiar bankers in, 36,
        93–94
    rural rebellion in, 94
    violence against Indians in, 94–95
Butalia, Urvashi, 114

Cairo
    al-Azhar mosque in, 71
    as centre of Islamic modernism, 71
    influence of, in Malay world, 71
Calcutta
    Partition refugees in, 115, 143
    poverty of, 143
Cambodia
    genocide in, 141, 188
    migration from, 169
    refugees from, in Thailand, 188
    refugees in Thailand from, 169
Capa, Robert, 98
capitalism. *See also* frontiers;
        globalization.
    and Chinese diaspora institutions,
        42
    and coercion, 10
    as cause of migration, 27, 47, 116
    in Asia's frontier regions, 25, 28,
        34
    shifts in nature of, since 1970s,
        154, 171, 185, 186
    uneven spread of, 5
Castles, Stephen, 162

censuses
  and identification of migrants, 13,
    24, 37
  as source for migration history, 13
Chandavarkar, Rajnarayan, 144,
  146
Chao Phraya, 29, 31
Chen, Ta, 81, 87, 181
China
  ban on emigration from, 75
  citizenship laws of, 123
  civil war in, 1945–9, 116
  Communist revolution in, 1949,
    117
  control over emigration from, 12,
    122
  Cultural Revolution in, 135
  economic development of, since
    1970s, 154
  ethnic minorities in, 133
  famines in, 99, 135
  First Opium War in, 1839–42, 26
  floating population in, 158, 159,
    172
  frontiers of, 50
  Great Leap Forward in, 1958–61,
    135
  hukou system in, 132, 157, 158
  internal migration after 1949, 132,
    134–35
  land rights in, 159
  migration of women in, 158, 172
  migration to frontiers, after 1949,
    132, 134
  nationalism in, 74–76
  political debates in, 76
  population growth in, 28
  population of, 50
  population resettlement after 1949,
    132, 136
  Qing dynasty, 12, 19
  refugees from, to Hong Kong, 122,
    135
  refugees in, 116
  revolution of 1911 in, 76
  social structure of North, 53

  Taiping Rebellion in, 5, 26–27
  treaty ports in, 26, 38
  urbanization in, since 1970s, 3, 5
  urbanization since 1970s, 157–59
Chinese Communist Party, 51, 97,
  102
  and 'Long March', 97
Chinese diaspora
  and Chinese nationalism, 74–75,
    76
  and education, 79–81
  and locality, 77
  and migration of women, 44, 45,
    46, 87
  and Sino-Japanese War, 101
  and social reform, 46, 86
  class distinctions within, 42, 43,
    44
  creolization in, 23, 42
  diversity of, 42
  early settlements in, 22, 23, 28
  economic activities of, 42–43
  experience under Japanese
    occupation, 104
  gender balance in, 44, 46
  indentured labour in, 41
  institutions of, 48, 49, 77–79, 101
  kinship in, 78
  kongsi in, 23, 48
  patterns of migration within, 4, 9,
    18, 30, 31, 38, 40–41, 45, 91
  political restrictions on, 46
  rituals of, 79
  role of *kongsi* in, 44
  social institutions of, 40
cities
  and slums, 159
  and use of public space, 84
  as site of cultural interaction, 62
  colonial and post-colonial, 145
  ecological vulnerability of, 155
  informal sector in, 146, 155
  mega-, 152, 157
  popular culture of, 64, 145
  port, 11
  representations of, 147

cities (*cont.*)
  residential segregation in, 145
  sources of employment in, 30,
    155
  squatter settlements in, 144, 145
citizenship
  definitions of post-colonial, 117,
    121
  diasporas and, 49, 81
Cold War, in Asia, 134, 154
colonization. *See also* capitalism;
    frontiers.
communications
  importance of, to migration, 7,
    151, 152
  telephone, 153, 179
Confucianism, 86
consumer culture, 173
coolies, definition of, 47
cosmopolitanism, 11, 195
Cribb, Robert, 118
cuisine, migration and changes in,
    198
cultural hybridity, 11

dams
  and population displacement, 130,
    134
  construction of, 128
Davis, Kingsley, 7, 32, 33
Davis, Mike, 143, 159, 164
decolonization
  and refugees, 112
  causes of, 90, 103, 112
  timing of, 112, 117
Delhi
  arrival of refugees in, 143
Deng, Xiaoping, 157
diasporas
  and nationalism, 72
  and social networks, 57
  and social reform, 86
  as conduit of ideas, 58, 63
  Chinese and Indian compared,
    46–49, 77, 82
  consciousness of, 72, 88

definitions of, 57
  formation of, 58, 87, 88
  institutions of, 88
  interaction of, 11, 12
  rituals of, 82, 85
  study of, 14
domestic work
  and labour movements, 175
  conditions of, 174
  in Hong Kong, 173
  migration for, 151, 173–75
Dong Du Movement, 61
Duara, Prasenjit, 54
Dubai
  and economic crisis of 2008–09,
    164
  conditions of migrant labour in,
    165–66
  construction industry in, 164
  labour protests in, 167
  transnational networks in, 167
Dutch East India Company, 21
  use of slaves by, 22

East India companies, 21
economic crisis
  and migrant flows, 89, 91, 159
  Great Depression, 8, 37, 89, 91, 92
  of 2008–09, 159, 170
economic development
  as theme in Asian history, 194
  aspirations for, 126
  changing patterns of, since 1970s,
    151, 153
  popular enthusiasm for, 127, 141
El-Niño Southern Oscillation, 28
environment
  and climate change, 6, 155
  as cause of migration, 6, 155
  impact of migration on, 136

family
  as engine of migration, 53, 178,
    196
  changing structure of, 87
  separation through migration, 181

famines
  as cause of migration, 28
  nineteenth century, 28
  twentieth century, 135
Fiji, Indian labour in, 73
First Sino-Japanese War, 1895, 59,
  75
food production
  expansion in nineteenth century,
  29
frontiers
  characteristics of, 28, 29
  closing of, 18, 24, 155
  in Second World War, 111
  location of Asian, 193
Frost, Mark Ravinder, 15
Fujian, emigration from, 38
Furnivall, J. S., 10, 11

Gandhi, Mahatma, 73
gender. See family; migration, of
  women.
Ghosh, Amitav, 89, 106
Gill, Simryn, 170
globalization
  as historical process, 153
  Asia's centrality to, 153
  characteristics of contemporary,
  8, 153
  definitions of, 7, 152
Gokhale, Gopal Krishna, 73
Gordon, Stuart, 20
Goscha, Christopher, 62
Guangdong
  economic development of, 158
  emigration from, 38
Gulf States
  citizenship laws of, 165
  dependence on migrant labour,
  164
  economic transformation of, 154
  patterns of migration to, 164–67
Guomindang, 97, 102, 116

hajj, 65–71
  and transfer of ideas, 69

expansion of, in nineteenth
  century, 66
financing of, 67
from Malay world, 66–67
numbers undertaking, 71
pilgrim guides during, 68
political implications of, 68
surveillance of, 66, 67
Hardy, Andrew, 140, 149
Harper, Tim, 62, 76
Harrell, Paula, 60
Harvey, David, 152
Hebei, migration to Manchuria
  from, 53
Ho Chi Minh, 62
Ho, Engseng, 120
Hong Kong
  British rule over, 26
  emigration from, 38
  refugee camps in, 188
housing. See also cities.
  shortages of, in post-colonial
  cities, 144
Hurgronje, C. Snouck, 68

imperialism
  European, in Asia, 18, 21
indentured labour, 55
  and contracts, 30
  compared with contemporary
  migration, 191–92
  end of, 37
  political mobilization against,
  73–74
India
  caste in, 130
  citizenship laws of post-colonial,
  123, 178
  control over emigration from, 37
  education and mobility in, 131
  effects of British rule in, 25, 29
  emigration from post-colonial,
  122
  emigration to Southeast Asia from,
  18, 30, 32, 33–38, 91
  famine prevention after 1947, 130

India (*cont.*)
  historical connections with
    Southeast Asia, 33
  industrialization in post-colonial,
    128, 130
  internal migration in, 33, 127, 129
  migration of women in, 129
  Mutiny/Rebellion in, 1857, 27
  Partition of, 1947, 90, 113–16
  patterns of emigration from, 32
  plantations in, 33
  population growth in, 28
  refugee crisis in, 1947–8, 113, 114,
    115, 143
  refugee crisis in, 1971, 119
  visions of development in post-
    colonial, 127
Indian diaspora
  caste in, 35, 83
  diversity of, 36
  experience under Japanese
    occupation, 104
  gender balance within, 35, 38
  institutions of, 82
  religious rituals of, 83, 84
Indian National Army, 104
  and Indian independence, 113
  Tamil labourers and, 105
Indian National Congress, 113, 127
Indian Ocean
  historical connections across, 17
  trading communities of, 20
indigenous peoples
  conflict between migrants and, 12,
    29, 94, 126, 147
  politics of defining, 95, 126, 150
Indonesia
  Chinese in post-colonial, 123, 124
  declaration of independence, 112
  Dutch colonial policy in, 29, 92,
    137
  environmental destruction in, 139
  military coup of 1965 in, 124
  political prisoners in, 139
  position of Chinese in colonial, 43
  transmigration policy of, 137–39

violence against Chinese in, 95,
    124
industrial revolution, 18, 28
industrialization, in post-colonial
    Asia, 126
Institute of Pacific Relations, 91
International Labour Organization
    (ILO), 169
internet
  development of, 153
  use by migrant groups, 16
Irrawaddy, 31
Islam. *See also hajj*; religion
  and cross-border networks, 65
  and mobility of teachers and
    scholars, 65, 70, 71
  diversity of, 72
  modernism in, 71

Jacoby, Annalee, 98
Japan
  and networks of prostitution,
    175
  emigration from, 59
  imperial expansion of, 27, 52, 59,
    96, 103
  Meiji Restoration in, 1867, 59
  post-war economic development
    of, 154
  rise as military power, 27, 59
Java
  fears of overpopulation in,
    137
  forced labour during Japanese
    occupation of, 108
Jewish Diaspora, 57, 120
Jia, Zhangke, 134
Jilin, growth of, 51

Kabir, Yasmine, 179
Kang, Youwei, 75, 86
kangany system, 40
    See also indentured labour;
    migration, free and forced.
  decline of, 92
Kapoor, Raj, 148

Kerala
  migration from, 151, 162
  return of migrants to, 184
Khan, Yasmin, 113
Khilnani, Sunil, 127
King, Anthony, 62
Korea
  division of, 117
  migration to Manchuria from, 50
Kuala Lumpur
  migration to, 145
Kwee, Tek Hoay, 86

labour. *See* migration
Lary, Diana, 132, 134, 136
Lasker, Bruno, 91
League of Nations, 46
Lee, Ching Kwan, 158
Lévi-Strauss, Claude, 143
Liang, Qichao, 75
Liberation Tigers of Tamil Eelam
  (LTTE), 189
Lim, Boon Keng, 76
Ludden, David, 1

Ma Bo, 131, 136
MacKinnon, Stephen, 97, 99
Malaysia
  British colonial rule in, 27
  detention of migrants in, 179, 189
  economic development of, 169
  Emergency in, 1948, 112, 125,
    143
  ethnic politics in post-colonial,
    125
  immigration controls in, 37
  Indian population of colonial, 37
  land legislation in colonial, 92
  migration to, since 1980s, 169
  nationalism in, 96
Manchuria
  as frontier region, 51
  Chinese migration to, 19, 31, 50,
    51, 52–55, 101
  Chinese migration to, after 1949,
    133

Chinese settlement in, 52
development of railways in, 51
economic activities of Chinese
  migrants in, 53
industrialization of, 52
Japanese conquest of, 52, 90, 96,
  97
Mao, Zedong, 97, 135
marriage
  as motivation for migration, 53,
    129, 185
  migration for, 176
McGee, Terence, 145
McKeown, Adam, 9
Mecca
  cultural diversity of, 68
  description of, nineteenth century,
    68–69
Mekong, 29, 31, 155
Middle East. *See* Gulf States;
  individual country entries
migrants
  agency of, 10, 55, 90, 194
  and non-migrants, 195
migration
  academic debates about, 9
  and cultural change, 3, 7, 11, 12,
    88, 185, 193
  and recruitment, 162
  and sojourning, 4, 32, 49, 95, 123,
    197
  and war, 3, 110–11, 116
  as political problem, 95
  causes of, 5–6, 19, 31, 47, 149,
    152, 200
  connections between types of, 2,
    30, 58
  controls over, 1, 4, 13, 32, 45, 92,
    110, 155, 162, 189, 193
  definition of, 2–3
  expansion of, in nineteenth
    century, 5, 8, 19, 25
  expansion of, since 1970s, 151, 155
  free and forced, 9–10, 48, 55–56,
    140, 191
  future prospects for, 200

migration (*cont.*)
  in early modern Asia, 5, 20
  industry, 162
  internal and international, 3, 8,
    118, 149, 152, 156
  networks of, 14, 36, 159, 178, 194
  of labour, 3
  of soldiers, 90
  of women, 7, 47, 87, 165, 171–72,
    173, 196
  over generations, 2, 58, 95
  periodization of Asian, 7–8,
    19, 31
  professional, 3
  seasonal, 3, 52
  skilled, 176–77
  undocumented, 13, 49, 141, 160,
    162, 171, 186, 189, 198
  war and, 5
Miller, Mark, 162
Mills, Mary Beth, 173
minorities
  creation of, by borders, 117,
    120
  Indians and Chinese as, 94, 96,
    122
Mistry, Rohinton, 117
modernity
  and high modernism, 140
  nineteenth century, 18
Mongolia, 50, 101, 133
Murphy, Rachel, 184
museums, representations of
  migrants in, 198
Mya Than Tint, 141

Nakahara, Michiko, 109
Natarajan, Subramania, 121
nationalism
  and history writing, 194
  transnational origins of, 194
Nehru, Jawaharlal, 122, 128, 148
Nepal
  migration from, 5, 161, 165
  traffic in women from, 175

newspapers. *See* printing press

oil crisis, 1973, 154, 161
oral history
  and study of migration, 15–16,
    114
Organization of Petroleum
  Exporting Countries (OPEC),
    154
Osella, Caroline and Filippo, 184
Overseas Chinese. *See* Chinese
  diaspora
Ozu, Yasujiro, 147

Pakistan
  Afghan refugees in, 187
  cross-border migration to,
    121
  migration from, 151, 179
Parry, Jonathan, 128, 150
passports
  in post-colonial Asia, 120–22
peasantry
  formation of, 29
Perdue, Peter, 24
Phan Boi Chau, 61
Philippines
  Chinese migration to, 43
  migration from, 160–61
  migration policies of, 161
  Muslim minority in, 137
  population resettlement in, 136
pilgrimage, connections with other
  kinds of mobility, 58, 70
plantations
  conditions of work on, 36
  organization of, 36
plural society, 11
population growth
  as cause of migration, 169
  in Asia, 118, 136, 142, 144
Portuguese Empire, expansion in
  Asia, 21
poverty
  agrarian, 143, 144

as cause of migration, 44
Pramoedya Ananta Toer, 112, 124, 139, 148
printing press
   and public spheres, 11
   and transfer of ideas, 15
prostitution. *See also* trafficking.
   and entertainment industry, 175
   in nineteenth century, 44
   networks of, 44–45

race
   colonial categorizations of, 12, 13, 58, 68
railways
   and migration, 25
   expansion of, in India, 25
Rakhain, 119
Ramasamy, Periyar E. V., 86
Rangoon
   communal riots in, 1930, 94
   housing in post-colonial, 144
Ray, Satyajit, 130
refugees, in Asia since 1970s, 187
religion
   and religious universalism, 194
   and sacred landscapes, 83, 198
   migration and changing practices of, 185
   syncretism of, 85
remittances
   as motivation for migration, 181
   investment of, in housing, 183, 184
   social meanings of, 181, 182
rice
   areas of cultivation, 24
   expansion in cultivation of, 29
Rida, Rachid, 71
Roff, William, 63
Rohingya, 119, 186
   refugees in Bangladesh, 188
rubber, 29
Russia, 20
Russo-Japanese War, 1904–5, 59

Sabah
   migration to, 170–71
   oil boom in, 171
Sarekat Islam, 96
Scott, James C., 24, 140
Second Sino-Japanese War, 1937–45, 90
   and Nanjing Massacre (1937), 96
   forced migration during, 101
   outbreak of, 96, 97
   refugee flight during, 97–99
Second World War
   and population resettlement, 109
   end of, 112
   fate of diasporas during, 103, 111
   forced labour in, 108–09
   Japanese conquest of Southeast Asia during, 90, 103
   mortality during, in Asia, 110
   Thai–Burma Railway in, 105, 108–09
Self Respect Movement, influence of, among the diaspora, 86
Shandong, migration to Manchuria from, 53, 135
Shanghai
   cosmopolitanism of, 64
   popular entertainment in, 64–65
   refugees in, 64, 98
Shapiro, Judith, 136
Shenzhen, growth of, 158
shipping
   and steam technology, 25
   containerized, 153
Siberia, 20, 50
Singapore
   centrality to migrant networks, 62–63
   migration to, since 1980s, 170
   print culture in, 63
slavery
   and European imperialism, 22
   and slave migration, 20
   and slave-raiding, 22

slavery (*cont.*)
  forms of, 21
  in Indian Ocean, 68
  persistence of, 22, 68
Southeast Asia
  economic crisis of 1997 in, 170
  Indians and Chinese in post-
    colonial, 122–23
  Japanese investment in, 154
  legacies of Japanese occupation of,
    103
  patterns of migration, since 1980s,
    160
  post-war economic development
    of, 154, 167
  regional inequalities within, 154
soy beans, 53
Spence, Jonathan, 27
Sri Lanka
  citizenship laws of, 125
  civil war in, 189
  migration of Indian labour to,
    34–35
  Tamil population in post-colonial,
    125, 126, 189
states
  interventionism of post-colonial,
    118, 140
  migrants as seen by, 13, 111
  power of, 6, 111, 194
Straits Chinese, political affiliations
    of, 77
students
  mobility of Asian, 59, 151, 178
SUARAM, 190
Suez Canal, 25, 66
Sugihara, Kaoru, 48
Suharto, Indonesian President,
    124
Sukarno, Indonesian President, 137
Sulu Zone, 171
Sumatra
  conditions of plantation labour in,
    42
  Javanese migration to, 137
Sun, Yat-Sen, 75

Taiwan
  arrival of Chinese refugees in,
    1949, 116
  marriage migration to, 176
  post-war economic developmet of,
    154
Tan Malaka, 108
Tan, Kah Kee, 101
Thailand
  centrality to trafficking networks,
    169, 175
  migration to and from, 169
  position of Chinese in, 95
  refugee camps in, 188
Tinker, Hugh, 105
Tokyo
  as place of political exile, 60
  Chinese students in,
    60–61, 76
  modernity of, 60
  pan-Islamists in, 61
Tongmenghui, 76
trafficking, routes of,
    175–76
transport. *See* air travel; railways;
    shipping
Tsai, Ming-Liang, 170

United Nations High Commission
    for Refugees (UNHCR), 186
United States of America, 150
urbanization, 3
  future prospects for, 157
  growth of, 8, 118, 142–45,
    157
  in contemporary Asia, 152,
    156–60
  patterns of, 157

Vertovec, Steven, 179
Vietnam
  and trans-border political
    networks, 62
  'culture of migration' in, 150
  declaration of independence, 112
  internal migration in, 139

refugees from, 188
rubber production in, 29
violence, against migrants, 89, 94

Wang, Jingwei, 97
war
    and displacement, 89, 90
    and migration, 90
Warren, James Francis, 44,
    171
Werbner, Pnina, 181
White, Theodore, 98

Williams, Catharina, 173
Wuhan, refugees in, 1930s, 99

Xinjiang, Chinese migration to, 133

Yan, Hairong, 172
Yangzi, 98
Young, C. Walter, 52
Yue, Meng, 64

Zamindar, Vazira, 121
Zheng, He, 23

For EU product safety concerns, contact us at Calle de José Abascal, 56–1°, 28003 Madrid, Spain or eugpsr@cambridge.org.